Java™

Java™ Data Objects

ROBIN M. ROOS

Addison-Wesley

An imprint of **Pearson Education**

London · Boston · Indianapolis · New York · Mexico City · Toronto
Sydney · Tokyo · Singapore · Hong Kong · Cape Town · New Delhi
Madrid · Paris · Amsterdam · Munich · Milan · Stockholm

Pearson Education Limited

Head Office: London Office:

Edinburgh Gate   128 Long Acre
Harlow CM20 2JE   London WC2E 9AN
Tel: +44 (0)1279 623623   Tel: +44 (0)20 7447 2000
Fax: +44 (0)1279 431059   Fax: +44 (0)20 7447 2170
Website: www.it-minds.com
           www.awprofessional.com
_____

First published in Great Britain in 2003

© Pearson Education Ltd 2003

The rights of Robin M. Roos to be identified as Author of this Work have been asserted by him in
accordance with the Copyright, Designs and Patents Act 1988.

ISBN 0-321-12380-8

British Library Cataloguing in Publication Data
A CIP catalogue record for this book can be obtained from the British Library.

Library of Congress Cataloging in Publication Data
Roos, Robin M., 1969-
   Java data objects / Robin M. Roos.
       p. cm.
   Includes bibliographical references and index.
   ISBN 0-321-12380-8 (pbk.)
    1. Java (Computer program language) 2. Application program interfaces (Computer
software) 3. Object-oriented programming (Computer science) 4. Computer
software--Standards. I. Title.
   QA76.73.J38 R67 2002
   005.13'3--dc21

                                                                         2002074864

The programs in this book have been included for their instructional value. The publisher does not
offer any warranties or representations in respect of their fitness for a particular purpose,
nor does the publisher accept any liability for any loss or damage arising from their use.

Many of the designations used by manufacturers and sellers to distinguish their
products are claimed as trademarks. Pearson Education Limited has made every
attempt to supply trademark information about manufacturers and their products mentioned
in this book.

Trademark Notice
Java™ is a registered trademark of Sun Microsystems.

10 9 8 7 6 5 4 3 2 1

Typeset by Pantek Arts Ltd, Maidstone, Kent
Printed and bound in the UK by Biddles Ltd of Guildford and King's Lynn

The Publishers' policy is to use paper manufactured from sustainable forests.

Contents

Acknowledgments

A number of people have been instrumental in my successful completion of this work. Specifically I would like to recognize the contributions I received from my editor, Simon Plumtree of Pearson Education, the support, encouragement and advice of my wife Catherine, and the patience of my daughter Genevieve.

My reviewers made invaluable contributions to the content, readability, accuracy, and overall quality of the manuscript. They were:

Andrew Roos, ExiNet

Eric Samson (JDO expert), LIBeLIS

Heiko Bobzin (JDO expert), Poet Software

John Cosby, Sun Microsystems

John Russell, Prism Technologies

Keiron McCammon (JDO expert), Versant

Leo Crawford

Matthew Adams (JDO expert), People Redesigned

Robert Hoeppe, Poet Software

Stephen Johnson (JDO expert), Prism Technologies

Trish Scott Deetz

Material for the summary of available implementations, presented in Chapter 12, was generously provided by:

Alexander Kraft, Object Industries

Eric Samson (JDO expert), LIBeLIS

Greg Chase (JDO expert), Poet Software

Heiko Bobzin (JDO expert), Poet Software

Keiron McCammon (JDO expert), Versant

Matthew Pope (JDO expert), HYWY Software

John Russell, Prism Technologies

Luca Garulli (JDO expert), Orient Technologies

Neelan Choksi, SolarMetric

Torsten Busch, Signsoft

David Tinker, Hemisphere Technologies

Srikanth Rukkannagari, ObjectFrontier

Thanks also go to all the members of the two most influential vendor-independent JDO discussion forums for their interesting, informative, and challenging postings:

JavaDataObjects

`http://groups.yahoo.com/group/JavaDataObjects/`

JDOcentral.com

`http://www.JDOcentral.com`

Finally, my thanks go to Craig Russell, JDO Specification Lead, and to all of the members of the JDO Expert Group, without whom JDO could not have been created.

Foreword

The JDO (Java™ Data Objects) standard has a long history, only some of which is visible by looking at the development of the standard itself. Its roots are in the ODMG (Object Data Management Group), which was an early attempt to standardize transparent access to databases from object oriented programming languages. The ODMG standard predates Java, having been developed when the biggest debate in the object development community was whether Smalltalk or C++ would be the dominant object oriented programming language. The debate turned out to be academic, as Java became the de facto standard for writing object oriented applications. And the ODMG responded by adapting its C++ and Smalltalk interfaces to Java.

The process of adapting the ODMG standard to Java was problematic. It was written when two-tier architectures were dominant. Application servers were difficult to model. And the standard had no compliance test; any vendor who had an implementation that looked anything like ODMG was free to claim compliance with the standard.

Enter the Java Community Process (JCP). At first glance, it appeared to solve the most immediate problems inherent in the ODMG process; the requirement for a reference implementation and compliance test suite. After further investigation, the process was adopted and the Java Specification Request was submitted and approved for development, with support from major database players, middleware vendors, and tools suppliers.

Development of the JDO standard proceeded in parallel with two other standards: the Java Connector Architecture (JCA), and container-managed persistence (CMP). The expert group felt strongly that keeping JDO in line with these two standards would be of primary importance, yet ease of use for simple applications was still an absolute objective.

The JCP requirements for a reference implementation and compliance test suite turned out to be the determining factor in the timing of the final release of the standard. The reference implementation was staffed with one full-time engineer, and the test suite with one contractor. By normal engineering standards, the projects were woefully understaffed. But this turned out to have a bright side, as commercial implementations were developed in parallel with the development of the reference implementation and test suite. While deficiencies were found in the standard by the reference implementation, even more were found in the attempt to adapt commercial database products to the standard. In fact, several products shipped even before the tests were complete, building more support for the standard-under-development.

I am gratified to see the adoption of JDO in the user community as well as in the vendor community. Its widespread availability in two- and multi-tier architectures and across database implementations brings new meaning to Java's promise of "write once, run anywhere."

Craig Russell
JDO Specification Lead
Sun Microsystems
Mountain View, California

April 2002

Preface

It's official! For the last two weeks, the executive committee of JCP has been considering the JDO specification and voting on it. JDO has now been approved as a standard, and as I write these words the first announcements of JDO 1.0 are being made on JavaDataObjects at Yahoo!Groups and on JDOcentral.com.

I believe that JDO will have a profoundly positive impact on the way that we architect, design, and implement Java applications. Conservative improvements of 20% in the development time (and therefore cost) of enterprise applications are being quoted, with some analysts suggesting that the actual savings may be much higher.

Support for the standard is considerable; there is already a significant number of products on the market, most of which target full compliance with JDO 1.0 in the immediate future.

Robin M. Roos
March 2002

What is JDO?

Java Data Objects is an interface-based definition of object persistence for the Java language, which describes the storage, querying, and retrieval of objects from data stores.

JDO is extremely compelling due to the notion of transparent persistence that it supports. This can be summarized briefly as follows:

- JDO transparently handles the mapping of JDO instances to the underlying data store; the so-called object-relational impedance mismatch.

- JDO is transparent to the Java objects being persisted; you do not have to add specific methods or attributes to your Java classes or alter the visibility modifiers of your class members. Fields with private visibility, and fields without get and set methods, are no problem for JDO!

- JDO can be used against a number of different data storage paradigms, including (but not limited to) relational databases, object databases, file systems, and XML documents. In due course JDO implementations will emerge for accessing persistent data held in legacy applications, for use in Enterprise Application Integration projects.

- JDO is transparent to the data store itself, so applications can be ported to any data store for which an appropriate JDO implementation is available. The binary compatibility of JDO instances, guaranteed by the JDO specification, means that this can be achieved without even recompilation, let alone any alterations at source code level.

- If an application references a persistent object and alters any of its persistent state in the memory, the JDO implementation will implicitly update the data store when the active transaction is committed. This relieves the developer of repeatedly coding explicit save operations.

To whom will JDO be important?

JDO will be important to *Java architects*, because they can use it to build flexible application architectures that integrate seamlessly with Java 2 Enterprise Edition (J2EE™). They will appreciate its portability across relational, object and other data storage paradigms, as well as JDO's applicability to enterprise, simple client-server, and – in due course – embedded Java 2 Micro Edition (J2ME™) environments.

JDO will be important to *Java designers*, because they can finally use all the good object modeling techniques (including interfaces and inheritance) that previously caused significant complication to the persistence infrastructure of their applications.

JDO will be important to *Java developers*, because it is intuitive and works at the domain object level – without them having to implement a persistence infrastructure for their applications. They will also appreciate the new Query Language with its Java-like syntax and semantics.

Finally, JDO will be important to *development and project managers*, because it will streamline the development of applications. Designers and developers can concentrate on the functional aspects of the application, without spending huge amounts of time and money implementing, and subsequently debugging, non-functional persistence infrastructures.

Who should read this book?

Although it has been written primarily for Java developers, this book's coverage of JDO will also be of significant interest to designers and architects.

I do expect my readers to have a good knowledge of the Java language and its syntax.

Traditionally, Java applications store data to relational databases using JDBC™ and SQL. JDO is capable of completely replacing both of these technologies. Therefore no knowledge of JDBC or SQL is required in order to learn JDO. Of course, developers with prior knowledge and experience in storing objects in databases will benefit from their background.

JDO can be used very successfully with or without a J2EE application server. It has application from standard Java clients, as well as web components (Servlets and JavaServer Pages) and enterprise components (Session, Message-Driven and Entity Beans).

Since JDO is applied largely to domain objects, I have placed significant emphasis on the design of flexible domain object models. This will be of interest to Java designers, who may then choose to skim through the syntactic examples.

Integration of JDO with the full suite of J2EE components will be of interest to Java architects as well as developers, and a chapter is dedicated to this topic. Chapter 11 begins with an explanation of each J2EE component for those not familiar with them. Thus no previous exposure to J2EE is necessary, although readers who do have such experience will naturally gain more insight than those without.

Organization

Chapter 1 Understanding object persistence
An introduction to the storage of objects in data stores, mentioning previous technology solutions.

Chapter 2 Developing a simple example
A step-by-step walk through a simple JDO example.

Chapter 3 JDO architecture
A look at essential architectural concepts, such as environments, transactionality, and identity.

Chapter 4 Instance lifecycle
Coverage of the lifecycle states of JDO instances, and the invocations which applications can make in order to initiate lifecycle transitions.

Chapter 5 Persistent object model
A detailed look at the manner in which JDO treats domain object models.

Chapter 6 Primary interfaces and classes
The essentials of JDO from a programmatic standpoint.

Chapter 7 Transaction management
How to manage transactions, with particular emphasis on optimistic transaction strategies.

Chapter 8 Queries with JDOQL
The new JDO Query Language.

Chapter 9 JDO exceptions
Exceptions defined by JDO.

Chapter 10 Persistence descriptor
A detailed look at the structure of XML persistence descriptors.

Chapter 11 J2EE integration
How to use JDO from EJB components (Session Beans, Entity Beans and Message-Driven Beans) and web components (Servlets and JavaServer Pages).

Chapter 12 JDO implementations
A summary of the available implementations. JDO is remarkably well implemented given its relative newness in the market.

Chapter 13 Epilogue
A look beyond JDO 1.0, considering features that might be expected in future versions of JDO.

Appendix A Properties for JDOHelper bootstrap
Useful property names for initializing JDO.

Appendix B Strings for supported options
Useful string constants.

Appendix C JDO persistence descriptor DTD
The DTD which constrains persistence descriptors.

Appendix D PersistenceManagerFactory
A list of the methods of the PersistenceManagerFactory, which has not been given in the text.

Appendix E JDOQL BNF
The formal grammar notation of JDOQL

A bibliography is also provided.

CD contents

The CD accompanying this book contains trial versions of the following JDO implementations:

- FastObjects™ by Poet
- Kodo JDO™ by Solarmetric
- LiDO™ by LIBeLIS
- OpenFusion JDO™ by Prism Technologies.

Each of these products is described in Chapter 12, "JDO implementations." Please refer to the CD's "readme.pdf" file for further information.

Source code for the significant examples from each chapter is available from the author's website:

```
http://www.OgilviePartners.com
```

JDO version information

This book covers JDO 1.0.
The Java examples are compliant with JDK 1.3.1_01 and J2EE 1.3.

About the author

Robin Roos studied at St. Andrews College and Rhodes University, South Africa, graduating with a B.Sc. in Computer Science and Physics, 1988, and a B.Sc. (Hons) in Computer Science in 1989. He worked extensively with relational databases and various procedural and object-orientated languages (including Forte) before learning Java in 1996. Since then, Robin has worked on numerous Java and J2EE projects. His experience of database access through Java using both JDBC and Entity Bean technology led him to believe there had to be a better way. He joined the JDO Expert Group (JSR12) during 2001.

Robin is Principal Consultant at Ogilvie Partners Ltd, a UK-based consulting company that delivers training, mentoring, and consultancy to an increasingly worldwide client base. Ogilvie Partners' focus on JDO is complemented by its project-related background in core Java J2EE technologies.

Robin has spoken on the topic of JDO at user groups and conferences across the UK, Europe and the USA. His contact details are:

Robin@OgilviePartners.com
http://www.OgilviePartners.com

About the cover illustration

The illustration on the cover of *Java Data Objects* is the work of Sara Connell based on a theme by the Author. The cover was designed by Mike Rogers. The coffee beans fed into the process represent ordinary Java classes. The process itself, culminating in a Delft coffee grinder that hangs in the Author's kitchen, represents JDO enhancement. Finally, the ground coffee obtained by turning the grinder's handle represents persistence-capable classes.

Understanding object persistence

1

Something fantastic is happening in the world of Java. For years, the supposedly straightforward task of loading and storing data has unnecessarily complicated the development of Java applications. However, the arrival of a new standard for object persistence will finally lay these issues to rest.

Java Data Objects (JDO) promises to revolutionize our industry. No longer the delicate coding of Java Database Connectivity (JDBC) and Structured Query Language (SQL) code, which has little or nothing to do with the business requirements for an application! No longer the complexities of the Entity Enterprise Java Beans (EJB) model of persistent data! No longer the lock-in to relational storage technology! Finally we have, in JDO, an interface-based standard for the storage and retrieval of data, so-called *object persistence*.

The standard is just that, a standard. Developers write code against the standard. The code is executed in conjunction with an implementation of the standard, called a JDO implementation. The choice of implementation will not be dictated by core functionality, which is mandated by the JDO specification. Instead this choice will be motivated by quality of service factors: performance, scalability, customer service, price, support for the target data store, and also the support provided for certain "optional" features of JDO, which are specified as such and may be relevant for certain applications. Binary compatibility, which the standard guarantees, facilitates the portability of an application from one JDO implementation to another. This includes portability from implementations targeting relational databases to others targeting object databases.

Writing applications that can be executed against relational or object databases without recompilation? This has *got* to be good!

As you will see throughout this book, the programming paradigm of JDO is very simple to use. As with all application programming interfaces (API), JDO has its complex aspects, but most of what developers require from a persistence infrastructure is achieved quickly. This ease of development is so significant that some Java architects are anticipating 20% reductions in development time for applications utilizing JDO instead of JDBC, SQL and Entity EJBs.

To cap it all, JDO can be fully integrated with J2EE application server technology and its declarative and distributed transaction model.

So let's get down to looking at JDO itself. The entire focus of JDO is the transparent persistence of Java objects. You're going to hear these terms repeatedly throughout all of the chapters, so it would seem appropriate to begin by establishing a common understanding of what they mean.

1.1   What is object persistence?

In Java (and other object oriented programming languages) an *object* is an instance of a class. As such it has state (its attribute values) and behavior (its methods). The collection of all class definitions that comprise an application is known as the application's *object model*. These classes perform a variety of functions: some render user interfaces; some manage system resources; some represent application events. However, within each object model there is usually a distinct set of objects that are direct abstractions of business concepts – typically with names to which non-technical business people would ascribe meaning. In an order processing application these may be "Customer," "Order," and "Product." For a financial application they might be "Client," "Account," "Credit Entry," and "Debit Entry." In each case these objects are modeling the business domain in which the specific application will operate, and thus they are collectively referred to as the *domain object model*.

The domain object model is of particular importance to application designers. It is these objects that represent the primary state and behavior available to the application. They will be the focus of many design workshops, since they represent concepts which the application's target user community understand, and in which they have specific expertise. Perhaps most importantly, it is these objects that typically need to be stored (somewhere and somehow) between invocations of the application and shared between multiple simultaneous users.

The storage of these objects, beyond the lifetime of the Java Virtual Machine (JVM) in which they were instantiated, is called *object persistence*.

There are, of course, other classes beyond those which fit naturally into the domain object model, which may require persistence services (e.g. log messages). Object persistence is by no means restricted to the domain object model, but it is here that we find the majority of classes for which persistence must be provided.

1.2   Current techniques for persistence

Persistence requires the storage of object state for future retrieval. Various underlying mechanisms are in use in the industry, but by far the most common approach is to use a relational database management system (RDBMS) accessed through a combination of JDBC and SQL. Alternative mechanisms include file system-based storage and object database management systems (ODBMS). A persistence infrastructure is often layered on top of the data store, examples being Entity Beans and Enterprise Application Integration (EAI) frameworks.

1.2.1   Relational databases

RDBMS technology has been widely adopted in the last 15 years because of its freeform definition of data (rows and columns), flexibility of ad hoc queries, and transactional reliability (begin, rollback, commit). Due to extensive standardization efforts in the RDBMS market, all such databases can be invoked using the SQL. Although variations exist in the SQL dialects used by various databases, support for the SQL-92 standard is relatively widespread.

What are transactions?

A transaction is a grouping of work that an application wants to happen all together, or not at all. Typically transactions include multiple updates to data, either in the same database or in different databases. However, it is also viable for a transaction to contain one or no updates to databases.

The application is responsible for demarcating transactions, i.e. specifying where they begin and end. All work performed between these two points is deemed to be part of the transaction.

When the transaction is committed, all of the updates made are written to the respective data stores. If any one of the updates cannot be performed, then all of the updates are undone. This allows data to be kept in a consistent state. The undoing of work is referred to a "rollback." As well as being a possible result of the commit process, the application can instruct a transaction to rollback instead of commit.

Transactions are said to have four properties, the so-called ACID properties:

- Atomic (all or none of the work is performed).
- Consistent (data consistency is maintained).
- Isolated (the degree to which updates in one transaction may be seen by reads in another transaction can often be controlled).
- Durable (work which is committed as part of a transaction remains committed).

Transaction management in JDO is covered in detail in Chapters 7 and 11.

Java applications using relational databases for persistence typically invoke the database by passing SQL commands to the database server through an API called Java Database Connectivity (JDBC). SQL statements are constructed as string objects, which are then passed to the database server for compilation and execution. The statements may be parameterized in certain circumstances, enabling the execution of that statement multiple times for the expense of a single compilation. Data retrieved from the database is returned to the Java application in the form of a **ResultSet**, containing multiple rows and columns.

Use of JDBC for the persistence of objects, although widespread, presents a number of difficulties. Firstly, the developer must know SQL and use it to implement every manipulation of persistent data. Secondly, the developer must map object attributes to the columns of one or more tables. This mapping is often non-intuitive, and is required because of the so-called "impedance mismatch" between the notions of an object and a database row. Thirdly, once implemented, the relative lack of portability offered by SQL may restrict the persistence code from working unaltered against an alternative RDBMS implementation, thereby locking the application into one vendor's technology. Finally, the weak type-checking and deferred compilation of SQL statements means that many errors cannot be detected at compilation time, although this can be mitigated when tools such as SQL/J are used.

1.2.2   File system

File systems are usually considered to be lightweight storage solutions. A file system is capable of storing data in files of a user-defined format, but does not inherently support transactions or automatic data integrity functions.

The one advantage that file systems *do* provide is that they require little by way of supporting services beyond the operating system itself. As such they are commonly used for persistence within embedded applications where system resources are constrained (e.g. the contact list on your mobile phone). However, they are generally not considered appropriate for business-critical transactional information.

Java applications storing data in a file system would usually do so with the **java.io** API, and may additionally use Java's object serialization facilities. This turns any **Serializable** object graph into a stream of bytes for network transmission or storage, from which a copy of the original object graph may later be reconstructed. Serialization techniques such as this suffer from the abject lack of any query capabilities, and are typically used only when the total data set can be conveniently held in memory.

1.2.3   Object databases

ODBMS are storage environments for objects. The internal representation in which each object is held is hidden from the application developer, who instead uses an API for persisting and retrieving objects. Although they can be extremely efficient at such activity, ODBMS have historically suffered from a lack of ad hoc query capabilities, or inefficiencies where such capabilities do exist. The lack of well-implemented standards for the invocation of persistence services, and the inevitable lock-in of an application to a proprietary vendor's product, have also constrained the adoption of this technology. The ODMG did put together a standard API for accessing object databases, but this has done relatively little to improve the industry's uptake of object database technology.

1.2.4   Entity beans

Entity beans are part of the J2EE EJB specification. They provide a standard way of representing persistent data application components that can be shared across many simultaneous remote and local client connections. Although the session bean and message-driven bean aspects of EJB have been widely successful, a variety of design flaws in the entity bean model hinder its suitability for the representation of persistent data.

Some of these flaws have been addressed in the EJB 2.0 specification (e.g. new local interfaces providing an alternative to the slower remote interface previously available). However, the semantic differences between local (pass by reference) and remote (pass by value) invocation introduce further issues. Other concerning aspects of entity beans remain (e.g. the lack of meaningful support for inheritance). Additionally, the persistence and query functions of entity beans must usually be coded by hand (in SQL with JDBC) or described by hand (in Enterprise JavaBean Query Language (EJBQL) which stems from SQL). Finally, the concurrency issues endemic in EJB's threading model, combined with the capability for gross inefficiency when manipulating large data sets, mean that entity beans have regularly failed to meet applications' requirements for object persistence.

1.3   Object persistence with JDO

JDO is different. Rather than providing the means for developers to write persistence infrastructure code that accesses a data store, JDO successfully eliminates the need for such development effort.

Developers first write the classes for which persistence services are required (the so-called *persistence-capable* classes) – typically this constitutes the domain object model. Then an eXtensible Markup Language (XML) document called the *persistence descriptor* is written. This text document, in its simplest form, merely identifies the names of the persistence-capable classes. An enhancement process is invoked which reads the XML descriptor, and adds into each nominated class the additional methods required for the setting and retrieving of attribute values by a JDO implementation.

Enhancement vs. hand-coding

Whilst all JDO instances must implement the `PersistenceCapable` interface, and this is the primary purpose of enhancement, JDO does not mandate that the enhancement tool be used for this purpose. It is perfectly legal for a developer to hand-code a class to implement the `PersistenceCapable` interface.

However, the corresponding method implementations must be coded very carefully, and there would appear to be no advantage to hand-coding over the transparency, accuracy, and ease of tool-based enhancement.

A side effect of the enhancement process may be the generation of Data Definition Language (DDL) scripts for the definition of the necessary storage in a specified data store. Some JDO vendors choose to provide a separate schema tool for this purpose, while it is common for object database implementations not to require such a step. Once these scripts have been executed, everything is in place for persistence to occur.

Naturally it tends not to be domain objects that invoke persistence services themselves, but rather it is application objects that do so in order to persist and retrieve instances of the domain objects. The application developer writes these invocations against a standard JDO interface called **PersistenceManager**. The invocations themselves are easy to use (see Chapter 2).

With the persistence descriptor written, the domain objects enhanced, the storage defined as required, and the application's invocation of the persistence manager written, the application is ready to run.

Notice that we have referred to a data store, but not stated what type of data store is in use. JDO itself provides the interfaces by which persistence services can be invoked. These services are invoked on a JDO implementation, which is a product purchased not directly for its functionality (since JDO defines that functionality) but rather for its quality of service against the target data store. For the application to execute against a particular relational database, we would define the storage in that database and use an appropriate JDO implementation. To use a different data store (perhaps an object database) we merely define the storage in that data store as required, and use an alternative JDO implementation. No developer effort is required (not even recompilation) when migrating a JDO-based application from one data store to another, even when moving across storage paradigms (e.g. between relational databases, object databases, and lightweight file systems for embedded usage).

Closure of instances

I have referred to the "closure of all persistent instances referenced from any one persistent instance," which warrants further explanation.

Imagine a simple banking object model where a **Client** has references to many **Account** objects, and each **Account** has reference to many **AccountActivity** objects (perhaps including **Deposit**, **Withdrawal**, and **ChequePayment** activities).

Given a particular client, the closure of instances includes all the **Account** instances referenced by the **Client**, plus all of the **AccountActivity**s referenced by each **Account**.

A group of objects that reference each other is called an *object graph*. Object graphs can be fairly large, particularly when considering the graph of objects reachable from the Bank object, which presumably holds references to every Client.

Of course, a persistence-capable class may have some fields that are themselves persistent, and other fields that are not. The default assignments can be overridden in the persistence descriptor by assigning field-level persistence modifiers of **persistent**, **transactional**, or **none**.

The closure of all persistent instances referenced from any one persistent instance is the object graph arising from traversal of persistent field references only (not those marked **transactional** or **none**).

JDO manages this transparently, allowing the application to believe that the entire persistent object graph is in memory, when actually it is in the data store and a small subset is present in the persistence manager's cache.

In Chapter 11, we will consider the serialization of JDO instances. You will see then that the serialized object graph contains instances referenced by all persistent fields except those fields that are "non-serializable." Non-serializable fields are defined with the Java modifier **transient**. Thus application designers can limit the size of serialized object graphs without impacting the transparent persistent features afforded by JDO.

When we say that JDO implements *transparent persistence*, one of the three meanings we ascribe the phrase is that which was conveyed above; portability across data storage paradigms and products. Another one is the illusion given to an application that it has in-memory access to the closure of all persistence instances referenced from any one persistent instance (despite the fact that most of this potentially large set of instances will be on disk and not actually in memory).

For me, however, the most important meaning is that of persistence being transparent to the domain object model: designers are largely free to design the domain model so that it most accurately abstracts the business domain, and can then apply persistence to that model, without having designed the model with persistence foremost in mind. The ability of JDO to persist graphs of objects including inheritance and implementation hierarchies, in much the same manner as an ODBMS but with the advantages of a standard API and a pluggable (potentially non-object oriented) data store, finally frees the designer to use all that is good in object modeling techniques.

Hopefully the power of this new technology is becoming apparent to you. Developers can write applications that exploit highly performant and transactionally robust persistence services:

- without writing any supporting infrastructure code;
- without lock-in to a particular data store vendor's product;
- without any requirement for SQL knowledge, let alone SQL expertise;
- with complete portability and binary compatibility across those data storage paradigms and products for which a JDO implementation is available;
- with transparency to the domain object model;
- with transparency to the state (in-memory or on-disk) of the closure of referenced persistent object instances;
- with a standard API by which applications can invoke persistence services.

As a result, developers are finally able to concentrate their efforts on the business domain aspects of the applications they write, instead of spending 40–60% of their time writing supporting infrastructure which is essentially non-functional. This focus on functional aspects is accentuated when JDO is combined with session and message-driven beans, in order to exploit the declarative security and transaction management afforded by J2EE-compliant application servers.

1.4   JDO positioning

Before we move on to discuss a simple JDO example, I present in Table 1.1 a brief comparison of the persistence mechanisms discussed above. This is intended to help position JDO with respect to alternative persistence APIs. The superscripts[1] through[4] refer to notes that appear beneath the table.

Table 1.1   Comparison of persistence technologies

	Serialization	JDBC	ODBMS	EJB	JDO
Transactional	✘	✔	✔	✔	✔
Query facility	✘	✔	✔	✔	✔
Standard API	✔ java.io	✔ JDBC	✘ ODMG[1]	✔ EJB	✔ JDO
Standard query language	✘	✘ SQL[2]	✘ OQL	✔ EJBQL	✔ JDOQL
Supported data store paradigm	File system	RDBMS	ODBMS	RDBMS, EAI	RDBMS, ODBMS, EAI, File system, others
Transparent to closure of persistent instances	✘	✘	✔	✘	✔
Transparent to domain model	✘	✘	✔	✘	✔
True object database	✘	✘	✔	✘	✘[3]
Supports existing table structure	✘	✔	✘	✘	✔[4]

Notes:
1. This standard is not widely implemented.
2. Although widely implemented, vendor-specific interpretations and extensions of the standard proliferate.
3. JDO queries only support the invocation of methods which (a) return a single persistent field value, and (b) are non-mutating. True object databases would support the invocation of any method. However, JDO is not an object database, but an object oriented interface to data storage which may or may not be implemented in the ODBMS paradigm. The restriction stated above facilitates the implementation of JDO against non-object data stores, and provides for extremely efficient query execution (as there is no need to instantiate objects in order to determine whether they fulfill query filter criteria).
4. Although this is not mandated or standardized by the JDO specification, all JDO vendors with implementations for relational databases expose the object-relational mapping to the developer.

What's next?

In the next chapter we will look at the Java code and XML persistence descriptor for a simple example of persisting objects with JDO.

Developing a simple example

2

I n this chapter we develop a single persistence-capable class and an application. The application uses JDO to create and persist instances of that class in the database and to list all instances of the class that have been persisted.

2.1 Order processing domain

The first thing we need for a simple example is a business domain within which to work. I have chosen to model an order processing application. In the fullness of time; our model will contain classes called "BusinessPartner," "Customer," "Order," "OrderLine," "Product," etc. However, in the first case we will start with just one business entity, the "BusinessPartner" class.

A **BusinessPartner** is an entity with which the user of the application does business. In our example this will represent a company or individual that places orders for our products. Simplistic treatments of this topic would call the class "Customer," but "Customer" is actually one of many roles that may be played by a business partner, hence my choice of class names.

The attributes of our **BusinessPartner** class will be partner number, name, and address. For now we will provide simple accessor (get) and mutator (set) methods for each attribute.

Please note that JDO does not require field accessor or mutator methods to be defined in persistence-capable classes. JDO reads and writes the values of persistent or transactional fields through methods of the **PersistenceCapable** interface, which all enhanced classes implement. We provide accessors and mutators in this example, but they are for the application's use and are not required by JDO. (Earlier attempts at persistence services for Java typically required such methods, which adversely affect both transparency and encapsulation.)

Using "property" notation (instead of listing each attribute and each accessor and mutator method independently), the Unified Modeling Language (UML) class diagram for **BusinessPartner** is shown on Figure 2.1.

The package structure used for this example, and throughout, is shown in Table 2.1.

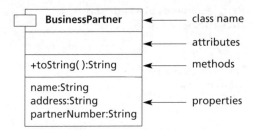

Figure 2.1 UML representation of **BusinessPartner**

Here is the Java code that implements the **BusinessPartner** class:

Table 2.1 Package structure

Package	Description
com.ogilviepartners.jdo	JDO support classes for use in your own projects
com.ogilviepartners.jdo.gui	Dynamic query window
com.ogilviepartners.jdobook	Examples specific to this book
com.ogilviepartners.jdobook.op	The order processing domain package
com.ogilviepartners.jdobook.op.pk	Primary key classes
com.ogilviepartners.jdobook.op.ex	Exception classes
com.ogilviepartners.jdobook.op.j2ee	J2EE components and helper classes
com.ogilviepartners.jdobook.other	Examples outside the order processing domain
com.ogilviepartners.jdobook.app	Text-based application code
com.ogilviepartners.jdobook.app.gui	GUI-based application code

BusinessPartner.java

```java
package com.ogilviepartners.jdobook.op;

public class BusinessPartner {

    protected String name;
    protected String partnerNumber;

    protected String address;

    public String toString() {
        return "BusinessPartner (number=" + partnerNumber
                            + "name=" + name +
                            "address=" + address + ")";
    }
}
```

```
        public void setName(String name) {
            this.name = name;
        }

        public String getName() {
            return name;
        }

        public void setAddress(String address) {
            this.address = address;
        }
        public String getAddress() {
            return address;
        }

        public void setPartnerNumber(String partnerNumber) {
            this.partnerNumber = partnerNumber;
        }

        public String getPartnerNumber() {
            return partnerNumber;
        }
    }
```

The application will manage the persistence lifecycle of **BusinessPartner** instances through the **PersistenceManager** interface. An instance of a class implementing the **PersistenceManager** interface is obtained from an appropriately configured **PersistenceManagerFactory**.

To obtain a reference to the **PersistenceManager** I make use of a supporting class called **JDOBootstrap**. This is not part of the **javax.jdo** package; it is one that I have provided, the source code for which is described later. This class reads properties from the file **jdo.properties** that defines the connection factory information required to initialize a **PersistenceManagerFactory**. It then provides a single method **getPersistenceManager()** that returns a **PersistenceManager** object. The JDO implementation I am using will store objects in any JDBC-compliant data store, so the properties passed to the **PersistenceManagerFactory** largely contain JDBC connection information. An example property file is shown below. The **JDOBootstrap** class will be discussed at a later stage.

jdo.properties

```
javax.jdo.PersistenceManagerFactoryClass=\
        com.prismt.j2ee.jdo.PersistenceManagerFactoryImpl
javax.jdo.option.ConnectionUserName=sa
javax.jdo.option.ConnectionPassword=
javax.jdo.option.ConnectionURL=jdbc:hsqldb:hsql://localhost
javax.jdo.option.ConnectionDriverName=org.hsqldb.jdbcDriver
```

(Note that the backslash character \ above indicates the first line should be continuous.)

The application itself will be run from the command-line. It will accept, as command-line arguments, values for each attribute of a **BusinessPartner** to be created. Since everything will happen within the application's **main()** method, all variables can be local to that method. We need to hold references to the **JDOBootstrap**, **PersistenceManagerFactory**, **PersistenceManager**, **Transaction**, and **BusinessPartner**.

```
JDOBootstrap bootstrap;
PersistenceManagerFactory pmf;
PersistenceManager pm;
Transaction t;
BusinessPartner bp;
```

First of all we instantiate the **JDOBootstrap**, which reads **jdo.properties** and configures a **PersistenceManagerFactory** object, and then we invoke its **getPersistenceManagerFactory()** method to obtain our reference to the factory. From this a persistence manager is acquired with a call to **getPersistenceManager()**. That done, a reference to the persistence manager's **Transaction** object is obtained.

```
bootstrap = new JDOBootstrap();
pmf = bootstrap.getPersistenceManagerFactory();
pm = pmf.getPersistenceManager();
t = pm.currentTransaction();
```

The command-line arguments are then used to construct and initialize a new **BusinessPartner** object. At this point the object is *transient* – it has not yet been made persistent and its lifetime is constrained by the lifetime of the JVM in which it was instantiated.

```
bp = new BusinessPartner();
bp.setPartnerNumber(args[0]);
bp.setName(args[1]);
bp.setAddress(args[2]);
```

Now it is time to begin a transaction and store (make persistent) the new **BusinessPartner** object. After doing this, the current transaction is committed.

```
t.begin();
pm.makePersistent(bp);
t.commit();
```

Having persisted the new **BusinessPartner** object, the application lists all persistent **BusinessPartner** objects from the data store. This is achieved using the **Extent** interface. An extent represents the complete set of all instances of a given class in the data store, optionally including or excluding subclasses. Extents have no filter facilities and as such are very distinct from queries.

Note that constructing the **Extent** object does not actually cause the retrieval or caching of any data store entities. An **Extent** is a small object that merely encapsulates information about the class hierarchy it represents, and provides methods for obtaining and closing **Iterator**s.

Here we get the **Extent** of all **BusinessPartner** objects (including sub-classes, even though there aren't any yet), obtain an **Iterator** of the extent and print each instance in turn. The **Iterator** is closed on the **Extent** at the end. Once again the **Transaction** is committed.

[handwritten annotation: t.begin();]

[handwritten annotation: t.begin();]

```
Extent extPartner = pm.getExtent(BusinessPartner.class, true);
Iterator i = extPartner.iterator();
System.out.println("Listing partners:");
while (i.hasNext()) {
    System.out.println(i.next());
}
System.out.println("Done.");
extPartner.close(i);//close the Iterator
t.commit();
```

Finally we close the **PersistenceManager** (so that it can neatly relinquish its resources) before allowing the application to exit. This should be placed into the **finally** block of a **try** statement, to ensure that it always occurs despite the throwing of any exceptions. This has been ignored here for brevity.

```
pm.close();
```

[handwritten annotation: I don't think we want to do this. Yes we do!]

The full source code for the application appears at the end of this chapter so that these extracts can be seen in context with the appropriate imports and so on.

Now that we have the domain object and the application, it's time to write the persistence descriptor. We will use a simple persistence descriptor that has the same name as the **BusinessPartner** class and merely identifies that class for enhancement.

BusinessPartner.jdo

```
<?xml version="1.0" encoding="UTF-8" ?>
<!DOCTYPE jdo SYSTEM "file:///jdowork/dtd/jdo.dtd">
<jdo>
  <package name="op">
    <class name="BusinessPartner" />
  </package>
</jdo>
```

The enhancement phase is next. I have encapsulated the enhancer invocation command into a simple script called "enhance" that takes a single persistence descriptor filename as an argument.

```
C:\jdowork\ex1-2>enhance BusinessPartner.jdo
Enhancing xml\BusinessPartner.jdo
Parsing JDO Descriptor File(s).
```

```
Analysing op.BusinessPartner
Analysis complete.
Enhancing op.BusinessPartner
Class Enhancement completed.
Populating Meta.
Writing Meta Classes.
Generating SQL Output.


C:\jdowork\ex1-2>
```

The enhancer I am using generates a DDL file called **load_all.sql**, which I then run in the SQL monitor of my database server in order to define the required tables and columns. Once this is done, the application can be executed:

```
C:\jdowork\ex1-2>java app.TestBusinessPartner 1 Robin
"Milton Keynes"
Persisting BusinessPartner (number=1 name=Robin
address=Milton Keynes)
Listing partners:
BusinessPartner (number=1 name=Robin address=Milton Keynes)
Done.


C:\jdowork\ex1-2>
```

A second execution proves that the first **BusinessPartner** has in fact been persisted:

```
C:\jdowork\ex1-2>java app.TestBusinessPartner 1 Cathy London
Persisting BusinessPartner (number=2 name=Cathy
address=London)
Listing partners:
BusinessPartner (number=2 name=Cathy address=London)
BusinessPartner (number=1 name=Robin address=Milton Keynes)
Done.


C:\jdowork\ex1-2>
```

2.2   Discussion

The book's accompanying CD contains trial versions of several JDO implementations, whilst the source code and the **enhance** and **compile** scripts that I used for the examples are available from my website:

```
http://www.OgilviePartners.com
```

I recommend you now install the software and compile, enhance, and execute this example.

It would now seem appropriate to discuss briefly what the application is actually doing and how it works; more detail will follow in the forthcoming chapters.

The first thing to notice is that we are using a relational database. However, the only information specific to this fact are the lines of the **jdo.properties** file pertinent to the connection factory (the **ConnectionURL** and **ConnectionDriver** properties). There is no JDBC code, there is no SQL, and the classes we have written could easily be executed against an alternative JDO implementation without recompilation, let alone any alteration at source code level.

The flow of activities described for this simple example shows the application being written before the enhancement phase. In this case there is no dependency between these actions. However, where more complicated domain object models are being used and the enhancer is responsible for generating primary key classes, the enhancement phase must be performed before the application can be compiled.

Note that this is only a requirement where the enhancer tool is generating class files that are referenced by the application, and only if the corresponding Object ID class is non-existent or the primary key fields have been altered. Class files do not have to be enhanced again when porting from one implementation to another, thanks to the binary compatibility mandated by the JDO specification.

2.2.1   Enhancement and PersistenceCapable

The enhancement tool has worked some magic on our **BusinessPartner** class. The enhancer actually reads one set of byte code and generates a new set of byte code, and so can be used without access to class source code. The enhanced **BusinessPartner** class implements an interface from the **javax.jdo.spi** package called **PersistenceCapable**. This interface, part of the service provider's interface (SPI) package, is internal to JDO and should never be referred to by the application. It provides methods by which a **PersistenceManager** can read and write the values of persistent and transactional fields.

Our simple persistence descriptor did not specify which fields of **BusinessPartner** were to be made persistent, so by default all fields (regardless of visibility) are persistent except for those defined with the Java modifiers **final**, **static**, or **transient**. In this case it is clear that the partner number, name, and address fields will all be persistent fields by default.

Attributes vs. fields

In Java we refer to classes having attributes and methods.

When using relational databases we refer to the columns of an individual table row as being its fields.

This name has been applied in JDO, and the persistent attributes of persistence-capable classes are referred to as persistent fields.

Although enhanced classes implement the **PersistenceCapable** interface, you can largely ignore it as you, the application developer, should *never* directly invoke methods of the **PersistenceCapable** interface on your domain objects.

2.2.2   JDOBootstrap and the PersistenceManagerFactory

Persistence manager instances are initially obtained from a persistence manager factory. JDO provides a standard mechanism for instantiating the factory that uses a **Properties** object to specify factory configuration information. The method used to achieve this is:

    JDOHelper.createPersistenceManagerFactory(Properties p)

There is no specific reason why an application should not invoke this method directly. However, I have chosen to encapsulate this method within the **JDOBootstrap** class, which obtains the property values from a text file **jdo.properties**. Neither the **JDOBootstrap** class nor the **jdo.properties** file are part of the JDO standard, although the names of the properties for use in configuring the factory most certainly are (see Appendix A). The source code for **JDOBootstrap** is included in the downloadable distribution (http://www.OgilviePartners.com) and I hope you will find it useful in your own JDO-based projects.

2.2.3   Transactions

We deal with JDO transactions in detail in Chapter 7, but for now you need to know that a single persistence manager has, at most, one active transaction. As such there is only ever one **Transaction** object associated with a given persistence manager. It is necessary for the developer to perform **begin()** and **commit()** method invocations against this **Transaction** object. Applications requiring multiple simultaneous independent transactions must obtain a corresponding number of persistence managers from the factory.

Transaction management gets significantly more involved when JDO is used within a J2EE application server, but that is an advanced topic that we will not discuss in detail until Chapter 11.

2.2.4   Transient vs. persistent

A transient object is one that does not directly reflect data in a data store. Most objects in your Java applications are transient, and when the **BusinessPartner** object is first instantiated, it too is transient (despite the fact that as an enhanced class it is persistence-capable).

A persistent object is one that *does* directly reflect data in a data store. The extent to which the data cached in the object is up to date with any recent modifications to the data store is dependent on the transaction management strategy being employed (more on that in Chapter 7). Alterations made to a persistent instance will normally be reflected in the data store on commit, or reversed on rollback of the current transaction.

To transition the new **BusinessPartner** object from being transient to being persistent we simply call the **PersistenceManager.makePersistent** (**Object pc**) method. The transient and persistent states, amongst others, are described in more detail in Chapter 4.

2.2.5   Iterating the extent

The simplest way to obtain all persistent instances of a given **PersistenceCapable** class is to obtain the extent of that class from the **PersistenceManager**. Extents represent all persistent instances of a given class or class hierarchy.

Extents are iterated through a **java.util.Iterator** obtained by invoking the **Extent's iterator()** method. Each call to the iterator's **next()** method returns the next object in the extent; in this case the next **BusinessPartner** object. Ordinarily one would cast the objects returned by **next()** into the appropriate class, but that is not necessary in this case as we are merely printing out each object by an implicit call to the **BusinessPartner.toString()** method.

JDO vendors should provide **Iterator** implementations that handle large volumes of data in an efficient manner. However, extents provide no filtering facilities; an extent is always the entire extent. The JDO Query Language provides comprehensive query facilities that we will cover in Chapter 8. Since this application does process every persistent instance, using the extent is appropriate and illustrates that **BusinessPartner** objects are indeed being correctly persisted to the data store.

2.3   Application source code

As promised, here then is the full source code for the application.

TestBusinessPartner.java

```
package com.ogilviepartners.jdobook.app;

import javax.jdo.*;
import com.ogilviepartners.jdo.JDOBootstrap;
```

```
import com.ogilviepartners.jdobook.op.BusinessPartner;
import java.util.Iterator;

public class TestBusinessPartner
{
    public static void main(String[] args) {
        JDOBootstrap bootstrap;
        PersistenceManagerFactory pmf;
        PersistenceManager pm;
        Transaction t;
        BusinessPartner bp;

        // check the arguments
        if (args.length != 3) {
            System.out.println("usage: java " +
                "TestBusinessPartner <partnerNumber> " +
                "<name> <address>");
            System.exit(1);
        }

        // instantiate the PersistenceManagerFactory and obtain
        // a PersistenceManager
        bootstrap = new JDOBootstrap();
        pmf = bootstrap.getPersistenceManagerFactory();
        pm = pmf.getPersistenceManager();
        try {
            // get a reference to the Transaction object
            t = pm.currentTransaction();

            // create a (transient) BusinessPartner
            bp = new BusinessPartner();
            bp.setPartnerNumber(args[0]);
            bp.setName(args[1]);
            bp.setAddress(args[2]);

            // persist the BusinessPartner
            System.out.println("Persisting " + bp);
            t.begin();
            pm.makePersistent(bp);
            t.commit();

            // obtain Extent of BusinessPartner and iterate
            // contents
            t.begin();
            Extent extPartner =
                pm.getExtent(BusinessPartner.class, false);
```

```
                        Iterator i = extPartner.iterator();
                        System.out.println("Listing partners:");
                        while (i.hasNext()) {
                            System.out.println(i.next());
                        }
                        System.out.println("Done.");
                        extPartner.close(i);
                        t.commit();
                    }
                    finally {
                        // close resources
                        pm.close();
                    }
                }
            }
```

What's next?

In the next chapter we will build on these concepts as we look into the JDO architecture in significantly more detail.

JDO architecture

3

In this chapter we discuss the JDO architecture. An understanding of the architectural points raised here is necessary to facilitate your correct use of JDO and your understanding of the more advanced topics covered later.

3.1   JDO implementations and vendors

The JDO package `javax.jdo`, which is freely available from Sun Microsystems, is largely made up of interface definitions. It also contains a few concrete classes, notably **JDOHelper** and the JDO exception classes. It is through these interfaces that applications have access to the functionality of object persistence. The most important one is **PersistenceManager**, through which transient instances can be made persistent, persistent instances deleted, and so on. However, we have already used two others, namely **Transaction** and **Extent**.

These standard interfaces, although a comprehensive description of persistence functionality, are not in themselves sufficient to actually implement persistence. What is needed is a set of concrete classes implementing the respective interface definitions, which will undertake persistence operations when invoked to do so. A set of such classes is known as a *JDO implementation*.

JDO implementations are data store-specific. Some work against any JDBC-compliant database. Others may work with only a specific relational database in order to exploit potential optimizations. Still others work with certain object databases, file system formats, or provide integration to specific enterprise applications. In some cases a spread of implementations for different data stores may be grouped together under a single product name.

A company that markets a JDO implementation is known as a *JDO vendor*. A selection of commercial and non-commercial JDO vendors and their JDO implementations is given in Chapter 12. I maintain and regularly update an online list of vendors and implementations on the Ogilvie Partners website, `http://www.OgilviePartners.com`. Another good source of information is `http://www.JDOcentral.com`.

Most JDO implementations are shipped with an enhancement tool. Technically this is unnecessary as the binary compatibility specified in the JDO specification allows any class that correctly implements **PersistenceCapable** (whether by hand or by enhancement) to be manipulated by any compliant JDO implementation. Therefore it should be sufficient to use the reference enhancement tool in all cases. However, each vendor tends to add value to the enhancement process through the use of <extension> tags in the descriptor, and the generation of DDL scripts to define the requisite storage in the target data store. Such scripts are extremely useful, and as a result it is common practice to use the vendor-provided enhancement tool.

3.2   JDO instances

In our simple example (see Chapter 2) we defined a single domain object **BusinessPartner**. This class was then enhanced according to its persistence descriptor. The enhanced class implements the **PersistenceCapable** interface and provides implementations of all the **PersistenceCapable** methods. We then used the enhanced class in our application.

The term *JDO instance* is used to describe any instance of a Java language class which implements the **PersistenceCapable** interface which the implementation is capable of managing. Some implementations, largely dictated by the underlying data store, require storage areas to be explicitly defined for each class before that class can be managed. This is more typical of object-relational mapping implementations (with an underlying relational database) than of object databases.

3.3   JDO environments

JDO is intended for use in two specific architectural spaces. The most straightforward environment is one in which an application directly invokes the services of an implementation. Our simple **BusinessPartner** example from Chapter 2 works in this way. This is the so-called *non-managed environment*.

The second environment is that in which the persistence functions of a persistence manager are invoked by application components running within a J2EE application server. This more complicated environment requires that vendors integrate their JDO implementations with the J2EE transaction and connector architectures. This is the so-called *managed environment*.

3.3.1   Non-managed environment

In the non-managed environment, an application is itself responsible for all interactions with the implementation. This includes configuring the **PersistenceManagerFactory**, obtaining the **PersistenceManager**, demarcating transactions (with appropriate **begin()**, **commit()** and **rollback()** invocations), and all persistence operations on instances. Architecturally this is shown in Figure 3.1.

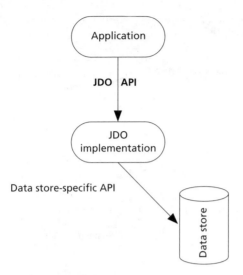

Figure 3.1 The non-managed environment

Applications using JDO in this manner generally configure a factory and obtain a **PersistenceManager** reference from the factory at startup and retain that reference until the application is closed. Heavily multithreaded applications, however, may rely on the pooling characteristics of the persistence manager factory, which maintains a pool of persistence managers. In such cases the application will get a persistence manager from the factory, use it, and then immediately return it to the pool by invoking its **close()** method.

3.3.2   Managed environment

In the managed environment JDO is integrated within a J2EE application server. Application components executing within the application server still invoke the **PersistenceManager** in the usual way. However, they would expect to obtain the **PersistenceManagerFactory** reference from the Java Naming and Directory Interface (JNDI) context of the application server.

All transaction management is coordinated between JDO and the application server. This enables components to exploit the declarative transaction demarcation model provided by J2EE, or to control it manually with bean-managed transactions (BMT) as appropriate. In the managed environment, applications tend to access data stores through JCA, providing maximum flexibility (Figure 3.2). Finally **PersistenceManager**s are pooled to reduce resource usage and facilitate scalability. Thus an application component using the services of a **PersistenceManager** should obtain it from the factory, use it, and close it immediately.

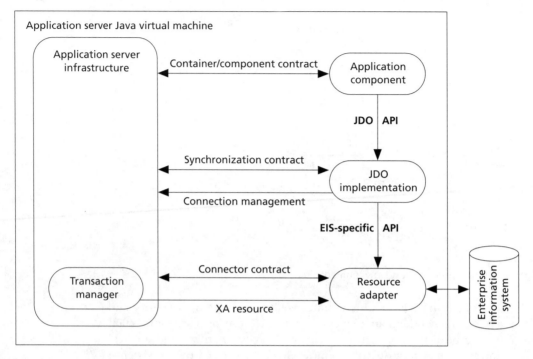

Figure 3.2 Managed environment

3.3.3   Comparison

Table 3.1 illustrates the most important differences between the two environments.

Table 3.1 Non-managed environment vs. managed environment

Non-managed	Managed
Invoked by an application that is outside a J2EE server	Invoked by application components inside a J2EE application server
Application must configure the factory	Application components obtain a pre-configured factory from JNDI
Application must demarcate transactions programmatically	Application components may use declarative (CMT) or programmatic (BMT) transaction demarcation
	Persistence managers are pooled and application components must not hold references to a persistence manager beyond business method invocations

3.4   Persistent vs. transient

JDO instances may be persistent or transient. When an instance is first instantiated via the new operator it is transient.

```
BusinessPartner bp = new BusinessPartner();
```

Such objects are no different to instances of the un-enhanced Java class (except in so far as they can have their state interrogated via the **JDOHelper** class; I'll discuss how in Chapter 6). Transient instances require no supporting persistence infrastructure. By this I mean that a **PersistenceManager** instance does not have to be present, although the JDO interfaces must be available through the **CLASSPATH**. Furthermore they can be serialized and the serialized form de-serialized into an instance of the un-enhanced class (possibly in a different JVM).

Transient objects do not directly reflect the data in the data store and are not ordinarily subject to JDO transactions. Changes made to transient objects will not be reflected in the data store unless the object is subsequently made persistent (or unless this object is part of the closure of objects referenced – at commit time – through the persistent fields of another instance which is made persistent; so-called *persistence by reachability*). Transient objects live only as long as they remain referenced within the JVM and the JVM continues running. If the last reference to a transient instance is discarded, through going out of scope or being set to an alternative value, the instance will be eligible for garbage collection. When the JVM is shut down, any remaining transient objects will be destroyed.

Persistent instances represent persistent data that logically exists in a data store. They have an inherent dependence upon the underlying JDO persistence infrastructure and hold a reference to a *local* (same JVM) **PersistenceManager** instance. Changes made to persistent instances will be reflected in the data store, unless subject to transactional rollback.

Upon serialization, a persistent instance (which directly represents data in a data store) is made transient. The data still exists in the data store, but the now transient instance no longer directly represents that data. Changes subsequently made to the instance will not be reflected in the data store.

OpenAMF

· *optimistic about changes whilst off line.*

· *but time sheet data may arrive.*

3.5   Transactional vs. non-transactional

As well as being transient or persistent, a JDO instance may be transactional or non-transactional.

A transactional instance is one whose persistent and transactional field values will be cached by the JDO implementation when the instance is first involved with a transaction. Upon **commit()** the cached field values will be discarded, but on **rollback()** the cached values will be restored into those fields.

Recall that the persistence descriptor can be used to declare a persistence modifier for each field, identifying that field as persistent, transactional, or none. Persistent fields are synchronized with the data store and are managed transactionally. Transactional fields are not synchronized to the data store but are managed transactionally. Hence the caching of field values and rollback processing applies to fields that are persistent and fields that are transactional.

A non-transactional instance is one that is not subject to transactional rollback. Its persistent and transactional field values are not cached or restored by the JDO implementation.

Most typically a transient instance would be non-transactional and a persistent instance would be transactional.

3.6   Support for transactional/persistent instances

JDO is a very thorough definition of object persistence. However, not all aspects of object persistence apply to all target data stores and applications. Thus, whilst the core features of JDO are *required*, many JDO features are declared to be *optional*. To be branded as JDO-compliant, an implementation must support all of the specification's required features. Vendors are at liberty to choose which optional features they will support in order to best serve their target customer base.

The JDO specification states that support is required for instances which are persistent transactional. This is necessary in order to store data transactionally. Transient non-transactional instances are supported by default, as they are effectively standard Java objects and do not require management by JDO. The other two combinations – transient transactional instances and persistent non-transactional instances – are optional in JDO. If you intend to use them, you must select a JDO implementation that explicitly provides the required support (Table 3.2).

Table 3.2 Support for JDO implementations

	Transient	Persistent
Non-transactional	Unmanaged	Optional
Transactional	Optional	Required

3.6.1   Transient transactional instances

A transient transactional instance is one that does not directly represent data in the data store but whose persistent and transactional field values the JDO Implementation will cache when the instance is first altered within a transaction. Upon `commit()` the cached field values will be discarded, but on `rollback()` the cached values will be restored into the instance's fields.

The *persistent* fields are those that were deemed persistent by the enhancer, whether explicitly (by individual mention in the persistence descriptor) or implicitly (defaults being applied to fields that are not explicitly mentioned). Despite use of the term *persistent*, these values are not actually stored whilst the instance is transient.

Transient transactional instances might be used whenever a non-persistent Java class, being altered within a transaction, must have its state kept in sync with the state of persistent transactional instances being manipulated in the same transaction.

If the JDO implementation in use does not support transient transactional instances, an alternative approach would be to make use of the synchronization capabilities of the transaction object. Such an approach is, however, far more restrictive.

3.6.2 Persistent non-transactional instances

A persistent non-transactional instance is one which exists in the persistence manager's cache but which is not necessarily consistent with the data store. They are used extensively in optimistic transactions.

The transaction interface, synchronization objects, and optimistic transactions are all discussed in Chapter 7.

3.7 JDO identity

Some form of persistent object identity is required for each instance. Applications use this to retrieve specific instances from the data store. Object identity can also be used to maintain uniqueness constraints over the domain objects where this is warranted (e.g. no two orders with the same order number).

In the Java language there are two forms of identity: *equality* and *equivalence*.

Equality is used to determine whether two Java references actually point to the same object in memory, and makes use of the **==** operator. Equality does not take into account the state (attribute values) of an object and cannot traverse JVM processes in distributed applications. As such it is limited in its application.

Equivalence compares two (potentially non-equal) objects to determine whether they both represent the same logical object, and makes use of the **equals()** method. Most applications already employ equality for their own comparisons.

In order to improve the transparency with which JDO can be applied to existing object models, JDO defines its own concept of identity. Both of the above techniques remain unaffected.

The three different types of identity defined by JDO are application identity, datastore identity, and non-durable identity. The desired identity for each instance is specified in the persistence descriptor.

Internally the JDO implementation is responsible for ensuring that there is, at most, one persistent JDO instance associated with a specific data store object per persistence manager. This process is referred to as *uniquing*. The object that encapsulates the identity of an instance is known as its *Object ID*, and the underlying class definition its *Object ID class*.

3.7.1   Datastore identity

Datastore identity is the default identity mechanism. Identity is ascribed to the object when it is made persistent. The manner in which this is achieved, and the nature of the Object ID Class, are internal to the JDO implementation and the data store. However, once the identity is determined it can be used in future requests to retrieve that particular object.

Datastore identity is typically used for dependent objects. For instance, an **Order** may have application identity (see 3.7.2) with a primary key comprised of its order number, and the **OrderLine** objects contained within the order may have datastore identity. Two **OrderLine** objects remain distinct from one another through their internally-assigned identity (Figure 3.3).

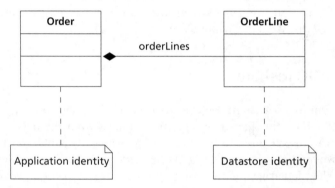

Figure 3.3 Order composition of **OrderLine**

Indeed this is such a common arrangement that it should be considered wherever the UML composition relationship, indicated by the solid black diamond, is used.

3.7.1.1 Example

In our simple example, the **BusinessPartner** class has datastore identity by default. The identity type can be specified explicitly with the **identity-type** attribute of the **<class>** tag, as shown below.

BusinessPartner.jdo

```xml
<?xml version="1.0" encoding="UTF-8" ?>
<!DOCTYPE jdo SYSTEM "file:///jdowork/dtd/jdo.dtd">
<jdo>
    <package name="com.ogilviepartners.jdobook.op">
        <class name="BusinessPartner"
                identity-type="datastore" />
    </package>
</jdo>
```

3.7.2 Application identity

With application identity the application is responsible for the identity of an instance, which is derived from the values of a subset of its persistent fields. The persistence descriptor is used to specify one or more persistent fields that will make up a primary key for the instance, alongside a name for the class that will act as the Object ID class. As such, application identity is often referred to as *primary key identity*, and the Object ID class for such an instance is often referred to as the *primary key class*. The application developer usually writes the primary key class, although some enhancer tools are capable of generating them when enhancing classes that use application identity.

Some restrictions exist regarding the primary key class. The class must be public and implement **java.io.Serializable**. A no-argument constructor and a string constructor must both exist. The **toString()** method must have been overridden so that the string it returns can be used as an argument to the string constructor, in order to create an equivalent instance of the primary key. (The actual format for this string is the developer's choice.) All non-static fields must be primitives, or references to **Serializable** classes, and must be public.

For every field identified in the persistence descriptor as a primary key field there must be a corresponding and identically named field in the primary key class; all of these (and only these) fields must be utilized by the primary key class's **equals()** and **hashcode()** methods for the determination of equivalence. There may be additional fields in the primary key class, but this is unusual as they would play no part in the uniquing process.

The restrictions above enable a JDO primary key class to be interchangeable with an Entity Bean primary key class, simplifying the integration of JDO with the EJB architecture. This integration is covered in detail in Chapter 11.

3.7.2.1 Example

By virtue of its default datastore identity, the uniquing of **BusinessPartner** instances has nothing to do with attribute values. Thus multiple **BusinessPartner** instances may share the same partner number. Each one will have its own unique Object ID assigned by the JDO implementation when it was made persistent.

We can now correct this by assigning application identity to the **BusinessPartner** class with a primary key comprised of its partner number. First of all, I show below the primary key class **BusinessPartnerPK**. I have chosen to put the primary key classes into a **pk** subpackage.

BusinessPartnerPK.java

```java
package com.ogilviepartners.jdobook.op.pk;

public class BusinessPartnerPK
{
    public String partnerNumber;

    public boolean equals(Object that) {
        try {
            return equals((BusinessPartnerPK) that);
        }
        catch (ClassCastException cce) {
            return false;
        }
    }

    public boolean equals(BusinessPartnerPK that) {
        if (that == null) return false;
        if (this == that) return true; // "equality" within
                                       // the JVM
        if (this.partnerNumber == null)
            return that.partnerNumber == null;
        return this.partnerNumber.equals(that.partnerNumber);
    }

    public int hashCode() {
        return partnerNumber.hashCode();
    }

    public BusinessPartnerPK(String arg) {
        this.partnerNumber = arg;
    }

    public BusinessPartnerPK() {
    }

    public String toString() {
        return partnerNumber;
    }
}
```

It is possible for an enhancer tool to generate Object ID classes when the developer has not already written these. I perceive this as a good approach and very rarely hand-write such classes. However, developers should be aware that applications tend to have compile-time dependencies on the primary key classes, and so the enhancement phase must have occurred prior to compiling the application classes.

Here then is the persistence descriptor that configures the application identity for **BusinessPartner**. The persistent fields that are part of the primary key must now be explicitly listed. Any unlisted fields will be made persistent or not according to the defaults mentioned in Chapter 2.

BusinessPartner.jdo

```
<?xml version="1.0" encoding="UTF-8" ?>
<!DOCTYPE jdo SYSTEM "file:///jdowork/dtd/jdo.dtd">
<jdo>
    <package name="com.ogilviepartners.jdobook.op">
        <class name="BusinessPartner"
                identity-type="application"
                objectid-class="com.ogilviepartners/
                .jdobook.op.pk.BusinessPartnerPK">
            <field name="partnerNumber"
                    primary-key="true" />
        </class>
    </package>
</jdo>
```

3.7.3   Non-durable JDO identity

Non-durable JDO identity is used for persistent objects where it is meaningless to try to distinguish one from another. Since the determination and creation of a data store key can be a resource-intensive operation, non-durable JDO identity is most often used to support the rapid persistence of new instances.

An example of this might be the implementation of a JDO instance that represents system alert messages. By using non-durable JDO identity these objects could be persisted very rapidly.

Many alerts, most of these duplicates of previously persisted alerts, may be created over a period of time. The semantics of manipulating instances with non-durable JDO identity are that if one is made persistent then there is one more persistent instance than there was before. Equally, if one is deleted then there is one fewer persistent instance than there was before.

Thus an application may facilitate the selection and deletion of a particular alert containing the message "Sales Transaction Abandoned." Once this operation has committed there will be one fewer alert with the message "Sales Transaction Abandoned" than there was previously. We are not in the least bit concerned with which particular one of potentially many such alerts (all with identical persistent field values) was deleted.

3.7.3.1 Example

Below is a sample persistence descriptor for a hypothetical **AlertMessage** class for which non-durable JDO identity is required:

AlertMessage.jdo

```
<?xml version="1.0" encoding="UTF-8" ?>
<!DOCTYPE jdo SYSTEM "file:///jdowork/dtd/jdo.dtd">
<jdo>
    <package name="com.ogilviepartners.jdobook.op">
      <class name="AlertMessage"
        identity-type="nondurable" />
    </package>
</jdo>
```

3.7.1   JDO identity comparison

Table 3.3 contrasts the three different JDO identity types.

Table 3.3 JDO identity comparison

	Datastore identity	Application identity	Non-durable identity
Is the default	✔	✘	✘
Uniquely identifies persistent instances	✔	✔	✘
Uses an Object ID Class	✔	✔	✘
Developer can provide Object ID class	✘	✔	✘
Identity determined by attribute values	✘	✔	✘
Subverts uniquing process for rapid persistence of transient instances	✘	✘	✔

What's next?

In the next chapter we will examine the lifecycle states and associated state transitions of JDO instances, and illustrate the Java code required to effect each state transition.

Instance lifecycle $\quad$ 4

"Here come the state transition diagrams!"

Robin M. Roos

The Java Data Objects Training Course

T he lifecycle of a JDO instance is governed by a series of states and associated state transitions. During this chapter we examine each of those
states, and the code that an application might use in order to effect
each state transition. By studying these you will learn how to manipulate
instances within your application, and gain a greater understanding of the
underlying technology.

4.1 Determining the state of an instance

The **PersistenceManager** internally knows the state of a JDO instance.
Although it is not possible for us to determine the state of an instance precisely
(some states being invisible to the application), we can get an excellent representation of an instance's state by using the **JDOHelper** class.

Five methods of **JDOHelper** give us information from which an approxima-
tion of an instance's state can be achieved. These are:

- `public static boolean isDeleted(Object pc)`
  Returns **true** if the object has been deleted in the current transaction.

- `public static boolean isDirty(Object pc)`
  Returns **true** if the object has had a persistent field value altered in the
  current transaction.

- `public static boolean isNew(Object pc)`
  Returns **true** if the object has been newly made persistent in the current
  transaction.

- `public static boolean isPersistent(Object pc)`
  Returns **true** if the object is persistent (as opposed to transient).

- `public static boolean isTransactional(Object pc)`
  Returns **true** if the object is transactional (as opposed to non-transactional).

In order to determine the approximate state of an object, I have encapsulated calls to each of these methods in a single method of a new class **StateHelper**.

StateHelper.java

```java
package com.ogilviepartners.jdo;

import javax.jdo.JDOHelper;

public class StateHelper
{
  public static String determineState(Object pc) {
    String s = "";
    s += (JDOHelper.isPersistent(pc) ? "Persistent":"Transient");
    s += (JDOHelper.isDirty(pc)      ? "-Dirty"    :"-Clean");
    s += (JDOHelper.isNew(pc)        ? "-New"      :"");
    s += (JDOHelper.isDeleted(pc)    ? "-Deleted"  :"");

    if (JDOHelper.isPersistent(pc)) {
      s += (JDOHelper.isTransactional(pc)   ? ""
                                      :"-Nontransactional");
    }
    else {
        s += (JDOHelper.isTransactional(pc) ?
                                "-Transactional":"");
    }

    return s;
  }
}
```

When invoked with a JDO instance as its parameter, this method returns strings such as

```
"Persistent-Clean"
"Persistent-New-Deleted"
"Transient-Dirty-Transactional"
```

As you will see, these are very similar to the names of the lifecycle states themselves.

4.2   Required lifecycle states

The JDO specification contains two categories of lifecycle states: those that are required by all compliant JDO implementations, and those that are optional and need be present only if the implementation supports the corresponding optional feature. The following are the lifecycle states required of all implementations.

4.2.1   Transient

Instances instantiated through a developer-written constructor with the **new** operator do not involve the persistence environment and behave like instances of the un-enhanced class. There is no JDO identity associated with a transient instance, and no intermediation on behalf of JDO to fetch or store persistent field values.

Transient instances exhibit no transactional behavior. The class will probably have fields that are persistent or transactional, as per explicit persistence modifiers in the persistence descriptor or the application of default persistence modifiers. However, because the instance is transient, these fields will not have their values cached and rolled back in sync with the persistence manager's transaction.

Persistence by reachability applies if this object is part of the closure of objects referenced through the persistent fields of another instance that is made persistent. In such a case the transient instance would become provisionally persistent (and therefore transactional). If it was still referenced at commit time, it would become persistent.

Method calls on transient instances do not throw any exceptions other than those defined by the developer (and the usual unchecked exceptions which have nothing to do with JDO). This is in contrast to non-transient instances, the methods of which might throw runtime exceptions from the JDO exception hierarchy. These exceptions are covered in detail in Chapter 9.

4.2.2   Persistent-New

This is the state of instances that have been made persistent during the current transaction. During the transition from transient to persistent, the associated persistence manager:

- becomes responsible for implementing state interrogation and further state transitions;
- saves persistent and transactional non-persistent field values for use during rollback;
- assigns a JDO identity to the instance.

4.2.3   Persistent-New-Deleted

JDO instances that have been newly made persistent and subsequently deleted, both within the current transaction, are assigned the state Persistent-New-Deleted.

Attempts to read any persistent fields of the instance will throw a **JDOUserException** unless the persistence-capable class employs application identity, in which case read access to the primary key fields is permitted.

4.2.4   Hollow

JDO instances that represent specific persistent data in the data store, but whose field values have not been read from the data store, are Hollow. Hollow instances have their JDO identity loaded, but not the values of their ordinary (as opposed to primary key) persistent fields. This state provides for the guarantee of uniqueness for transactional instances between transactions.

A JDO Implementation is permitted to effect a legal state transition from Hollow at any time, as if a field had been read. Therefore the Hollow state may not be visible to the application.

4.2.5   Persistent-Clean

JDO instances that represent specific transactional persistent data in the data store and whose values have been read in the current transaction, but not altered, are Persistent-Clean.

If no field values had been read in the current transaction then the instance is more likely to be Hollow.

4.2.6   Persistent-Dirty

JDO instances that represent persistent data that was changed during the current transaction are Persistent-Dirty.

If a field of a Persistent-Clean instance is modified, but the new value equals the old one, the JDO vendor may choose whether to transition to Persistent-Dirty. If no modification was made to any field, the instance will not be transitioned to Persistent-Dirty. If a modification was made to any field which changed that field's value, the instance will be transitioned to Persistent-Dirty.

An instance can be made dirty through the **makeDirty()** method of the **JDOHelper** class. This is useful only when recording changes made to persistent fields of array type, since JDO does not mandate the automatic tracking of changes for array fields. This technique and the **JDOHelper** class are discussed in Chapter 6.

When the transaction is committed or rolled back, the state to which Persistent-Dirty instances transition is dependent upon the setting of the **RetainValues** and **RestoreValues** flags of the transaction. These flags can be set on the **Transaction** object before the transaction has been begun, as long as the implementation provides support for the corresponding optional features.

The **RetainValues** flag indicates whether instances should remain cached after commit. Upon commit, the dirty instance transitions to Hollow if **RetainValues** is **false**, and to Persistent-Nontransactional if **RetainValues** is **true**.

The **RestoreValues** flag indicates whether instances should remain cached after rollback. Upon rollback, the dirty instance transitions to Hollow if **RestoreValues** is **false**, and to Persistent-Nontransactional if **RestoreValues** is **true**.

The state transition diagrams that follow throughout this chapter presume that both flags are **false**.

4.2.7   Persistent-Deleted

JDO instances that represent specific persistent data in the data store, and that have been deleted in the current transaction, are Persistent-Deleted. (Note that if the deleted instance had been newly made persistent in the current transaction, it would instead transition to Persistent-New-Deleted.)

Read access to primary key fields is permitted for an instance in this state, but access to other persistent fields will throw a **JDOUserException**.

On commit, such an instance transitions to Transient, having had its state cleared (persistent fields set back to their default values) and its JDO identity removed.

4.3   Required lifecycle state transitions

Now that we've met the different states we can examine the transitions between them. These will each be illustrated with a code snippet that would effect the transition.

4.3.1   Persisting a transient instance

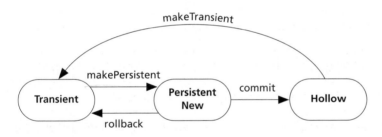

retain values = false

Figure 4.1 Persisting a transient instance

To persist a transient instance, pass it to the **makePersistent()** method of a **PersistenceManager** (Figure 4.1). This is essentially a request to create a new entity in the data store. Where application identity is used this request will fail if the primary key already exists in the datastore. With data store identity the entity will be persisted even if another persistent entity already exists with identical persistent field values, as the JDO identities (created by the implementation when each instance is made persistent) will be different.

Test

```
// assume pm references a PersistenceManager
Transaction t = pm.currentTransaction();
t.begin();
BusinessPartner bp = new BusinessPartner();
pm.makePersistent(bp);
t.commit();
```

— now hollow

4.3.2 Create/delete in one transaction

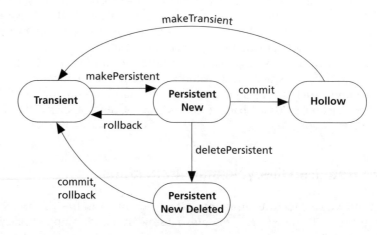

Figure 4.2 Create/delete in one transaction

When an instance is both made persistent and deleted within the same transaction, it transitions to the Persistent-New-Deleted state (Figure 4.2). Upon commit, the Persistent-New-Deleted instance transitions to Transient since the Java object no longer directly represents a persistent entity in the data store.

```
// assume pm references a PersistenceManager
BusinessPartner bp = new BusinessPartner(); // partner
                                             // is Transient
Transaction t = pm.currentTransaction();
t.begin();
pm.makePersistent(bp);    //transition to Persistent-New

// potentially other code, as long as it does not commit the
// current transaction

pm.deletePersistent(bp); // transition to Persistent-
                         // New-Deleted

t.commit();              // transition to Transient
```

4.3.3 Reading field values

When field values of a Hollow instance are first read, the instance transitions to Persistent-Clean. Upon commit, a Persistent-Clean instance transitions to Hollow.

```
// assume pm references a PersistenceManager
// assume c references a BusinessPartner in the Hollow state
```

```
Transaction t = pm.currentTransaction();
t.begin();
c.getName(); // transition to Persistent-Clean
t.commit();
```

4.3.4   Eviction

Please refer to Figure 4.3. Occasionally an application may wish to notify the **PersistenceManager** that it is no longer using a particular instance, in order that the **PersistenceManager** may more efficiently manage its instance cache. This can be done with a call to the **evict()** method. However, it should be noted that this merely gives a hint to the **PersistenceManager**; whether or not any action is taken in response to that hint is implementation-specific.

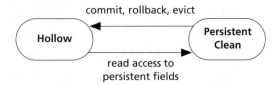

Figure 4.3 Reading field values and evicting instances

Eviction is most commonly used when an application is serially processing a large number of instances, such as when iterating an extent.

```
// assume pm references a PersistenceManager
Transaction t = pm.currentTransaction();
t.begin();
Extent extPartner = pm.getExtent(BusinessPartner.class, false);
Iterator I = extPartner.iterator();
while (i.hasNext()) {
    BusinessPartner bp = (BusinessPartner) i.next();
    // do something useful with bp
    pm.evict(c);
}
extPartner.close(i);
t.commit();
```

Do not use eviction if you will later access persistent field values of the same instance within the same transaction. Doing so would cause the implementation to read the entity from the data store again, with the performance degradation that would imply.

4.3.5   Updating field values

When the field values of an instance are first changed in the current transaction, it transitions to Persistent-Dirty (Figure 4.4).

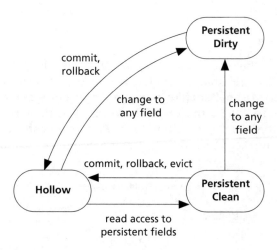

Figure 4.4 Updating field values

In the code example below, the name field is first read, effectively forcing a transition to Persistent-Clean, before the value is changed and the instance transitions to Persistent-Dirty. This is not necessary; it is perfectly legitimate to alter a field without first reading its value in the current transaction. Upon commit, a Persistent-Dirty instance transitions to Hollow.

```
// assume pm references a PersistenceManager
// assume bp references a BusinessPartner in the Hollow state
Transaction t = pm.currentTransaction();
t.begin();
String s = bp.getName(); // transition to Persistent-Clean
bp.setName(s + "!");     // transition to Persistent-Dirty
t.commit();              // transition to Hollow
```

4.3.6   Refreshing field values

When an instance's field values are changed it transitions to Persistent-Dirty. Usually upon commit the changes are synchronized to the data store and the instance transitions to Hollow. However, it is sometimes necessary to reverse the changes made to an instance during the current transaction without rolling back the transaction as a whole. This can be achieved by refreshing the instance. The instance's persistent field values are reset to their values as at the start of the transaction, and the instance transitions back to Persistent-Clean (Figure 4.5).

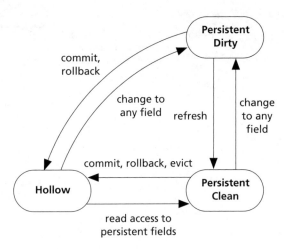

Figure 4.5 Refreshing field values

```
// assume pm references a PersistenceManager
// assume bp references a BusinessPartner in the Hollow or
// Persistent-Clean states
Transaction t = pm.currentTransaction();
t.begin();
String name = bp.getName();
bp.setName(name + "!");     // transition to Persistent-Dirty
pm.refresh(bp);             // transition to Persistent-Clean
t.commit();                 // transition to Hollow
```

4.3.7   Deleting a persistent instance

When an instance which was persistent prior to the current transaction is found and deleted, it transitions to the Persistent-Deleted state (Figure 4.6). Upon commit the deletion will be synchronized with the data store and the instance will transition to Transient.

```
// assume pm references a PersistenceManager
// assume bpId is the JDO Object ID of a BusinessPartner to
// be deleted
Transaction t = pm.currentTransaction();
t.begin();
BusinessPartner bp;
= (BusinessPartner) pm.getObjectById(bpId);
pm.deletePersistent(bp); // transition to Persistent-Deleted
t.commit();              // transition to Transient
```

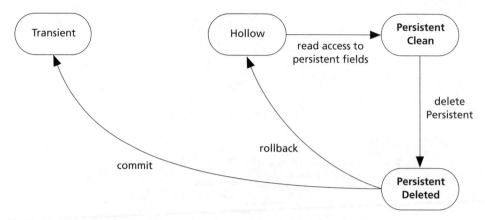

Figure 4.6 Deleting a persistent instance

4.3.8   Deleting a Persistent-Dirty instance

When an instance which was persistent prior to the current transaction is found, altered, and subsequently deleted in one transaction, it transitions from Persistent-Clean to Persistent-Dirty and then to Persistent-Deleted (Figure 4.7).

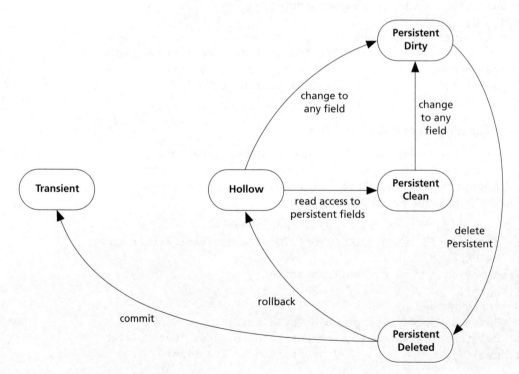

Figure 4.7 Deleting a Persistent-Dirty Instance

Upon commit the deletion will be synchronized with the data store and the instance will transition to Transient.

```
// assume pm references a PersistenceManager
// assume bp references a BusinessPartner in the Hollow or
// Persistent-Clean states
Transaction t = pm.currentTransaction();
t.begin();
String name = bp.getName();  // transition to Persistent-Clean
                             // if it was Hollow
bp.setName(name + "!");      // transition to Persistent-Dirty
pm.deletePersistent(bp);     // transition to Persistent-Deleted
t.commit();                  // transition to Transient
```

4.3.9 Making an instance transient

Despite the fact that the core focus of object persistence is on making transient objects persistent, it is occasionally useful to make a persistent instance transient again (Figure 4.8). This is particularly useful when an instance is being sent to another JVM for some purpose, and occurs implicitly during the serialization process.

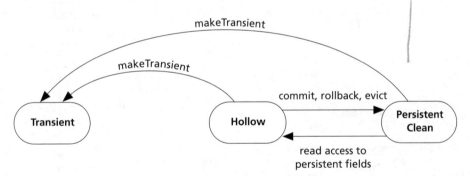

Figure 4.8 Making an instance transient

Note that making an instance transient does not affect the underlying data store entity in any way. Making the instance transient does not delete the data; it merely disassociates the instance from the data store. Any subsequent changes to the instance will not be synchronized with the data store.

```
// assume pm references a PersistenceManager
// assume bp references a BusinessPartner in the Hollow or
// Persistent-Clean states
Transaction t = pm.currentTransaction();
t.begin();
pm.makeTransient(bp);      // transition to Transient
bp.setName("new name");  // this change will not be synchronized
                         // to the data store
```

```
                                    // since the instance is transient,
                                    // not persistent
          t.commit();
```

If the instance were later passed as an argument to **makePersistent()**, the JDO implementation would attempt to create a new data store entity corresponding to the field values of the instance. The attempt to make the transient instance persistent again may result in an exception if application identity is being used and the primary key field values are identical to those of a currently persistent instance.

I mention this because it is a common misconception that a persistent instance can be altered by making it transient (possibly via serialization), altering its field values, and then making it persistent again. This would serve to create a new data store entity and could not update the existing one. Essentially, the instance loses its JDO identity in the transition from any persistent state to transient.

The correct way in which to update a persistent instance is to alter its persistent field values (by making calls on its public methods), and then commit the persistence manager's transaction. The alteration of field values makes the instance Persistent-Dirty, and the commit causes these values to be flushed to the data store.

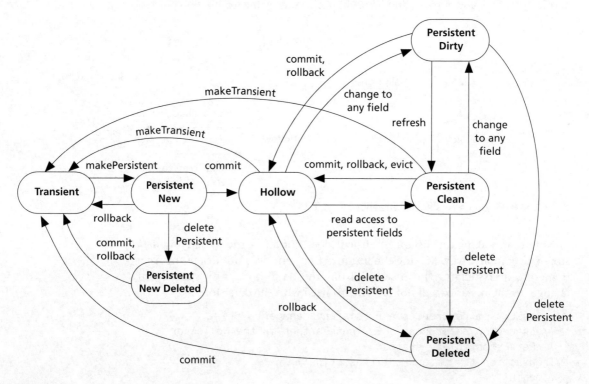

Figure 4.9 All required state transitions

4.3.10 All required state transitions

We have now completed our discussion of those lifecycle state transitions that are required by the JDO specification. Before we discuss the optional transitions, I have included a transition diagram (Figure 4.9) that combines those discussed. Please note that not every possible transition is necessarily represented here.

4.4   Optional lifecycle states

All JDO implementations must support the required states detailed so far. The following optional states, however, are defined in support of various optional features of the specification. Only those JDO vendors providing support for the associated feature will implement these states.

4.4.1   Persistent-Nontransactional

This state is used in the implementation of optimistic transaction management. It is applied to JDO instances that represent specific persistent data in the data store, whose field values are currently loaded but are not necessarily transactionally consistent. It allows persistent instances to be managed as a cache of instances that are updated asynchronously. There is a JDO identity associated with such instances.

4.4.2   Transient-Clean

The states Transient-Clean and Transient-Dirty are used in the implementation of transient transactional instances.

Transient transactional JDO instances, whose persistent and transactional field values have not been changed in the current transaction, are Transient-Clean. (Note that although the persistence-capable class may have "persistent" fields, they will not be synchronized with the data store, as the instance is transient.)

4.4.3   Transient-Dirty

Transient transactional instances whose values have been changed in the current transaction are assigned the state Transient-Dirty.

4.5   Optional lifecycle transitions

The following state transitions involve optional states and apply only to implementations where the associated optional feature is supported.

4.5.1   Optimistic transactions

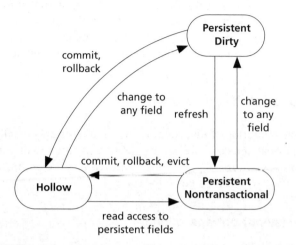

Figure 4.10 Optimistic transactions

Support for optimistic transactions is implemented with the state Persistent-Nontransactional (Figure 4.10). Whereas a Persistent-Clean instance has its state constantly synchronized with the data store, a Persistent-Nontransactional instance may remain unaltered in the persistence manager's cache even though the underlying data entity has been altered.

When optimistic locking is in use, the reading of field values from a Hollow instance causes a transition to Persistent-Nontransactional. Only when a field value is altered (within a transaction) does the transition to Persistent-Dirty occur. At that point the state of the instance is cached for rollback purposes and to verify the optimistic concurrency assumptions when the transaction is later committed.

On commit, if the optimistic concurrency assumptions are correct (i.e. no other transaction has committed changes to the data store entity since the instance became Persistent-Nontransactional), the data is written and the transaction completed. If the concurrency assumptions turn out to be invalid (because the underlying data *has* been changed), a **JDOUserException** is thrown and the transaction rolled back.

```
// assume pm references a PersistenceManager
// assume bp references a BusinessPartner in the Hollow state
Transaction t = pm.currentTransaction();
t.setOptimistic(true);   // the implementation must support
                         // this optional feature
t.begin();
String s = bp.getName(); // transition to Persistent-
                         // Nontransactional
bp.setName(s + "!");     // transition to Persistent-Dirty
```

```
t.commit();              // throws JDOUserException if
                         // optimistic concurrency
                         // assumptions prove to be invalid
```

4.5.2   Persistent access outside transactions

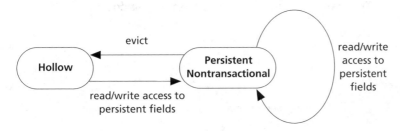

Figure 4.11 Persistent access outside transactions

Support for non-transactional access to persistent instances is optional in the JDO specification (Figure 4.11). If supported, this is once again implemented using the lifecycle state `Persistent-Nontransactional`. As long as there is no transaction active, fields may be read and written non-transactionally.

As soon as a field value is read within a data store transaction, or updated within an optimistic transaction, the instance will become transactional again.

In the example below, a persistent **BusinessPartner** instance, is made nontransactional. It is then altered, firstly outside a transaction and secondly within a transaction. The transaction is subsequently rolled back. The comments in this example in this example illustrate the instance's behavior as it transitions between the appropriate states.

```
// assume pm references a PersistenceManager
// assume bp references a BusinessPartner in the Hollow or
// Persistent-Clean states with the name "Genevieve".
// assume NontransactionalRead and NontrasactionalWrite-enabled
Transaction t = pm.currentTransaction();

pm.makeNontransactional(bp);   // transition to Persistent-
                               // Nontransactional
String name;
name = bp.getName();           // read outside a transaction,
                               // no transition
System.out.println(name);      // prints "Genevieve"
bp.setName("Cathy");           // alter outside transaction,
                               // no transition
```

```
t.begin();
bp.setName("Robin");          // transition to Persistent-
                              // Dirty
t.rollback();
name = bp.getName();
System.out.println(name);     // prints "Cathy"
```

4.5.3   Transactional access to transient instances

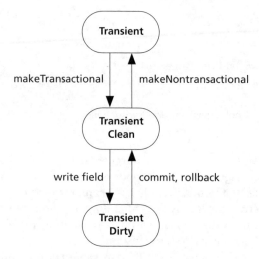

Figure 4.12 Transient transactional instances

Support for transactional access to transient instances is optional in the JDO specification. If supported by the implementation, it involves the optional life-cycle states Transient-Clean and Transient-Dirty (Figure 4.12).

A transient non-transactional instance that is made transactional, transitions to Transient-Clean. (For fun, try reading the previous sentence out loud!) When any field value is altered it transitions to Transient-Dirty, after having had its field values cached before the update was applied.

Upon commit, a Transient-Dirty instance merely transitions to Transient-Clean and the cache of field values is discarded. Upon rollback, a Transient-Dirty instance has its field values restored from the cache and transitions to Transient-Clean. Upon being made non-transactional, a Transient-Clean instance transitions to Transient.

```
// assume pm references a PersistenceManager
BusinessPartner bp = new BusinessPartner ();
// bp is newly instantiated, so Transient
```

```
bp.setName("Robin Roos");
Transaction t = pm.currentTransaction();

t.begin();
pm.makeTransactional(bp);          // transitions to Transient-
                                   // Clean and caches
                                   // field values in case
                                   // of rollback
String name;
name = bp.getName();// read field, no transition
System.out.println(name);          // prints original field
                                   // value: Robin Roos
bp.setName(name + "!");            // alter name, transition
                                   // to Transient-Dirty
System.out.println(bp.getName());  // prints altered field
                                   // value: Robin Roos!
t.rollback();                      // restore values from
                                   // cache and transition
                                   // to Transient-Clean
System.out.println(bp.getName());  // prints original field
                                   // value: Robin Roos
// we've illustrated a Transient Transactional instance, but
// just to complete the
// process let's make the instance Transient
// (but no longer Transactional) again.
pm.makeNontransactional(bp);       // transition to Transient
```

4.6   InstanceCallbacks

The above discussion about the required and optional states and state transitions should have given you a good feel for the way an application invokes the **PersistenceManager** in order to manipulate instances. We will look at this in more detail in Chapter 6. The final topic for this chapter illustrates how instances can be made aware of specific lifecycle events occurring to them, so that the application developer can invoke an appropriate action if required.

InstanceCallbacks is itself an interface containing four method signatures. Classes implementing the interface must provide implementations of the callback methods explicitly – the enhancer will not undertake this task. The JDO implementation will then invoke the callback methods as appropriate. The UML for the **InstanceCallbacks** interface is shown in Figure 4.13.

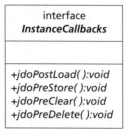

interface
InstanceCallbacks
+jdoPostLoad( ):void
+jdoPreStore( ):void
+jdoPreClear( ):void
+jdoPreDelete( ):void

Figure 4.13 UML for InstanceCallbacks interface

4.6.1   Post load

The post load callback **void jdoPostLoad()** is invoked on the instance after the default fetch group fields have been loaded. If the instance uses application identity then the primary key fields, which must not be part of the default fetch group, will already have had their values loaded.

This method is a suitable place to initialize any non-persistent fields in the instance. However, it should be noted that it is illegal to attempt access to fields other than primary key fields and those in the default fetch group. Additionally, access to other persistent JDO instances is disallowed. If present, this method is not modified during enhancement.

4.6.2   Pre store

The pre store callback **void jdoPreStore()** is invoked immediately before the persistent fields of a persistent instance are synchronized (i.e. written) to the data store. Persistent fields whose values are dependent on other (perhaps non-persistent) fields should have their values assigned here. Access to other persistent JDO instances is allowed.

This method, if present, is modified during enhancement so that alterations made to persistent fields are correctly reflected in the data store.

The **preStore()** method is also a useful place for the validation of data within the instance. Code in this method could throw a **JDOUserException** if the validation failed, and so cause the transaction to rollback.

4.6.3   Pre clear

The pre clear callback **void jdoPreClear()** is invoked immediately before persistent field values are cleared, and occurs during the transition to the Hollow state.

During this method any non-persistent non-transactional fields should have their values reset to appropriate defaults, otherwise such state may be "inherited" by the next data store entity that happens to be represented by that particular instance. Additionally, any references to runtime objects (e.g. threads) should be set to null.

This method, if present, is not modified during enhancement.

4.6.4 Pre delete

The pre delete callback **void jdoPreDelete()** is called immediately before a transition to the Persistent-Deleted or Persistent-New-Deleted states. Access to persistent field values is valid from within this method, but is not valid subsequently.

Pre delete is typically used to implement delete restrict and delete cascade behavior. To implement delete restrict, evaluate the condition under which deletion is disallowed and throw an instance of **JDOUserException** to prevent the deletion from proceeding. When a UML Containment is being modeled, delete cascade is implemented by passing all contained child instances as arguments to a **deletePersistent()** invocation on the persistence manager.

An example is shown below which illustrates both delete restrict and delete cascade functionality.

```
public void jdoPreDelete() {
    System.out.println("joPreDelete called for Order" +
                                        orderNumber);
    if (isDispatched()) {
        System.out.println("Order is Dispatched!");
        throw new JDOUserException("cannot delete order" +
                orderNumber + "as it has been dispatched.");
    }

    // deletion will proceed - delete contained instances

    System.out.println("Deleting OrderLines");
    JDOHelper.getPersistenceManager(this).
                            deletePersistentAll(orderLines);
}
```

The example above is an extract from a class **Order**, which maintains a **Collection** (implemented as a **HashSet**) of **OrderLine**s. The implementation of **jdoPreDelete()** restricts the deletion if the order has been dispatched by testing the value of a boolean property. If the deletion is to proceed, all contained **OrderLine** instances (i.e. the contents of the **orderLines** collection) are also deleted.

To delete the order lines, a reference to a **PersistenceManager** is required. This is obtained through the **JDOHelper**'s **getPersistenceManager(Object pc)**, which returns a reference to the **PersistenceManager** associated with the designated instance. By passing this to the method we obtain a reference to the specific **PersistenceManager** responsible for this instance. The method **deletePersistentAll()** is used to delete an entire collection of instances in one invocation.

What's next?

We've now studied the lifecycle states (required and optional) and the associated state transitions, and have seen code extracts which illustrate how an application can effect these state transitions on instances it is manipulating. We will see further syntactic detail of this in Chapter 6.

In the next chapter we examine the persistent object model implemented by JDO. We specifically cover the notion of first- and second-class objects, showing how the developer can specify this in the persistence descriptor and illustrating how first- and second-class objects interact with each other.

Persistent object model 5

The term *persistent object model* is used to describe the set of rules that constrains the allowable types and configurations of objects managed by a **PersistenceManager** and specifies the ways in which they interact.

JDO has been designed so that domain object models can be persisted without having been specifically designed with persistence in mind. However, it is necessary for you to understand the intricacies of JDO's persistent object model in order to apply the technology appropriately.

5.1 Transparency

Generally it is objects of the domain object model that will be persisted by an application. These objects typically reference each other to the extent that the closure of referenced instances represents the entire contents of the data store. Whilst the application is running, its JVM will contain many transient instances. Most of these will be normal (non persistence-capable) objects. Some, however, will be (or will reference) instances of persistence-capable classes.

Each JDO persistence manager maintains an active cache of instances. As an application navigates a reference from one instance to another that is not in the cache, JDO loads the required instance into the cache

This is illustrated in Figure 5.1. A single JVM process is active in which an application is using JDO. The application has a number of transient object instances. Some of these reference persistent instances currently loaded in the JDO cache. Some transient objects, and some of the cached persistent instances, reference other persistent instances which are not yet instantiated in the cache, but which will be upon demand.

In order that persistent objects may be stored in or retrieved from a given data store, a mapping function exists between the object definitions and the storage. Every implementation must provide a suitable mapping, although the mapping itself is implementation-specific and not standardized by JDO.

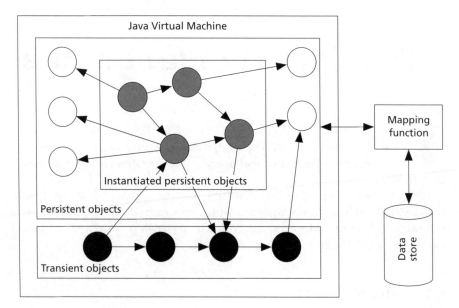

Figure 5.1 Transparency

5.1.2 Transparent persistence

The term *transparent persistence* refers to:

1 The illusion that all persistent instances are in memory and immediately available.

2 The implicit update of dirty persistent instances with the data store upon transaction commit.

3 The automatic mapping of Java types to the native types of the underlying data store.

Transparent persistence

People ascribe various meanings to the phrase *transparent persistence* depending upon their perspective, and there is no definitive list. I asked people for their interpretations in a message posted on JDOcentral.com, and here are some of those that were suggested:

- Automatic caching of a before-image of instance which is changed within a transaction, according to the transaction properties.
- Automatic change-tracking of instances, so they become dirty when they are changed.

- Automatic synchronization of dirty instances with the data store upon commit (so that applications do not have to explicitly save changes).

- Automatic construction of instances in the persistence manager's cache when an application navigates to them over a persistent reference.

- Automatic retrieval of data from the data store when fields not in the default fetch group are accessed.

- Automatic mapping of Java types to the field types of the underlying data store.

- Automatic persistence of transient objects, which are referenced by persistent fields of an object newly made persistent, when the transaction commits.

- This and everything else JDO does to make the database seem to disappear: the application can primarily operate on instances in memory and traverse the object model without any concern for the database, yet it is still there and being accessed "under the covers."

Thanks to David Ezzio, Keiron McCammon, Heiko Bobzin, and David Jordan who contributed to this thread at JDOcentral.com.

5.2   JDO instances

JDO instances may have persistent and non-persistent fields. The persistence descriptor dictates whether or not specific fields are persistent. By default, any fields declared to be of supported or persistence-capable types and not **static**, **final** or **transient** are made persistent. However, this can be set explicitly on a field-by-field basis.

Non-persistent fields are not directly managed by the JDO persistence infrastructure, and there are no restrictions as to the specific Java types that are permissible for such fields.

Persistent fields are managed by JDO. All Java modifiers are supported, i.e. persistent fields may be any valid combination of **private**, **public**, **protected**, package/friendly, **static**, **transient**, **abstract**, **final**, **synchronized**, and **volatile**. In order to facilitate this management there are various restrictions that apply to the permissible Java types for such fields. Some of these restrictions depend on optional features support by your chosen implementation.

JDO differentiates between those classes that, through enhancement or by hand-coding, implement the **PersistenceCapable** interface and those that do not. Most of the domain objects you write will implement **PersistenceCapable**. Most of your application classes will not, as these tend to represent processing to be undertaken whilst the application is running, instead of persistent state.

Most system classes (e.g. packages `java.lang`, `java.io` and `java.net`) represent aspects of the runtime environment (e.g. threads, I/O streams and network sockets) that cannot be persisted. Such runtime context would not be valid at an arbitrary later point in time when the objects were retrieved from the data store.

However, some standard Java classes, such as those that represent large numbers, locale information, and collections of other objects, do warrant persistence. The JDO specification dictates a set of standard classes for which persistence must be supported by all compliant implementations. Beyond that list, support for other standard Java classes is optional in the specification. Thus it is important to note that, although the `Collection` interface must be supported by an implementation, not every concrete `Collection` class is necessarily supported. Indeed, the only concrete `Collection` class that JDO requires all implementations to support is `HashSet`.

5.3   First- and second-class objects

JDO divides instances into first-class and second-class objects. There are specific differences between the operation of shared instances when those instances are first or second class, and the developer must appreciate these differences.

First-class objects are instances of `PersistenceCapable` classes, which have a JDO identity and therefore support uniquing in the `PersistenceManager`'s cache. Recall that uniquing is the process by which the `PersistenceManager` ensures that only one cached persistent instance of a particular `PersistenceCapable` class exists with a given identity.

When field values of a first-class object are altered, that object is transitioned to an appropriate dirty state (e.g. from Hollow or Persistent-Clean to Persistent-Dirty). A first-class object may usefully be referenced by multiple other first-class objects (e.g. a single Customer could be referenced by multiple Order objects).

A second-class object is an instance of a `PersistenceCapable` class or, in the case of standard Java classes, an instance of a class which does not implement `PersistenceCapable` but for which specific persistence support has been provided by the implementation.

Second-class objects do not have a JDO identity and therefore do not support uniquing. They are only ever stored as part of a first-class object. When a second-class object is altered it does not itself assume a dirty state. Instead it conveys the fact that it has changed to its owning first-class object, which becomes dirty.

To see how this works, let's consider the UML composition between the `Order` and `OrderLine` classes as shown on Figure 5.2.

Figure 5.2 Order composition of OrderLine

Let us implement the composition using the concrete **Collection** class **HashSet**. Thus the **Order** class would contain a line of code similar to:

```
private Collection orderLines;
```

At some point, when a new Order is instantiated (i.e. in the Order constructor), we would expect to see

```
orderLines = new HashSet();
```

The persistence descriptor for the **Order** class will annotate the **orderLines** field as a persistent field that is a collection of **OrderLine** objects. Below is an extract from the persistence descriptor to this effect:

```
<field name="orderLines" default-fetch-group="true">
    <collection element-type=
    "com.ogilviepartners.jdobook. op.OrderLine" />
</field>
```

Facilities would exist by which **OrderLine** objects could be instantiated and added to the **orderLines** collection, but these ordinary Java methods are not shown here.

In terms of first- and second-class objects, the **Order** and **OrderLine** classes would be enhanced to be **PersistenceCapable**. These are first-class objects (more on why later). The instance of **HashSet** is, at this point, an ordinary (transient) instance of an un-enhanced standard Java class.

When the Order object is made persistent, the implementation will detect that the **orderLines** field references an instance of **HashSet**. In order to persist the contents of the **HashSet** a new instance will be created of a class that has all the functionality of a **HashSet** but is persistable. Furthermore this new class has been specifically implemented so that it will notify its owning first-class object if the collection content is altered.

We now have a situation where the JDO cache contains the Order object, now persistent, a persistent **HashSet** (not the original **HashSet** instance but an instance of a vendor-supplied persistence-capable **HashSet**), and potentially a number of **OrderLine** objects. Recall that through *persistence by reachability*, when a **PersistenceCapable** object is made persistent, the entire graph of **PersistenceCapable** objects reachable from that one instance is made persistent.

The persistent **HashSet** is a second-class object. This means that it has no JDO identity of its own. We may search for an **Order** by its identity and, if appropriate, we might search for an **OrderLine** by its identity. However, the **HashSet** which, although an object, represents a field of the **Order**, is not something we would wish to search for. Since it has no identity, the persistent **HashSet** does not support *uniquing*. Thus two distinct Order objects could have identical collections of **OrderLine**s without this causing a problem. Again, since the **HashSet** object is merely representative of a single field of the Order, this is appropriate.

5.3.1   Visibility of changes

The final thing to note is that the original transient **HashSet** may still exist in memory but is no longer referenced by the now-persistent **Order** object. If the application retained its own references to the **HashSet**, alterations to its contents would not be reflected in the JDO cache and subsequently in the data store. This is referred to as the second-class object "losing its Java identity," typically upon commit of the transaction.

The most significant difference between first- and second-class objects is the visibility of changes made to shared objects. Naturally second-class objects are intended for use in situations where they are not shared, but are associated with a single first-class object. However, to illustrate the loss of identity, consider the following examples with reference to Figure 5.3.

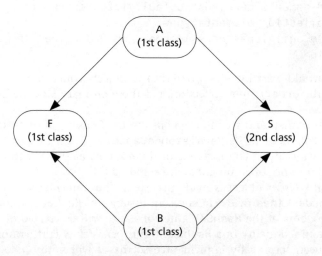

Figure 5.3 Visibility of changes

If a first-class object F is shared between (i.e. referenced by) two transient **PersistenceCapable** classes A and B, which are then made persistent, changes subsequently made to F (which is now persistent thanks to *persistence by reachability*) will be seen by both A and B.

On the other hand, presume that a second-class **HashSet** S is shared between (i.e. referenced by) two transient **PersistenceCapable** classes A and B, which are then made persistent. As part of the commit process two new second-class instances will be instantiated to represent the **HashSet**. In the JDO cache, each of the first-class objects will have a reference to its own second-class instance. Changes subsequently made to S will not be seen by either A or B. Furthermore, changes made to the persistence-capable **HashSet** referenced by A would not be seen in the persistence-capable **HashSet** referenced by B, and vice versa.

5.3.2   PersistenceCapable classes as second-class objects

I mentioned earlier in this chapter that persistence-capable classes, although usually first-class objects, could also be second-class objects. This is decided by the persistence descriptor of the owning first-class object. For the purpose of illustrating this point, consider that the **BusinessPartner** class contains a reference to an **Address** object. Figure 5.4 is the UML class diagram illustrating this, and a sample persistence descriptor. Since the persistence descriptor describes more than one persistence-capable class it is named after the package.

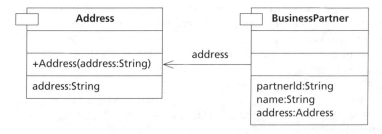

Figure 5.4 UML for BusinessPartner references Address

op.jdo

```
<jdo>
  <package name="com.ogilviepartners.jdobook.op">
    <class name="Address" />
    <class name="BusinessPartner">
      <field name="address"
             embedded="true" />
  </class>
  </package>
</jdo>
```

The persistence descriptor specifies that the **Address** is an embedded object within the **BusinessPartner**. As a result the address of a **BusinessPartner** will be persisted as a second-class object; it will have no JDO identity of its own and address changes will be conveyed to the **BusinessPartner**, which will assume the dirty state.

Consider now the following code extracts:

```
// assume pm references a PersistenceManager instance
Address a = new Address("Milton Keynes, United Kingdom");
pm.makePersistent(a);
```

In the first extract, an **Address** object is constructed and persisted. This will be persisted as a first-class object. It has its own (datastore) identity and when altered itself becomes dirty.

```
// assume pm references a PersistenceManager instance
BusinessPartner bp = new BusinessPartner();
Address a = new Address("London, United Kingdom");
bp.setAddress(a);
pm.makePersistent(bp);
```

In the second extract, the address is persisted only because it is referenced by the **BusinessPartner**. Since the reference is stated in the persistence descriptor to be embedded, **Address** will be persisted as a second-class object (with no JDO identity of its own, and conveying changes to the **BusinessPartner** object which will assume the dirty state).

Thus it is possible to have a single class (in this case **Address**) of which some persistent instances are first-class and some persistent instances are second-class. The judicious definition of instances as second-class objects allows significant optimization to be performed by the implementation. Second-class objects do not have an Object ID so the cost (in performance terms) of establishing unique IDs is avoided. They may be stored in the same data store entity as the fields of the owning first-class object (specifically where one-to-one relationships exist), thus reducing the associated data store interaction when instances are fetched and stored.

> ### Should all dependent objects be second class?
>
> I define dependent objects as those which cannot exist for longer than the owning object, and which cannot be shared between multiple owning objects. They are typically referenced in one of two ways: singleton reference from the owning object, or a UML composition relationship implemented with a Collection class.
>
> Dependent objects are certainly candidates for embedded objects, but can this be applied as a rule? The answer here is most definitely "no."
>
> *Cost*
>
> Second-class objects do not have a JDO identity, and therefore they cannot be independently retrieved from the persistence manager by Object ID. Instead the owning parent must be obtained and its persistent fields navigated to reach the second-class object.
>
> This issue comes down to a design choice as to whether Object IDs are desirable for the dependent objects.

5.4   "Third-class" objects – arrays

The JDO specification does not use the term "third-class," but I have coined it here to describe array support in JDO. Support for array objects is not required in JDO, it is an optional feature. Where arrays are supported by an implementation, the change tracking feature, by which second-class objects notify their owning first-class objects of changes, is itself optional. Thus, although a particular vendor may provide an array implementation that does fulfill the change tracking semantics of second-class objects, this behavior should not be relied upon. Portable applications that make use of array persistence must implement functionality by which changes to the array contents is reflected by explicitly making the owning first-class object dirty. This can be achieved by calling the `makeDirty(Object pc)` method of the **JDOHelper** class.

5.5   Type restrictions for persistent fields

The XML Document Type Definition (DTD) for the persistence descriptor allows individual fields of a persistence-capable class to be marked as **persistent**, **transactional**, or **none**. Fields that are persistent are by default transactional as well.

5.5.1   Non-persistent non-transactional fields

For non-persistent non-transactional fields there are no type restrictions, and such fields in a persistence-capable class may be of any allowable Java type. JDO does not manage the values of such fields in any way.

5.5.2   Transactional non-persistent fields

For non-persistent but transactional fields, there are once again no type restrictions. JDO will manage these fields' values only in so far as they are cached at the beginning of a transaction, and the cached values restored on transaction rollback.

5.5.3   Persistent fields

In the remainder of this section we discuss the allowable Java types for persistent fields.

5.5.3.1 Primitive types

All Java primitive types are supported. The Java primitives are: **boolean**, **byte**, **short**, **int**, **long**, **char**, **float**, and **double**.

5.5.3.2 Immutable object class types

Immutable classes are those whose objects encapsulate values that cannot be altered after instantiation. All implementations support the following immutable class types as persistent fields:

Package java.lang:
  `Boolean`, `Character`, `Byte`, `Short`, `Integer`, `Long`, `Float`, `Double`, `String`

Package java.util:
  `Locale`

Package java.math:
  `BigDecimal`, `BigInteger`

Although support for these class types is required, the implementation may choose to support them as first- or second-class objects. Portable applications should not rely upon a particular implementation's choices. Thus you should not habitually rely upon different persistent fields referencing the same immutable object.

5.5.3.3 Mutable object class types

Support for the following mutable object classes as types for persistent fields is required of all JDO implementations:

Package java.util:
  `Date`, `HashSet`

Support for the following mutable object classes is optional:

Package java.util:
  `ArrayList`, `HashMap`, `Hashtable`, `LinkedList`, `TreeMap`, `TreeSet`, `Vector`

Once again, implementations may choose whether support for these class types is to be provided as first-class or second-class objects. Note that **HashSet** is the only **Collection** class for which support can be guaranteed across all implementations. Support for the other common collections (**ArrayList**, **Vector** and **HashMap**) is, however, widespread across implementations. For details of this support refer to Table 12.1 (page 196).

What about the other concrete Collections?

To be JDO compliant an implementation must support the Collection and Set interfaces and the **HashSet** class.

However, as Table 12.1 illustrates, there is widespread support for the other Collection interfaces and classes, specifically the **List**, **ArrayList**, **Vector**, **Hashtable** and **TreeSet**.

The required set of Collections was limited to more easily facilitate the application of JDO, and the porting of JDO-compliant applications, to embedded environments using J2ME, where the Java 2 Collections hierarchy is not present.

5.5.3.4 PersistenceCapable class types

All implementations must support persistent fields of types that are themselves **PersistenceCapable** classes. Support must be provided as first-class objects. Support for these types as second-class objects, as per the embedded attribute in the persistence descriptor, is optional, with implementations at liberty to store as first-class objects instead.

Applications using second-class persistence-capable types, with embedded= "true," should not rely on the second-class treatment of such objects.

Can I subclass the concrete Collections?

Let's discuss this with reference to **HashSet**, although the discussion also applies to the other concrete Collections.

In JDO, if you persist an instance which references a **HashSet** object, then the implementation is at liberty to substitute its own persistence-capable subclass of **HashSet** for use whenever you access that particular field. We will refer to this class as **VendorHashSet**.

Now presume that you have subclassed **HashSet** to create **MyHashSet** and added specific functionality to that class. You now persist a transient instance that references an instance of **MyHashSet**. Since your class is an "instance of" **HashSet**, the implementation *might* substitute it with an instance of **VendorHashSet**, in which case your added functionality would no longer apply to that field.

To get around the issue, you could enhance **MyHashSet** so that it becomes persistence-capable in its own right. Fields defined as type **MyHashSet** (and not just **HashSet**) should now be persisted correctly. However, it is evident that an element of transparency has been lost, as such fields must be defined as the concrete class type instead of the interface type.

5.5.3.5 Example – BusinessPartner references Customer

Simplistic object models, dealing with the order processing domain, might model customers as representing some or other entity that places orders, and ascribe to the Customer object attributes such as Name, Address, etc. Such a design is illustrated in Figure 5.5.

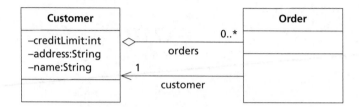

Figure 5.5 Inflexible design – Customer aggregates Order

Unfortunately this approach has many limitations. How do we model a supplier, which also has a Name and Address but which does not place Orders? How do we cope with a supplier that is also a customer? The solution to these problems lies in making Customer and Supplier roles, which are played by a **BusinessPartner**. Thus a single business partner may be a customer and/or a supplier. The **BusinessPartner** provides the central class where common features, such as Name and Address, are modeled.

To illustrate attributes that reference persistence-capable classes we will introduce a Customer role into our object model. The UML is shown in Figure 5.6.

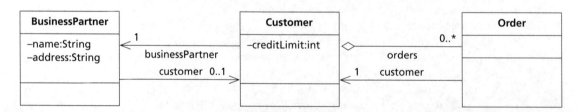

Figure 5.6 Customer is now a role played by a BusinessPartner

Every **BusinessPartner** references zero or one **Customer** objects. Each Customer in return holds a reference (cardinality: exactly one) to its **BusinessPartner**. These are dependent objects, in that the life of the **Customer** is entirely constrained by the life of the **BusinessPartner** to which it relates. Specific attribution that pertains only to the customer role of the **BusinessPartner** is ascribed to the **Customer** class, e.g. credit limit.

In order to complete the picture, **BusinessPartner** is the factory for creating **Customer** objects through a **makeCustomer()** method. The complete UML notation for these classes is shown in Figure 5.7.

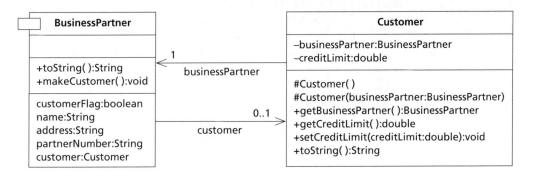

Figure 5.7 Completed UML for BusinessPartner and Customer role

Here is the source code for the **Customer** object. There is nothing unusual here – just standard Java methods with no JDO specifics whatsoever.

Customer.java

```java
package com.ogilviepartners.jdobook.op;

public class Customer
{
    private BusinessPartner businessPartner;
    private double creditLimit;

    protected Customer() {
    }

    protected Customer(BusinessPartner businessPartner) {
        this.businessPartner = businessPartner;
    }

    public BusinessPartner getBusinessPartner() {
        return businessPartner;
    }

    public double getCreditLimit() {
        return creditLimit;
    }

    public void setCreditLimit(double creditLimit) {
        this.creditLimit = creditLimit;
    }
```

```
public String toString() {
        return "Customer (partnerId=" +
        businessPartner.getPartnerNumber() +
            "partnerName=" + businessPartner.getName() + ")";
    }
}
```

Here then is the **BusinessPartner** source code. We see that **BusinessPartner** holds a reference to **Customer** (the reference is the attribute "customer") and that in its **makeCustomer()** method the **BusinessPartner** constructs a **Customer** object and stores its reference. Once again there is nothing JDO-specific.

BusinessPartner.java

```
package com.ogilviepartners.jdobook.op;

public abstract class BusinessPartner {

    protected String name;
    protected String partnerNumber;
    protected String address;
    protected boolean customerFlag;
    protected Customer customer;

    public String toString() {
            return "BusinessPartner (number=" + partnerNumber
            + "name=" + name +
                "address=" + address + "customerFlag=" +
                getCustomerFlag() + ")";
    }
    public boolean getCustomerFlag() {
            return customerFlag;
    }

    public void setName(String name) {
            this.name = name;
    }


    public String getName() {
            return name;
    }

    public void setAddress(String address) {
            this.address = address;
    }
```

```
    public String getAddress() {
            return address;
    }

    public void setPartnerNumber(String partnerNumber) {
            this.partnerNumber = partnerNumber;
    }

    public String getPartnerNumber() {
            return partnerNumber;
    }

    public Customer getCustomer() {
            return customer;
    }

    public void makeCustomer() {
            if (customer == null) customer = new Customer(this);
            if (!customerFlag) customerFlag = true;
    }
}
```

In order to make this object model persistence-capable we write the appropriate persistence descriptor and enhance the classes. All we need to do is make sure that both **BusinessPartner** and **Customer** are enhanced to become persistence-capable. We do not have to declare the reference between them to JDO in any way.

op.jdo

```
<jdo>
  <package name="com.ogilviepartners.jdobook.op">
     <class name="BusinessPartner" />
     <class name="Customer" />
  </package>
</jdo>
```

Once the classes have been enhanced the object graph can be persisted through JDO. Here is an extract from an application that works with these two objects illustrating their persistence.

```
JDOBootstrap bootstrap;
PersistenceManagerFactory pmf;
PersistenceManager pm;
BusinessPartner bp;
Transaction t;
Object oid;
```

```
// initialize everything
bootstrap = new JDOBootstrap();
pmf = bootstrap.getPersistenceManagerFactory();
pm = pmf.getPersistenceManager();
t = pm.currentTransaction();

// create a new (therefore transient) BusinessPartner
bp = new BusinessPartner();
bp.setName("Ogilvie Partners");

// persist the BusinessPartner and get its Object ID
t.begin();
pm.makePersistent(bp);
oid = pm.getObjectId(bp);
System.out.println("Is bp a Customer?" +
    bp.getCustomerFlag());
t.commit();

// make the BusinessPartner a Customer
t.begin();
bp.makeCustomer();
t.commit(); // no need to "save" bp - that's part of
            // transparent persistence

bp = null;

// retrieve the BusinessPartner by Object ID and see that it
// is a Customer
t.begin();
bp = (BusinessPartner) pm.getObjectById(oid);
System.out.println("Is bp a Customer?" +
    bp.getCustomerFlag());
t.commit();
```

a number of discrete transactions w/ one pm [handwritten annotation]

5.5.3.6 Object class type

All implementations are required to support persistent fields of type **Object**. However, the treatment of these as first- or second-class objects is an implementation choice. Most implementations will restrict the set of types that can be stored in such fields (e.g. restriction to only persistence-capable types for which storage has been defined in the data store). In such cases, a **ClassCastException** will be thrown for an invalid type assignment.

5.5.3.7 Example – BusinessPartner references Customer through Object reference

We can illustrate the use of object class type for persistent fields very simply. To do this we alter the **BusinessPartner** class so that its **Customer** reference is in fact defined to be an **Object** reference. So the declaration

```
protected Customer customer;
```

is replaced by

```
protected Object customer;
```

A few (Customer) typecasts must be added wherever methods of the Customer class were to be invoked. The developer should beware of **ClassCastException**s should incompatible (or compatible but non persistence-capable) objects be assigned to the reference. However, since this is a runtime (un-checked) exception I have not caught it here.

```
public Customer getCustomer() {
      return (Customer) customer;
}
```

The persistence descriptor remains unaltered.

Use of **Object** references in this manner is not something that I would recommend when the actual type of the reference is known (**Customer** in this case). It is presented here to illustrate JDO's capability to operate across generic **Object** references when required to do so.

5.5.3.8 Collection interface types

All implementations are required to support persistent fields of the following interface types:

Package java.util:

Collection, **Set**.

implementations may optionally support the following interface types:

Package java.util:

Map, **List**

This is shown in Figure 5.8, which provides a simplified class diagram for the Java 2 Collections (all classes shown belong to the java.util package).

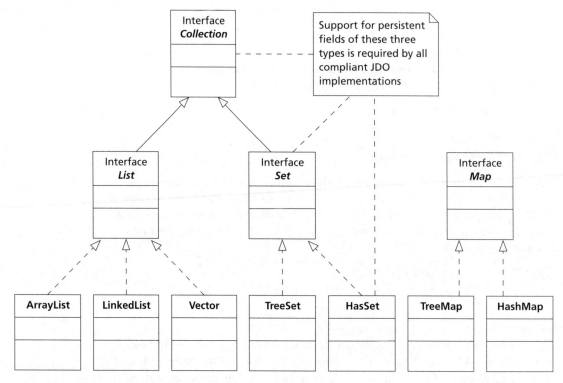

Figure 5.8 Simplified UML class diagram for the Java 2 Collections

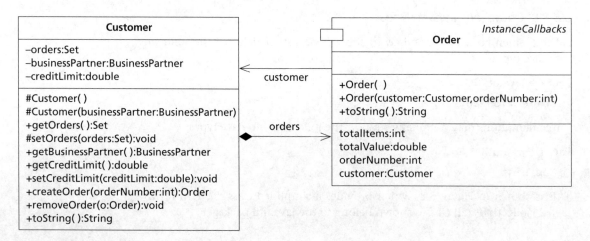

Figure 5.9 UML for Customer aggregates Order

5.5.3.9 Example – Customer references Order

To illustrate persistent fields of **Collection** type we will implement the notion that customers manage collections of orders. The **Order** class is not very complicated; for now it will merely encapsulate an order number, number of items, and order value (Figure 5.9).

Here is the source code for our simple **Order** class:

Order.java

```java
package com.ogilviepartners.jdobook.op;

public class Order {
    private int orderNumber;
    private int totalItems;
    private double totalValue;
    private Customer customer;

    public Order() {
    }

    public int getTotalItems(){
        return totalItems;
    }

    public void setTotalItems(int totalItems){
        this.totalItems = totalItems;
    }

    public double getTotalValue() {
        return totalValue;
    }

    public Order(Customer customer, int orderNumber) {
        this.customer = customer;
        this.orderNumber = orderNumber;
    }

    public int getOrderNumber() {
        return orderNumber;
    }

    public String toString() {
        return "Order (number=" + orderNumber + ")";
    }
```

```
        public Customer getCustomer() {
            return customer;
        }
    }
```

The customer class now has an attribute of type **Collection** called "orders."
When the **Customer** is instantiated by a developer using the
Customer(BusinessPartner bp) constructor, the **Collection** is initialized to
be a new **HashSet**. The no-argument constructor, which will be used by the JDO
implementation when introducing new Customer instances to the cache, does
not initialize the orders collection. This is because the implementation will
retrieve the appropriate collection from the data store.

Customer.java

```
package com.ogilviepartners.jdobook.op;

import java.util.HashSet;
import java.util.Set;
import java.util.Collections;

public class Customer
{
    private Set orders;
    private BusinessPartner businessPartner;
    private double creditLimit;

    protected Customer() {
    }

    protected Customer(BusinessPartner businessPartner) {
        this.businessPartner = businessPartner;
        orders = new HashSet();
    }

    public Iterator orders() {
        // return an iterator of an unmodifiable collection
        // of orders to maintain encapsulation
        return getOrders().iterator();
    }

    public Set getOrders() {
        // return an unmodifiable collection of orders to
        // maintain encapsulation
        return Collections.unmodifiableSet(orders);
```

```
    }

    public BusinessPartner getBusinessPartner() {
        return businessPartner;
    }

    public double getCreditLimit() {
        return creditLimit;
    }

    public void setCreditLimit(double creditLimit) {
        this.creditLimit = creditLimit;
    }

    public Order createOrder(int orderNumber) {
        Order o = new Order(this, orderNumber);
        orders.add(o);
        return o;
    }

    public void removeOrder(Order o) {
        orders.remove(o);
    }

    public String toString() {
        return "Customer (partnerId=" +
                businessPartner.getPartnerNumber() +
                "partnerName=" + businessPartner.getName() + ")";
    }
}
```

[handwritten margin note: Cf. create Schedule(project) in Diary]

New orders may be added to the collection by invoking the **makeOrder(int orderNum)** method. An **Iterator** of orders is obtained by calling the **orders()** method. The actual collection is entirely encapsulated within the **Customer** class. Many developers try to achieve this, but unwittingly break encapsulation rules by providing a public method that returns a reference to the actual collection. That reference could be used by an application to directly manipulate the supposedly encapsulated data. Here deliberately construct an un-modifiable **Set**, which is then exposed. Thus, even attempts to execute **remove()** methods on the returned **Set** or its **Iterator** will not affect the underlying collection.

Notice that I have implemented the orders collection using **HashSet**, the only concrete **Collection** class for which support is required by all compliant implementations. If your domain object model involves **ArrayList**, **Vector** or other **Collection** implementations, you should establish that your vendor supports these classes explicitly.

The persistence descriptor must now explicitly identify those fields that will hold collections of persistence-capable objects. Additionally, since collections in Java are not typed (they hold **Object**s, not specifically **Order**s or some other designated class), the persistence descriptor specifies the name of the class type, instances of which will comprise the collection.

op.jdo

```
<jdo>
  <package name="com.ogilviepartners.jdobook.op">
    <class name="Customer" identity-type ="datastore">
      <field name="orders" default-fetch-group="true">
        <collection element-type =
        "com.ogilviepartners.jdobook.op.Order"/>
      </field>
    </class>

    <class name="Order"
       identity-type="application"
       objectid-class=
       "com.ogilviepartners.jdobook.op.pk.OrderPK">
    </class>
  </package>
</jdo>
```

In this case the objects held in the orders collection are all instances of the **Order** class. However, if warranted by the domain object model, such collections could contain objects spanning an inheritance hierarchy or an implementation hierarchy. For inheritance hierarchies, the type ascribed to the collection would be the common superclass. For implementation hierarchies, the type ascribed to the collection would be the common interface.

Here is a simple application that illustrates persistence of the collection.

```
JDOBootstrap bootstrap;
PersistenceManagerFactory pmf;
PersistenceManager pm;
Customer c;
Transaction t;
Object oid;

// initialize everything
bootstrap = new JDOBootstrap();
pmf = bootstrap.getPersistenceManagerFactory();
pm = pmf.getPersistenceManager();
t = pm.currentTransaction();
```

```
// create a new (transient) BusinessPartner, make it a
// Customer and add 2 Orders
BusinessPartner bp = new BusinessPartner();
bp.setName("Ogilvie Partners");
bp.makeCustomer();
Customer c = bp.getCustomer();
c.createOrder(1);
c.createOrder(2);

// persist the current object graph
t.begin();
pm.makePersistent(bp);
oid = pm.getObjectId(bp);
t.commit();

// in a separate transaction, add another Order
t.begin();
c.createOrder(3);
t.commit();

bp = null;

// find the BusinessPartner by Object ID and print its Orders.
t.begin();
bp = (BusinessPartner) pm.getObjectById(oid);
Iterator i = bp.getCustomer().orders();
while (i.hasNext()) {
    System.out.println(i.next());
}
t.commit();
```

5.5.3.10 *Other (non-Collection) interface types*

All implementations will support persistent fields of all non-Collection interface types. implementations may restrict the set of allowable objects that can be assigned to persistent fields of such types, and will throw a **ClassCastException** as appropriate. Typically the implementation will only support the assignment of objects that implement the interface type as well as implementing **PersistenceCapable** and for which appropriate storage has been defined (if appropriate).

5.5.3.11 Example – OrderLine references SellableItem interface

An order needs products that can be ordered. This is most simplistically achieved by introducing an **OrderLine** class and a **Product** class. Each order is composed of zero or more **OrderLine** objects, and each **OrderLine** object references a specific product that is being ordered. Such a design is illustrated in Figure 5.10.

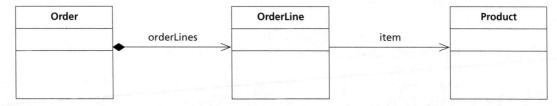

Figure 5.10 OrderLine references Product directly

Such a design is too rigid for most real-world domains. What happens when new items are added to the catalog which aren't exactly products but which must be orderable? The simple solution of subclassing **Product** is not usually sufficient. A more flexible design would be to introduce an interface describing all things that are sellable, and the **OrderLine** object should reference this interface. **Product** is altered to implement this interface. Subsequently, new things can be made orderable without requiring them to be subclasses of **Product**.

In the UML diagram in Figure 5.11 I have introduced a new interface, **SellableItem**. **Product** implements this interface, as does a new class **ServiceContract** (also orderable, but not strictly a physical product). Finally **OrderLine** holds a reference to the **SellableItem** interface, instead of the **Product** class.

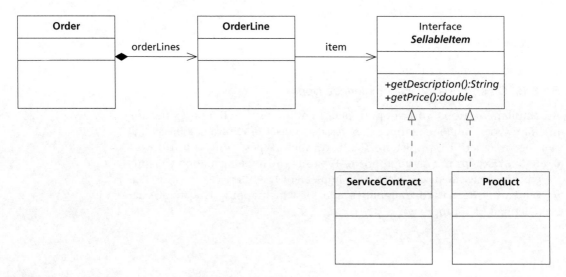

Figure 5.11 OrderLine references SellableItem interface

Here is one final design note. Experienced designers, particularly those well versed in the work on UML modeling of Peter Coad and his colleagues [*Java Modeling in Color with UML* (Coad et al., 1999)], will notice that **OrderLine**, itself a moment-interval, should not ordinarily hold a direct reference to **Product**, but rather to a role played by **Product** called **ProductInSale**. Such a design would be significantly more flexible than that described above. However, since this book is on the topic of JDO and not on UML design, I have chosen to keep the domain model only just complex enough to illustrate the various capabilities of JDO.

Further reading on object modeling

If you enjoy reading about good design practices in a bid to improve your object modeling skills, I would recommend two further books.

Firstly, *Java Design* (Coad et al., 1999) gives a thorough grounding in the design principles involved in common Java application tasks. Secondly, *Streamlined Object Modeling, Patterns, Rules and Implementation* (Nicola et al., 2002) builds on Coad's work with the four archetypes and the domain neutral component and distils a core set of analysis patterns.

The management of **Order**'s collection of **OrderLine**s is as per the aggregation of Order by Customer. What is illustrative here is the reference from **OrderLine** to **SellableItem** (Figure 5.12).

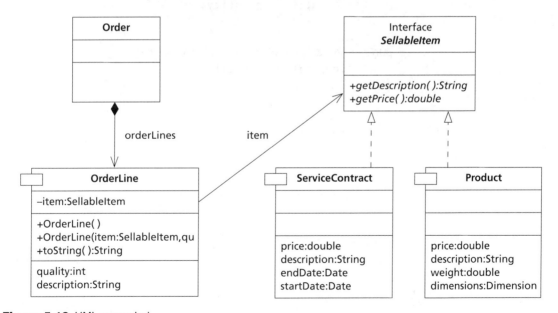

Figure 5.12 UML expanded

SellableItem.java

```java
package com.ogilviepartners.jdobook.op;

public interface SellableItem
{
    public double getPrice();
    public String getDescription();
}
```

OrderLine.java

```java
package com.ogilviepartners.jdobook.op;

public class OrderLine {

    private SellableItem item;
    private int quantity;
    public OrderLine() {
    }

    public OrderLine(SellableItem item, int quantity) {
        this.item = item;
        this.quantity = quantity;
    }

    public void setQuantity(int quantity) {
        this.quantity = quantity;
    }

    public int getQuantity() {
        return quantity;
    }

    public String getDescription() {
        return item.getDescription();
    }

    public String toString() {
        return "OrderLine (description=" + getDescription() +
                            "quantity=" + quantity + ")";
    }
}
```

For brevity, the **Product** and **ServiceContract** classes have not been shown here. Suffice it to say that these classes will explicitly implement the **SellableItem** interface, and that they will be enhanced to become persistence-capable.

Here is the persistence descriptor that describes the classes:

op.jdo

```
<jdo>
  <package name="com.ogilviepartners.jdobook.op">
    <class name="OrderLine" />
    <class name="Product" />
    <class name="ServiceContract" />
  </package>
</jdo>
```

Why is it so simple? Don't we have to identify the "item" field of the **OrderLine** class as a reference to an interface with persistence-capable implementations? The answer is no, you don't have to do this. The JDO implementation does not need any information beyond that in the classes themselves. All you have to do as a developer is watch out for potential **ClassCastException**s if you assign to the "item" field an instance of a class which does implement the **SellableItem** interface, but which is not persistence-capable.

5.5.3.12 Array types

Support for arrays is an optional feature of implementations. If supported, the vendor may implement arrays as first- or second-class objects. If implemented as second-class objects, the requirement to track changes and notify the owning first-class object (which is mandatory for all other second-class objects) is optional in the case of arrays.

5.5.3.13 Example

Very few object modelers regularly use arrays in their designs. The restriction that array size must be known when the array is instantiated and cannot be altered thereafter means that the far more flexible Collection classes are used almost to the exclusion of arrays.

To illustrate array persistence I have generated a small example below. This does not have anything to do with the order processing domain. Instead I have defined a simple class that maintains an array of five string objects. The class is called **FiveHolder** (Figure 5.13).

FiveHolder
–content:String[ ]
+FiveHolder(s1:String,s2:String,s3:String,s4:String,s5:String +setItem(index:int,s:String):void +toString( ):String

Figure 5.13 UML for FiveHolder

Here is my implementation of the class.

FiveHolder.java

```
package com.ogilviepartners.jdobook.other;

import javax.jdo.JDOHelper;

public class FiveHolder {
    public FiveHolder(String s0, String s1, String s2,
    String s3, String s4) {
        content = new String[5];
        content[0] = s0;
        content[1] = s1;
        content[2] = s2;
        content[3] = s3;
        content[4] = s4;
    }

    public void setItem(int index, String s) {
        // instruct JDO that the field "content" is about
        // to be altered
        JDOHelper.makeDirty(this,"content");
        content[index] = s;
    }

    public String toString() {
        System.out.println("FiveHolder: 0=" + content[0] +
        "1=" + content[1] +
        " 2=" + content[2] + "3=" + content[3] + "4=" +
        content[4]);
    }

    private String[] content;
}
```

In order to persist instances of the **FiveHolder** class we have the persistence descriptor.

FiveHolder.jdo

```
<jdo>
  <package name="com.ogilviepartners.jdobook.other">
    <class name="FiveHolder" />
  </package>
</jdo>
```

Arrays

Notice that the program **FiveHolder.java** includes a compile-time dependency on the **javax.jdo** package. This is because the class must notify its persistence manager whenever the contents of the array may be changed. This is one area where the transparency of JDO to the object model falls short.

Remember that the call to **makeDirty()** must occur *before* the array contents are changed, to ensure that the original values are correctly restored on transaction rollback.

5.5.3.14 Strings

Strings are immutable system classes and are therefore likely to be stored as second-class objects by the implementation. The above example could easily have been implemented with an array of some persistence-capable object (e.g. **Product**), but the Java code and persistence descriptor would not have been substantially different.

5.6   Inheritance

JDO's support for implementation and inheritance hierarchies is a major benefit of the technology. It enables the design of domain object models that closely represent the business domain.

The support for inheritance is particularly flexible. A class might be persistence-capable even if its superclass is not. Equally, that class's subclasses may be persistence-capable or not as required by the developer. Thus, in an inheritance hierarchy, classes may be independently persistence-capable and non-persistence-capable.

When one class in an inheritance hierarchy is defined as persistence-capable in a persistence descriptor, the persistence modifiers ascribed to its fields (**persistent**, **transactional** or **none**) are inherited by subclasses. Thus fields identified as **persistent** will be persistent in the subclasses, fields identified as **transactional** will be transactional in the subclasses, and fields identified as **none** will be neither persistent nor transactional in the subclasses. Furthermore, the identified fields must be defined in that class, and not inherited from a superclass. This allows the **PersistenceManager** to take control of field values, and not have to rely on behavior in a superclass.

Please note that the current version of JDO does not automatically persist fields of non-persistence-capable superclasses. If a persistence-capable class has a superclass that is not persistence-capable, then fields defined in the superclass will not be synchronized to the data store by JDO. If the values of these fields must be stored, you should define the superclass to be persistence-capable if possible. This is by far the easiest and most logical option in most cases. If the superclass cannot be made persistence-capable, you must redefine in the subclass those fields of the superclass which are to be persisted. It is then up to you to guarantee that these new, but identically named, fields are updated whenever the corresponding fields in the superclass are updated – a tricky and sometimes impossible task.

5.6.1   Complicated inheritance scenario

Warning: Do not try this at home!

The discussion which follows considers a hypothetical case where an inheritance hierarchy will indeed have alternately persistence-capable and non-persistence-capable classes. This is an unusual scenario. Indeed, in object orientation terms, it is probably nonsensical for this to be the case. The entire situation is massively simplified if the least-derived class of the hierarchy is persistence-capable (even though it may be abstract) and all of the subclasses are as well.

I do not recommend that you implement inheritance hierarchies in the manner I am about to describe. By all means read through the discussion, but then focus your attention on the "solution," which is to make the entire hierarchy persistence-capable. Such an inheritance hierarchy is discussed in the example "BusinessPartner as an abstract superclass" given on page 86.

To illustrate our discussion we will use the hypothetical inheritance hierarchy illustrated by the UML class diagram in Figure 5.14. Furthermore, we will presume that we wish to store instances of classes **Two** and **Four** in our data store, and not instances of classes **One** or **Three**.

To achieve this we will write a persistence descriptor for the package. We'll use the notional package name 'inherit.' The enhancer will use this descriptor to enhance classes **Two** and **Four**. This is achieved by specifying the appropriate superclass for all but the least-derived (topmost) persistence-capable class. Note that since **One** and **Three** are not to be made persistence-capable, they will not be described in the descriptor.

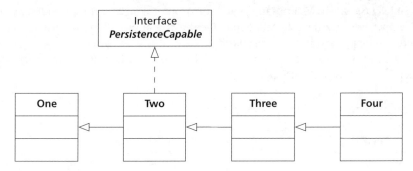

Figure 5.14 UML for hypothetical inheritance hierarchy

inherit.jdo

```
<jdo>
  <package name="com.ogilviepartners.jdobook.inherit">
    <class name="Two" />
    <class name="Four"
      persistence-capable-superclass="Two" />
  </package>
</jdo>
```

The situation we have described is as follows. Class **Two** is persistence-capable, and its fields have appropriate default persistence modifiers. Class **Four** is persistence-capable, and its fields have appropriate default persistence modifiers. It has a persistence-capable super class of class **Two**, so all fields of class **Two** will have their persistence modifiers inherited. Thus whenever an instance of **Four** is persisted or retrieved, the values for fields inherited from class **Two** will be managed appropriately by JDO according to the inherited persistence modifiers.

5.6.1.1 Determining persistability

Note that in the hierarchy, the top-most persistence-capable class will implement the **PersistenceCapable** interface (in this case class **Two** will do so after enhancement; the implementation was shown in the UML diagram as a reminder). This class and all subclasses thereof are therefore instances of **PersistenceCapable** (as per the **instanceof** operator). The fact that a class is an instance of **PersistenceCapable** is not sufficient to determine whether it can be stored via JDO (e.g. class **Three**). This is true of all **PersistenceCapable** classes, but is most evident in inheritance hierarchies of independently persistence-capable and non persistence-capable classes.

Any non-persistence-capable class that is the direct superclass of a persistence-capable class which does not have a no-argument constructor must itself have a no-argument constructor. This is because the enhanced persistence-capable class will have a no-argument constructor which, if not provided by the developer, will by default call **super()** and the appropriate constructor must therefore be present in the superclass.

Let us now add some attributes to the inheritance hierarchy in order to consider a specific case (Figure 5.15).

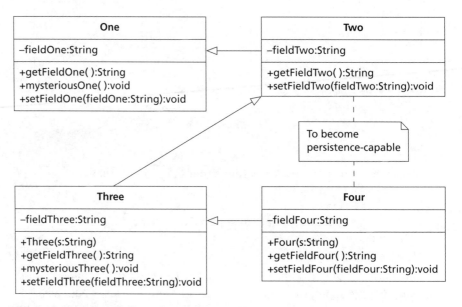

Figure 5.15 Hypothetical inheritance hierarchy with attributes

Each of the four classes (**One**, **Two**, etc.) now has a single attribute (**fieldOne**, **fieldTwo**, etc.). The persistence descriptor will be the same as **inherit.jdo** shown above. Enhancement of the classes as shown above is not viable as neither class **Four**, nor its immediate superclass **Three**, have a no-argument constructor. To remedy this, a no-argument constructor must be added to either one – the choice of which is up to the designer.

After enhancement, JDO will manage the value of **fieldTwo** in instances of **Two**. In class **Four**, JDO will manage the values of **fieldFour** (specific to that class) and **fieldTwo** (inherited from **Two**). However, it becomes apparent that fields **fieldOne** and **fieldThree** remain unmanaged despite being inherited through the hierarchy. Thus, values assigned to **fieldOne** in instances of class **Two**, and **fieldOne** and **fieldThree** in instances of class **Four**, will not be persisted to, or ultimately retrieved from, the data store.

The problem arises because only fields defined in a class can be described in its deployment descriptor. Thus class **Two** can have persistence modifiers set for its field **fieldTwo**, but not for the inherited field **fieldOne**. This can be remedied in part by redefining **fieldOne** as an attribute of class **Two**. The persistence modifier can then be set in the descriptor for class **Two**. The field's values will then be persisted as part of persistent instances of class **Two**. Also, through the inheritance of persistence modifiers, the same field's values will be stored as parts of persistent instances of class **Three**.

Unfortunately our workaround, the redefinition of fields in a subclass, is not universally applicable. When **fieldOne** is declared in class **Two**, it is a new field that replaces the inherited field of the same name. Manipulation of the attribute within methods of class **One** will affect the value of the original field (scoped to class **One**) and not the new and persistent field (scoped to class **Two**). If access to **fieldOne** by methods of class **One** is always made through accessor methods (also defined in class **One**), the situation can be corrected by implementing these accessor methods in the subclass **Two**. However, if methods of class **One** might manipulate the value of **fieldOne** directly, it is not possible to persist **fieldOne** reliably without making class **One** itself a persistence-capable class.

The final UML class diagram is shown in Figure 5.16.

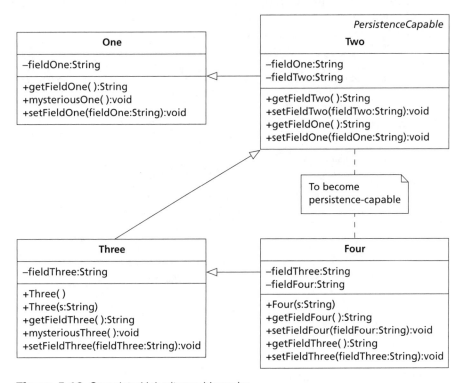

Figure 5.16 Completed inheritance hierarchy

The no-argument constructor has been added to class **Three**, and attributes **fieldOne** and **fieldThree** have been added to classes **Two** and **Four** respectively. Unfortunately it is not possible to guarantee that methods **mysteriousOne** and **mysteriousThree**, which potentially update the values of **fieldOne** and **fieldThree** directly in each class, will correctly update field values in instances of

Two and **Four** and mark these instances as dirty. This consideration exists because of the unusualness of the hierarchy. In situations where the least-derived (topmost) class is itself persistence-capable, as are all subclasses, the situation does not arise.

5.6.1.2 Example – BusinessPartner as an abstract superclass

In order to illustrate inheritance we turn once more to the order processing domain. **BusinessPartner**s may have a **Customer** role that aggregates **Order** objects on that partner's behalf. So far a **BusinessPartner** has been some entity that has a name and an address. Now we add further detail to this concept by making the **BusinessPartner** class **abstract**, and subclassing it with a number of concrete classes which will themselves be persistence-capable.

The concrete implementations will be **Individual**, **Company**, and **Charity**. Each of these is a **BusinessPartner** (in that they can place orders on our order processing system). However, they each have elements of common and unique attribution. This makes them ideal candidates for an inheritance hierarchy. The UML diagram is shown in Figure 5.17.

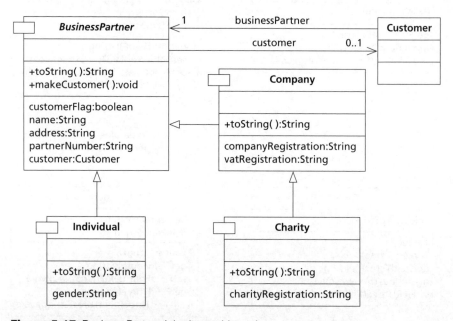

Figure 5.17 BusinessPartner inheritance hierarchy

BusinessPartner has been made abstract (note the use of *italics* for its name in Figure 5.17). Otherwise it is largely unchanged. It still maintains the **Customer** role.

Individual, **Company**, and **Charity** each add attribution specific to themselves. I have assumed that every charity is a company, and hence **Charity**

extends **Company**. This is probably not correct in all cases, but does serve to illustrate a non-trivial inheritance hierarchy.

BusinessPartner is the topmost persistence-capable class in the hierarchy, despite the fact that it is abstract. This way it is not possible to instantiate a **BusinessPartner**; you must instantiate one of the concrete subclasses instead. However, you can obtain the extent of **BusinessPartner**. This extent will include instances of the various subclasses as appropriate. Having **BusinessPartner** persistence-capable also gives us this flexibility of querying through JDOQL (see Chapter 8).

Here is a persistence descriptor that correctly specifies the inheritance.

op.jdo

```
<jdo>
  <package name="com.ogilviepartners.jdobook.op">
    <class name="BusinessPartner"
           identity-type="application"
           objectid-class="com.ogilviepartners/
           .jdobook.op.pk.BusinessPartnerPK">
    <field name="partnerNumber"
    primary-key="true"/>
  </class>

  <class name="Individual"
         identity-type="application"
         persistence-capable-superclass=
             "com.ogilviepartners.jdobook.op.BusinessPartner"
         objectid-class=
         "com.ogilviepartners. jdobook.op.pk.IndividualPK" />

  <class name="Company"
         identity-type="application"
         persistence-capable-superclass=
             "com.ogilviepartners.jdobook.op.BusinessPartner"
         objectid-class=
         "com.ogilviepartners. jdobook.op.pk.CompanyPK" />

  <class name="Charity"
         identity-type="application"
         persistence-capable-superclass=
             "com.ogilviepartners.jdobook.op.Company"
         />
  </package>
</jdo>
```

The inheritance hierarchy illustrated above is a typical usage of JDO's inheritance support. Because the entire hierarchy is persistence-capable, everything is very straightforward and manageable.

Note that with **BusinessPartner** now abstract, its primary key class **BusinessPartnerPK** will itself be abstract. Furthermore, each persistence-capable class which inherits from an abstract persistence-capable class must define its own concrete primary key class, which inherits from the abstract primary key class. This is illustrated in the persistence descriptor above, where **Individual** and **Company** have their own Object ID classes identified. In the case of **Charity**, however, it will use the Object ID class of the non-abstract **Company** from which it inherits.

5.7   Interlude: order processing GUI

The object model for the order processing domain is now complete. Before we move on to the next chapter I need to introduce a graphical user interface (GUI) application which allows users to manage objects in the model.

You will find this most useful for creating and persisting order processing objects. You can later use these to practice your grasp of the JDO Query Language with the Dynamic Query Window, which is introduced at the end of Chapter 8.

The GUI application is called **Explorer** and belongs to the package **com.ogilviepartners.jdobook.op.gui**. Two sample windows are shown. Figure 5.18 shows the Explorer window listing all persistent **BusinessPartner** instances. JDO's support of inheritance is well illustrated, as the list includes **Company**, **Individual**, and **Charity** instances. The "New" button is disabled because the **BusinessPartner** class is **abstract**.

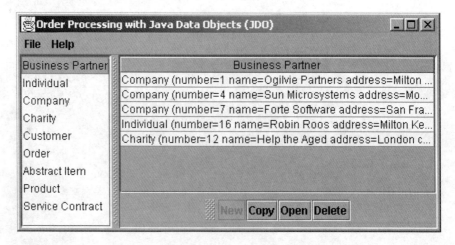

Figure 5.18 Explorer window listing BusinessPartners

Figure 5.19 shows a Viewer window in which the Company "Forte Software" is being created.

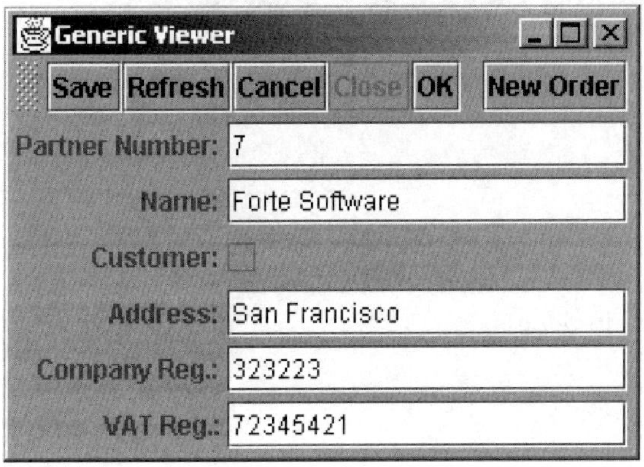

Figure 5.19 Company Viewer window

Other windows facilitate the construction of the remaining objects in the model.

What's next?

The next chapter discusses in detail the classes and interfaces of the `javax.jdo` package.

Primary interfaces and classes

6

The JDO package is comprised of a number of Java interfaces and classes which applications use to achieve persistence. In this chapter we examine the most important of these in detail.

6.1 JDOHelper

JDOHelper is a concrete class that facilitates the bootstrapping of a JDO implementation. It also provides applications with methods to interrogate the state of JDO instances. Although it contains a constructor, all of the methods it defines are static and are commonly executed on the class name directly without first obtaining a **JDOHelper** instance.

The UML for **JDOHelper** is shown in Figure 6.1.

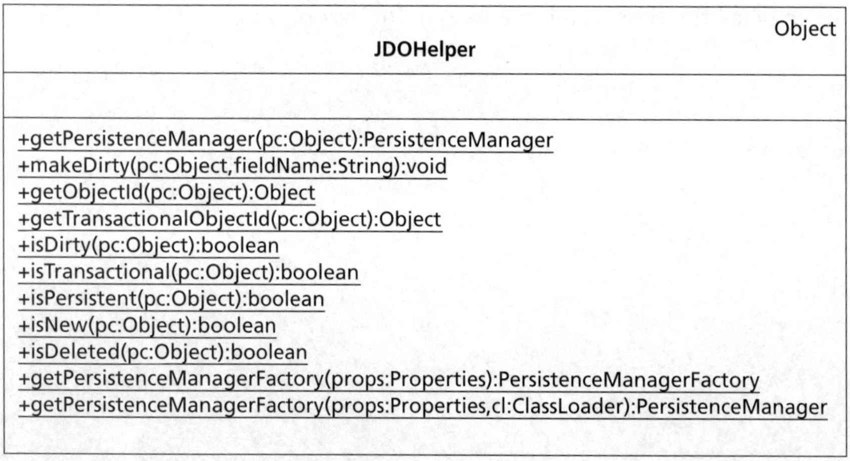

JDOHelper	Object
+getPersistenceManager(pc:Object):PersistenceManager	
+makeDirty(pc:Object,fieldName:String):void	
+getObjectId(pc:Object):Object	
+getTransactionalObjectId(pc:Object):Object	
+isDirty(pc:Object):boolean	
+isTransactional(pc:Object):boolean	
+isPersistent(pc:Object):boolean	
+isNew(pc:Object):boolean	
+isDeleted(pc:Object):boolean	
+getPersistenceManagerFactory(props:Properties):PersistenceManagerFactory	
+getPersistenceManagerFactory(props:Properties,cl:ClassLoader):PersistenceManager	

Figure 6.1 UML for JDOHelper

6.1.1 State interrogation

The following methods are used to determine the state of an instance:

- `isDirty(Object pc)`

  Returns **true** for persistence-capable instances that have been changed in the current transaction. If the argument is null, references an instance that is transient or references an object that is not persistence-capable, then the method returns **false**.

- `isTransactional(Object pc)`

  Returns **true** for persistence-capable instances that are associated with the current transaction. If the argument is null, references an instance that is transient or references an object that is not persistence-capable, then the method returns **false**.

- `isPersistent(Object pc)`

  Returns **true** for persistence-capable instances that are in a persistent state and therefore represent persistent data in the data store. If the argument is null, references an instance that is transient or references an object that is non-persistence-capable, then the method returns **false**.

- `isNew(Object pc)`

  Returns **true** for persistence-capable instances that have been newly made persistent in the current transaction. If the argument is null, references an instance that is transient or references an object that is non-persistence-capable, then the method returns **false**.

- `isDeleted(Object pc)`

  Returns **true** for persistence-capable instances that have been deleted in the current transaction. If the argument is null, references an instance that is transient or references an object that is not non-persistence-capable, then the method returns **false**.

6.1.2 Administrative functions

The following methods help applications to administer their managed instances.

- `getPersistenceManager(Object pc):PersistenceManager`

  This method returns a reference to the persistence manager responsible for managing the instance. If the argument is null, references an instance that is transient or references an object that is non-persistence-capable, then the method returns null.

- `getObjectId(Object pc)`

  This method returns the JDO identity of the instance. If *application identity* applies, the returned object will be of the class identified as the Object ID Class in the persistence descriptor. Some implementations support the changing of application identities, an optional feature. This facilitates the alteration of primary key fields of persistent instances. This particular method will return the identity as it was at the start of the transaction, regardless of any primary key field changes that have already been made during the transaction.

If *datastore identity* applies, the object returned will be of a class determined by the implementation. Such classes are not standardized, and different implementations are likely to use different classes for this purpose.

If the argument is null, references an instance that is transient or references an object that is non-persistence-capable, then the method returns null.

- **getTransactionalObjectId(Object pc)**

This method is the same as **getObjectId()** above, except that when application identity applies it will return the current identity, taking into account any alterations made to primary key fields during the current transaction.

The code extract below illustrates the difference between these two methods. It alters the primary key of an instance with application identity and then, during the same transaction, invokes **getObjectId()** and **getTransactionalObjectId()** and displays the results.

```
package com.ogilviepartners.jdobook.app;

import javax.jdo.*;
import com.ogilviepartners.jdo.JDOBootstrap;
import com.ogilviepartners.jdobook.op.BusinessPartner;
import java.util.Collection;

public class ChangeApplicationIdentity {

    final String changeIdentity =
            "javax.jdo.option.ChangeApplicationIdentity";

    public static void main(String[] args) {
        JDOBootstrap bootstrap;
        PersistenceManagerFactory pmf;
        PersistenceManager pm;
        BusinessPartner bp;
        BusinessPartnerPK oldKey;
        String newPartnerNumber;
        Collection supportedOptions;

        Bootstrap = new JDOBootstrap();
        pmf = bootstrap.getPersistenceManagerFactory();
        SupportedOptions = pmf.supportedOptions();

        // is changing of application identity supported?
```

```
        if (!supportedOptions.contains(changeIdentity)) {
            System.err.println("This JDO implementation does
                not support the " +
                        "changing of application identities");
        }
        if (args.length != 2) {

            System.err.println
              ("usage: java ChangeApplicationIdentity " +
                "<oldPartnerNumber> <newPartner Number>");
            System.exit(1);
        }

        oldKey = new BusinessPartnerPK(args[0]);
        newPartnerNumber = args[1];

        pm = pmf.getPersistenceManager();
        t = pm.currentTransaction();
        t.begin();

        // find the BusinessPartner
        bp = (BusinessPartner) pm.getObjectById(oldKey);

        // change the primary key field
        bp.setPartnerNumber(newPartnerNumber);

        // print out the ObjectId and TransactionalObjectId
        System.out.println("ObjectId=" + pm.getObjectId(bp));
        System.out.println("TransactionalObjectId=" +
                            pm.getTransactionalObjectId(bp));
        // done
        t.commit();
        pm.close();
    }
}
```

The essential results of executing this application are shown below, presuming that a persistent **BusinessPartner** exists with the partner number 6, but none exists with the partner number 7.

```
C:>java ChangeApplicationIdentity 6 7
ObjectId=6
TransactionalObjectId=7
```

● **makeDirty(Object pc, String fieldname)**

This method call marks the specified field name as dirty and transitions the instance to an appropriate dirty state. If the object reference is null, references an instance that is transient, references an object that is non-persistence-capable, or if the names field is not managed by JDO, then the method returns silently without having any effect. Optionally the field name may be fully qualified by package and class names.

The example below illustrates how **makeDirty()** might be used when manipulating a persistence-capable instance through direct field access from another class which is not persistence-capable.

Account.java

```
package com.ogilviepartners.jdobook.other;

public class PersistentAccount {
    double balance; // package level ("friendly") visibility

    public setBalance(double balance) {
        this.balance = balance;
    }
}
```

ChangeAccount.java

```
package com.ogilviepartners.jdobook.other;
                                    // Same package as Account

    public class ChangeAccount {
        public incrementBalance(Account a) {
            JDOHelper.makeDirty(a,"balance");
            // now JDO knows it is dirty
            a.balance++;
        }
    }
```

Account.jdo

```
<jdo>
  <package name="com.ogilviepartners.jdobook.other">
    <class name="Account"/>
  </package>
</jdo>
```

Persistence-aware classes

The use of **JDOHelper.makeDirty()** in **ChangeAccount.java** has unde-sirably introduced a compile-time dependency on the **javax.jdo** package. However, since no array manipulation is involved, this is unnecessary. Rather than alter the source code of **ChangeAccount.java** we could enhance the class to be persistence-aware.

Persistence-capable classes are capable of having their state persisted in a data store. The **Account** class above is persistence-capable.

Classes which are not persistence-capable, but which manipulate persistence-capable instances through direct attribute manipulation (as opposed to method invocations), should be made persistence-aware. Persistence-aware classes cannot have their state persisted, but they are aware of other persistence-capable instances and automatically invoke the appropriate **makeDirty()** method whenever direct attribute manipulation occurs.

To make a class persistence-aware you do not declare it in the persistence descriptor – doing so would instead make it persistence-capable. Instead, the name of the class is generally passed as a command-line argument to the enhancer. The exact manner in which this is done will be detailed in the documentation for your JDO implementation.

6.1.3   Bootstrapping functions

There are several different ways of obtaining a persistence manager within an application, a process I refer to as *bootstrapping* the JDO implementation. Of the available methods, some are required features of the specification and can be guaranteed to work with all compliant implementations. Others are optional features that depend upon support by the particular implementation in use.

The only standard bootstrapping methods are:

1 Use **JDOHelper** to construct a **PersistenceManagerFactory** configured according to properties defined in a properties object.

2 Obtain a pre-instantiated **PersistenceManagerFactory** instance from a naming service via JNDI, and invoke its **getPersistenceManager()** method.

In addition to these, the following non-standard methods could be used in a non-managed environment if necessary:

3 Construct an instance of the implementation's concrete class that implements the **PersistenceManagerFactory** interface according to the documented public constructors. Set the necessary properties individually and then invoke its **getPersistenceManager()** method.

4 Construct an instance of the implementation's concrete class that implements the **PersistenceManager** interface according to the documented public constructors.

6.1.3.1 Bootstrapping with JNDI lookups

The JNDI lookup of a **PersistenceManagerFactory** is the accepted approach when JDO is used in a managed environment, within EJB (session, entity and message-driven) or web components (servlets and JavaServer Pages). An example of this is shown in Chapter 11.

6.1.3.2 Bootstrapping with JDOHelper

JDOHelper provides two methods for obtaining a **PersistenceManagerFactory**. These provide the most commonly used method for bootstrapping JDO in the managed environment.

```
getPersistenceManagerFactory(Properties p)
getPersistenceManagerFactory(Properties p, ClassLoader cl)
```

These methods are used to instantiate appropriately configured **PersistenceManagerFactory** instances. If no class loader is explicitly provided, the current thread's default class loader is employed. The configuration of the **PersistenceManagerFactory** is dictated by property settings contained in the properties object. The returned **PersistenceManagerFactory** will then return correspondingly configured **PersistenceManager** instances when its **getPersistenceManager()** method is called.

This approach is the standard method of persistence manager factory construction. The names of the standard properties are detailed below.

It is, however, permissible for implementations to define additional properties. To support this and yet retain portability, implementations will ignore any properties with unrecognized names. Many of the properties invoke support for optional JDO features. If the implementation does not support the corresponding feature, the call to **getPersistenceManager()** will throw a **JDOFatalUserException**.

The **PersistenceManagerFactory** obtained in this manner is non-configurable; all of its property mutator (set) methods will throw an exception if invoked.

6.1.3.3 Bootstrapping with explicit PersistenceManagerFactory construction

The explicit construction of a **PersistenceManagerFactory** instance is an alternative to using the **JDOHelper** methods described above. Although the specification does not guarantee that the factory will have a no-argument constructor, one is present in most, if not all, implementing classes. The application must know the name of this class (usually as a property value) and must also know how to obtain (from JNDI) or construct an appropriate **ConnectionFactory** for the underlying data store.

6.2 JDO properties explained

The standard **JDOHelper** bootstrap properties are explained here. The property names are additionally listed in Appendix A for your quick reference.

It is permissible for implementations to support additional properties with names that are not standard. Details of these will be provided in the appropriate product documentation.

javax.jdo.PersistenceManagerFactoryClass

This is the fully package-qualified class name of the JDO implementation's class implementing the **PersistenceManagerFactory** interface.

javax.jdo.option.Optimistic

If this property is set to **true**, the returned **PersistenceManagerFactory** will employ optimistic transaction management.

javax.jdo.option.RetainValues

If this property is set to **true**, the automatic eviction of persistent instances on transaction completion is suppressed. This may decrease the number of times that a particular persistent instance must be loaded into the cache at the expense of a much larger cache size.

javax.jdo.option.RestoreValues

Transactional rollback is essential in most transactional applications. However, it brings with it overheads such as the caching of instance field values for use during rollback.

If the **RestoreValues** property is set to **true**, instances do have their transactional (and persistent) field values restored when transaction rollback occurs. However, some applications will not refer to instances after completion. If **RestoreValues** is **false**, instances do not have such fields restored on rollback. When the **false** value is used, the implementation can achieve significant performance gains: instance field values are not cached when the instance becomes involved with a transaction, and are not restored if the transaction is rolled back.

Note that this does not affect the transactional behavior of the data store. The persistent data will still be restored on rollback. However, the instance in memory will not have its field values restored.

javax.jdo.option.IgnoreCache

If set to **true**, this property provides a hint to the JDO implementation that JODQL queries may be resolved without reference to changes present in cached instances but not yet synchronized to the data store. The implementation may choose to ignore this property value and always return exact query results including changed cached instances.

javax.jdo.option.NontransactionalRead

If this property is set to **true**, applications may cause persistent instances to be read outside a transaction, typically by executing Querys or by reading (or navigating through) as yet unloaded persistent field values. If set to **false**, the execution of Querys or the reading of as yet unloaded values outside a transaction will throw a **JDOUserException**.

javax.jdo.option.NontransactionalWrite

If this property is set to **true**, non-transactional instances may be changed outside a transaction. Otherwise updates to such instances must be performed within a transaction, despite being unaffected by any subsequent rollback of that transaction.

javax.jdo.option.Multithreaded

This property is used to enable or disable the synchronization of calling threads within a persistence manager. If set to **true**, the **PersistenceManagerFactory** will subsequently return persistence managers which internally synchronize calling threads, thus relieving the application of such responsibility. If your application will potentially invoke the services of a persistence manager from multiple threads, you must set the **Multithreaded** property to **true**. However, if your application has only a single thread, or itself performs the appropriate synchronization between multiple threads, the value can be set to **false**. This will reduce unnecessary synchronization overheads within the **PersistenceManager** object.

Note that in Swing/JFC applications there are typically at least two threads – the main thread and the Abstract Windowing Toolkit thread – and appropriate care should be taken.

javax.jdo.option.ConnectionDriverName

This is the fully package-qualified name of the driver class for the underlying data store.

javax.jdo.option.ConnectionUserName

This is the username to be used for authentication against the data store. It is used by the connection factory when instantiating connections.

javax.jdo.option.ConnectionPassword

This is the password to be used for authentication against the data store. It is used by the connection factory when instantiating connections.

javax.jdo.option.ConnectionURL

The **ConnectionURL** will be used by the connection factory when instantiating connections. It should correctly identify the protocol, network location, port number and name of the data store. The exact format of these uniform resource locator (URL) strings is dependent on the underlying driver that the connection factory will employ.

Here is an example URL for connecting to an Hypersonic SQL database running on its default port number on the local host:

```
jdbc:hsqldb:hsql://localhost
```

Here is an example for connecting to an Oracle database with name "jdotest1" on host "Ogilvie-1" at port 1521:

```
jdbc:oracle:oci8:@(description=(address=(host=ogilvie-
1)(protocol=tcp)(port=1521))(connect_data=(sid=jdotest1)))
```

javax.jdo.option.ConnectionFactoryName

This property identifies the JNDI name of a pre-instantiated **ConnectionFactory** to be used by the persistence manager. Its use supercedes and negates the other connection properties (**ConnectionUserName**, **ConnectionPassword** and **ConnectionURL**). This has most relevance in the managed environment where factories are typically obtained through a naming service.

javax.jdo.option.ConnectionFactory2Name

Within the managed environment, standard connection factories always return connections that are registered with the current J2EE transaction. This is not appropriate when working with optimistic transaction management. The **ConnectionFactory2Name** property is for the identification of an alternative JNDI connection factory name to be used by the persistence manager in these circumstances.

6.2.1   ConnectionFactory properties

Many JDO implementations will be layered on top of standard Connector implementations. These are likely to provide additional bootstrap property names that correspond to the **ConnectionFactory** configuration parameters. Such facilities will include the setting of the connection pool size properties (**MinPool** and **MaxPool**) amongst others.

The JDO specification does not standardize the names used for such properties.

6.2.2   Bootstrapping JDO implementations

Now that we have examined the standard properties for bootstrapping a persistence manager factory through **JDOHelper**, it's time to look at a concrete example. During the early chapters we used a class called **JDOBootstrap** for this purpose (Figure 6.2). It is not part of the standard but the source code is shown below and included on the downloadable distribution.

The purpose of **JDOBootstrap** is to locate a property file called "**jdo.properties**," construct a properties object from the contents of that file, and then use the **JDOHelper** class to instantiate a **PersistenceManagerFactory**. The properties file is located (by looking firstly in the **CLASSPATH** and subsequently in the file system) when the **JDOBootstrap** instance is constructed. The **getPersistenceManagerFactory** method returns a **PersistenceManager-Factory** instance. (The method itself appears in the UML diagram as a property called "persistenceManagerFactory" in the bottom compartment.)

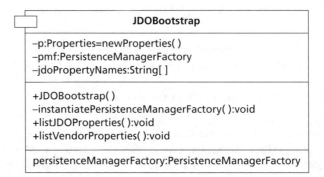

Figure 6.2 UML for JDOBootstrap

Actual instantiation of the persistence manager takes place in the private method **instantiatePersistenceManagerFactory**.)

The two remaining methods list property values. The **listJDOProperties** method prints those standard properties that are present in the **jdo.properties** file. Only standard properties are listed so that any misspelling of property names is easily evident to the developer. However, even non-standard properties will be passed on to the **JDOHelper**. The **listVendorProperties()** method prints out two properties that identify the implementation: the **VendorName** and the **VersionNumber**. These values can be determined only after instantiation of the **PersistenceManagerFactory**, so instantiation takes place when this method or the **getPersistenceManagerFactory** method is called, whichever occurs sooner.

JDOBootstrap.java

```
package com.ogilviepartners.jdo;

import java.io.*;
import javax.jdo.PersistenceManagerFactory;
import javax.jdo.JDOHelper;
import java.util.Properties;
import java.util.Enumeration;

public class JDOBootstrap
{
    private Properties p = new Properties();
    private PersistenceManagerFactory pmf;
    private String[] jdoPropertyNames = {
        "javax.jdo.PersistenceManagerFactoryClass",
        "javax.jdo.option.Optimistic",
        "javax.jdo.option.RetainValues",
```

```
        "javax.jdo.option.RestoreValues",
        "javax.jdo.option.IgnoreCache",
        "javax.jdo.option.NontransactionalRead",
        "javax.jdo.option.NontransactionalWrite",
        "javax.jdo.option.ConnectionDriverName",
        "javax.jdo.option.ConnectionUserName",
        "javax.jdo.option.ConnectionPassword",
        "javax.jdo.option.ConnectionURL",
        "javax.jdo.option.ConnectionFactoryName",
        "javax.jdo.option.ConnectionFactory2Name",
        "javax.jdo.option.Multithreaded"};

public JDOBootstrap() throws BootstrapException {
    // try classpath
    InputStream propStream = getClass().getResourceAsStream
        ("/jdo.properties");
    if (propStream == null) {
        // try local
        propStream = getClass().getResourceAsStream
        ("jdo.properties");
        if (propStream == null) {
            throw new BootstrapException("Could not " +
            "locate or read 'jdo.properties' which should " +
            " be in CLASSPATH or the working directory");
        }
    }

    try {
        p.load (propStream);
        propStream.close();
    }
    catch (java.io.IOException ioe) {
        ioe.printStackTrace ();
            throw new BootstrapException("Could not load " +
                "properties from 'jdo.properties'\n" + ioe );
    }
}

private void instantiatePersistenceManagerFactory() {
    pmf = JDOHelper.getPersistenceManagerFactory(p);
}

public void listJDOProperties() {
    Collection c = new ArrayList();
```

```
            for (int i=0; i<jdoPropertyNames.length; i++) {
                c.add(jdoPropertyNames[i]);
            }
            System.out.println("Listening standard JDO properties");
            for (Enumeration e = p.propertyNames();
                                    e.hasMoreElements(); ) {
                String s = (String) e.nextElement();
                if (c.contains(s))
                    System.out.println(s + "=" + p.getProperty(s));
            }
            System.out.println("Listening standard JDO properties");
            for (Enumeration e = p.propertyNames();
                                    e.hasMoreElements(); ) {
                String s = (String) e.nextElement();
                if (c!contains(s))
                    System.out.println(s + "=" + p.getProperty(s));
            }
            System.out.println();
        }

    public void listvendorProperties() {
        if (pmf == null) {
            System.out.println(
                "Instantiating PersistenceManagerFactory");
            instantiatePersistenceManagerFactory();
            System.out.println();
        }
        System.out.println("Listing JDO vendor properties");
        System.out.println("vendorName=" +
            pmf.getProperties().getProperty("vendorName"));
        System.out.println("VersionNumber=" +
            pmf.getProperties().getProperty("VersionNumber"));
        System.out.println();
    }

    public PersistenceManagerFactory getPersistenceManagerFactory()
    {
        if (pmf == null)
            instantiatePersistenceManagerFactory();
        return pmf;
    }
}
```

BootstrapException.java

```
public class BootstrapException extends Exception {
    public BootstrapException(String s) {
        super(s);
    }
}
```

6.2.2.1 Example

Applications use this class by first instantiating it and then optionally listing the two sets of properties before calling **getPersistenceManagerFactory()**, as shown in the code extract below.

```
JDOBootstrap bootstrap = new JDOBootstrap();
bootstrap.listJDOProperties();   // useful debug info
bootstrap.listvendorProperties(); // useful debug info
PersistenceManagerFactory pmf =
                    bootstrap.getPersistenceManagerFactory();
```

6.3   PersistenceManagerFactory

An instance of a concrete class implementing the **PersistenceManagerFactory** interface is provided as a part of each JDO implementation. This is the usual source from which **PersistenceManager** instances are obtained. Although it is possible to construct a **PersistenceManager** directly without doing so through a factory, as noted earlier, this approach is less common.

The **PersistenceManagerFactory** interface details accessor and mutator methods for each of its properties. The accessor (get) methods can be used at any time to determine the corresponding property values which are assigned to persistence managers obtained from a particular factory instance.

The mutator (set) methods may be used to configure the factory only until the first persistence manager has been obtained from it (which occurs when the **getPersistenceManager()** method is invoked). Afterwards any attempt to alter the configuration of the factory by invoking its mutator (set) methods will throw an exception.

Note that if the factory was obtained through **JDOHelper**, with its configuration dictated by a properties object, the factory cannot be reconfigured even before its **getPersistenceManager()** method has been called.

The 17 "set" methods and 16 "get" methods (the **ConnectionPassword** property is write-only, so the single method **setConnectionPassword()** is provided) are not listed here. The full set of **PersistenceManagerFactory** configuration methods is tabled in Appendix D. The meanings of the property names have already been described in section 6.2.

The most important non-configuration methods are detailed below.

```
PersistenceManager getPersistenceManager()
PersistenceManager getPersistenceManager
   (String user, String password)
```

These methods return an appropriately configured **PersistenceManager** instance. The configuration is determined by the values of the various properties of the **PersistenceManagerFactory** itself. Property values may have been set by explicit calls to corresponding set methods prior to the first invocation of either **getPersistenceManager** method, or by a properties object passed to a **getPersistenceManagerFactory** method in the **JDOHelper** when the factory instance was originally obtained.

The method that takes user and password as parameters will return a persistence manager with an appropriately configured connection to the data store. Note that specifying user details in this way may subvert both the pooling of connections by the connection factory and the pooling of persistence managers by the persistence manager factory.

Properties getProperties()

The return value from this method is a properties object describing the configuration of the factory.

6.3.1   Optional feature support

Since the JDO specification contains a large number of optional features, a means is required by which a particular implementation's support for optional features can be determined. This is achieved through the factory's **supportedOptions()** method.

Collection supportedOptions()

The return value of this method is a collection comprised of string objects. JDO defines a set of strings that may be present in the returned collection to indicate support for the corresponding optional feature.

For example, if the implementation supports application identity, the string **"javax.jdo.option.ApplicationIdentity"** will be present in the collection. If the implementation supports datastore identity, the String **"javax.jdo.option.DatastoreIdentity"** will be present in the collection. (Recall that to be JDO compliant, an implementation must support at least one of these.)

The full list of supported option strings is provided in Appendix B.

6.3.1.1 Example – optional feature support

Below is an example application that bootstraps a JDO implementation and then lists the optional features it supports.

OptionalSupport.java

```java
package com.ogilviepartners.jdobook.app;

import javax.jdo.*;
import com.ogilviepartners.jdo.JDOBootstrap;
import java.util.Collection;
import java.util.Iterator;

public class OptionalSupport
{
    public static void main(String[] args) {

        // instantiate the PersistenceManagerFactory
        JDOBootstrap bootstrap = new JDOBootstrap();
        bootstrap.listJDOProperties();
        bootstrap.listVendorProperties();
        PersistenceManagerFactory pmf =
                    bootstrap.getPersistenceManagerFactory();

        // determine and print supported optional features
        System.out.println("Supported Optional Features:");
        Collection c = pmf.supportedOptions();
        Iterator i = c.iterator();
        while (i.hasNext()) {
            System.out.println(i.next());
        }
    }
}
```

6.4   PersistenceManager

see also ch 4

The **PersistenceManager** interface is the application developer's primary means of affecting the state of persistence-capable instances. In Chapter 4, I presented examples illustrating the use of a persistence manager's state management methods (**makePersistent**, **deletePersistent**, **makeTransient**, **evict**, **refresh**, etc.). We will now examine the **PersistenceManager** interface in more detail, but without unnecessarily reproducing Chapter 4's examples.

The **PersistenceManager** interface presents overloaded variants of most cache management and instance lifecycle methods. One of these manipulates a single instance, whilst others perform the same manipulation to collections or arrays of instances, and potentially another applies the manipulation to all applicable instances in the cache. The precise meanings of these overloaded methods will be described only for the eviction methods.

6.4.1   Cache management

The following methods allow an application to influence the management of a persistence manager's cache.

6.4.1.1 Evict

`void evict(Object pc)`

Evict the identified persistence-capable instances from the cache.

`void evictAll(Collection c)`

Evict all members of the identified collection of persistence-capable instances from the cache.

`void evictAll(Object[] o)`

Evict all members of the identified array of persistence-capable instances from the cache.

`void evictAll()`

Evict all cached persistence-capable instances from the cache.

Eviction is a hint to the persistence manager that an instance should be removed from its cache. Under usual circumstances this happens automatically during transaction completion, and it is not necessary for an application to programmatically evict instances.

The persistence manager will ignore requests to evict instances that are in an inappropriate state, e.g. those that are dirty.

6.4.1.2 refresh

`void refresh(Object pc)`
`void refreshAll(Collection c)`
`void refreshAll(Object[] o)`
`void refreshAll()`

The instance's persistent field values are reset to their values as at the start of the transaction, and the instance transitions back to Persistent-Clean if it was Persistent-Dirty. Persistent-Nontransactional (e.g. optimistically locked) instances have their fields refreshed but remain in the same state. See Chapter 7, for more information about optimistic transaction strategies.

6.4.1.3 retrieve

```
void retrieve(Object pc)
void retrieveAll(Collection c)
void retrieveAll(Object[] o)
```

The retrieve methods cause the instance's as yet unread fields to be read from the data store.

If your application has a reference to a **Collection** of JDO instances (perhaps reference called **orders** to a **HashSet** containing **Order** objects) and you are about to iterate through the **Collection**, you might consider calling **retrieveAll(orders)**. This will cause the implementation to read all the field values of each referenced **Order** instance. This minimizes subsequent data store activity as the application accesses each **Order**.

Avoid doing so if your **Collection** is known to contain an enormous number of instances, or if you do not intend to work through the whole of its contents.

6.4.2　Instance lifecycle

The following methods are used by an application to alter the state of a JDO instance.

6.4.2.1 makePersistent

```
void makePersistent(Object pc)
void makePersistentAll(Collection c)
void makePersistentAll(Object[] o)
```

This is a request to create a new entity in the data store.

Where *application identity* is used and the primary key already exists in the data store, the instance cannot be persisted. Depending on the implementation, an exception will be thrown either when **makePersistent()** is called or when the transaction is committed.

With *datastore identity* the entity will be persisted even if another persistent entity already exists with identical persistent field values, as the JDO identity for each object (created at persist time by the implementation) will be different.

At the time that a transient instance is made persistent, the implementation marks any other transient instances that are referenced by persistent fields of the newly persistent instance as being provisionally persistent. This occurs recursively, until the closure (complete set) of transient instances referenced by such persistent fields is provisionally persistent. At commit time, those provisionally persistent instances which are still part of this closure are made persistent. This is called *"persistence by reachability"*.

By way of an example, consider a transient **Order** instance that holds a collection of references to (transient) **OrderLine** instances. When the **Order** is passed as a parameter to **makePersistent()**, each referenced **OrderLine** will be made *provisionally persistent*. However, it is still possible to alter the **order-lines** collection before the transaction is committed. At commit time, only those **OrderLine** instances which are referenced by the **Order** will be made persistent. Any **OrderLine** instances which were referenced at the time of **makePersistent()**, but are no longer referenced at the time of **commit()**, will remain transient.

When to use makePersistent()

Readers with a background in relational databases will be used to "inserting" new entities into the data store. This is essentially what **makePersistent()** does, although with a little more flair (e.g. persistence by reachability).

However, if you had to call **makePersistent()** every time you instantiated a new object that was to be stored, you would quickly find JDO to be less than transparent!

The truth is that applications only rarely need to invoke **makePersistent()**. Most of the time, newly created (and therefore transient) instances are referenced by existing persistent instances, either via singleton references or membership of a collection. In such cases, the new instance will be transparently made persistent when the transaction is committed.

Two occasions when you will nevertheless call **makePersistent()** are:

● when you are persisting an instance which is not immediately being referenced by another persistent instance;

● when you need to obtain the Object ID for your new Instance before the transaction has been committed.

6.4.2.2 deletePersistent

```
void deletePersistent(Object pc)
void deletePersistentAll(Collection c)
void deletePersistentAll(Object[] o)
```

These methods delete persistent instances from the database. They must be called in the context of an active transaction (albeit an optimistic transaction). The instance transitions to Persistent-Deleted or Persistent-New-Deleted as appropriate. After the transaction has been successfully committed it transitions to Transient. The Java object thus remains, but no longer represents the persistent data store entity, which has been deleted.

Please note that **deletePersistent()** is not the exact opposite of **makePersistent()**. Persistence by reachability permits the **makePersistent()** call to persist a closure of instances. However, JDO merely specifies that **deletePersistent()** will delete the particular instance (or instances if a collection is given).

JDO vendors may choose to add value to their implementations by specifying deletion constraints, which cause deletes to cascade to dependent objects. However, there is no guarantee that the set of objects deleted in this manner would be the same as the set of objects that would have been persisted through reachability. Furthermore, portable applications should not rely on such delete cascade functionality, which is beyond the JDO specification and may not be supported by alternative implementations.

difference btwn makeP deleteP

6.4.2.3 makeTransient

```
void makeTransient(Object pc)
void makeTransientAll(Collection c)
void makeTransientAll(Object[] o)
```

Make a persistent instance transient again. Note that this does not affect the underlying data store entity in any way. Making the instance transient does not delete the data; it merely disassociates the instance from the data store. Any subsequent changes to the instance will not be synchronized with the data store.

Please note that when an instance is passed as a parameter to **makeTransient()**, only that instance transitions to the transient state. If it holds references to other persistent instances, they do not become transient. In this way **makeTransient()**, like **deletePersistent()**, is not the opposite of **makePersistent()**.

6.4.2.4 makeTransactional

```
void makeTransactional(Object pc)
void makeTransactionalAll(Collection c)
void makeTransactionalAll(Object[] o)
```

Make a non-transactional instance transactional, so that its persistent and transactional field values become subject to transaction rollback.

6.4.2.5 makeNontransactional

```
void makeNontransactional(Object pc)
void makeNontransactionalAll(Collection c)
void makeNontransactionalAll(Object[] o)
```

Make a transactional instance non-transactional.

The state Persistent-Nontransactional applies to persistent instances whose field values are not necessarily in sync with the data store. This applies to persistent instances whose field values have been read, but not yet altered, in an optimistic transaction.

A Persistent instance can explicitly be made Persistent-Nontransactional through the persistence manager's **makeNontransactional()** method, although it is unlikely that an application would choose to do so. As soon as field values are read in a data store (pessimistic) transaction, or as soon as field values are updated in either type of transaction, the instance transitions to Persistent-Dirty.

Applications will, however, make transient instances transactional. The `makeNontransactional()` method is intended for applications to reverse that process.

6.4.3   Working with JDO identities

`PersistenceManager` provides two methods for determining the identity of an instance. They are identical to the equivalent static methods of the `JDOHelper` class. Where they are used, the methods must be invoked on the particular `PersistenceManager` instance that is responsible for managing the persistence-capable instance. Since many `PersistenceManager`s may be active in a complex application (particularly likely when multiple data stores are accessed), it is more usual for the `JDOHelper` methods to be used.

Class getObjectIdClass(Object pc)

This method returns the class descriptor for the class that forms the JDO identity of the specified persistence-capable instance. Where application identity applies, this will be the class identified in the persistence descriptor. Where datastore identity applies, this will be the class chosen for that purpose by the implementation.

Object getObjectId(Object pc)

This method returns the JDO identity of the instance.

Object getTransactionalObjectId(Object pc)

This method is the same as **getObjectId** above, except that where application identity applies it will return the current identity, taking into account any alterations made to primary key fields during the current transaction.

Object newObjectIdinstance(Class cls, String representation)

It is a requirement of Object ID classes that they support a **toString()** method outputting a string representation of the key, and a string constructor that can accept such a representation and equivalently initialize an appropriate Object ID instance.

The **newObjectIdinstance** method accepts the class descriptor for a persistence-capable class, and a string representation of an Object ID. The method identifies the appropriate Object ID class for the indicated persistence-capable class, and returns a new instance initialized from the string representation.

6.4.4   Administrative functions

The following functions facilitate an application's administration of persistence managers.

void close()

void isClosed()

When an application has finished using a `PersistenceManager` instance it should call the **close()** method. After **close()** has been called, any further invocation of its methods throws a **JDOFatalUserException**, apart from the **isClosed()** method that returns **true**.

When a persistence manager is closed, the implementation may choose what to do with it. In a non-managed environment the object is likely to be discarded (and subsequently garbage-collected), whilst in a managed environment the object is likely to be returned to a pool of free persistence managers.

setUserObject(Object o)

Object getUserObject()

These methods allow an application to associate any single but arbitrary object with a persistence manager. This may be used by an application framework for infrastructure or administrative purposes.

PersistenceManagerFactory getPersistenceManagerFactory()

This method returns a reference to the factory from which the persistence manager was originally obtained.

Transaction currentTransaction()

This method returns a reference to the persistence manager's transaction object (an instance of **javax.jdo.Transaction**). Each persistence manager has only one such object, through which the application can demarcate transactions serially. If separate transactions are required in parallel, separate persistence managers will have to be used.

void setMultithreaded(boolean multithreaded)

boolean getMultithreaded()

These methods allow manipulation of the **Multithreaded** option within a persistence manager. If supported by the implementation, setting **Multithreaded** to **true** enables the application to invoke its methods from multiple threads simultaneously, at the expense of added thread synchronization overheads within the persistence manager.

void setIgnoreCache(boolean ignoreCache)

boolean getIgnoreCache()

These methods allow the manipulation of the **IgnoreCache** option. If **IgnoreCache** is set to **true** then the implementation is permitted (but not required) to optimize query execution by ignoring optimistically locked instances that have been changed in the current transaction.

6.4.5   Obtaining instances

Extent getExtent(class cl, boolean subclasses)

Given the class descriptor for a persistence-capable class, this method returns the extent of all persistent instances of that class. If the subclasses parameter is **true**, the extent includes all persistent instances of that class and its subclasses.

Extent query cost more than getObjectById

```
Object getObjectById(Object id)
```

This method retrieves a single persistent instance from the data store based on the identified Object ID instance.

It is possible for an application to determine an instance's identity from a persistence manager of a particular implementation, and to subsequently attempt to get the corresponding instance using the **getObjectById()** method of another persistence manager that is part of a different implementation. In such cases, the Object ID is guaranteed to be portable only if the JDO instance has application identity. For datastore identity the actual class acting as Object ID is an implementation choice, and portability across implementations is not even likely, let alone guaranteed.

6.4.6   Query factory methods

A persistence manager acts as the factory for JDO Query objects. This is provided through nine overloaded variants of the method **newQuery()**. Each of these will be discussed in Chapter 8.

6.5   Extent

The extent of a class (the so-called *candidate class*) represents the complete set of all persistent instances of that class. In pure object oriented terms, an extent actually contains all classes that are instances of the candidate class, although JDO allows the construction of an extent to optionally include or exclude subclasses of the candidate class.

Extents without subclasses

There are a number of JDO experts, myself included, who believe that the concept of an extent of a candidate class without subclasses does not make sense in terms of object orientation.

We recognize that extents without subclasses do facilitate performance improvements with some Implementations. However, it is our opinion that the subclasses = **false** setting should be considered as a hint to the implementation that it may optimize execution by ignoring any subclasses, rather than a mandatory requirement to specifically exclude any persistent subclasses which may exist.

I present this argument in more detail in Chapter 13.

An extent is merely a holder for the class descriptor, subclasses flag, and a collection of open **Iterator** objects. In this regard the JDO specification does not expect the obtaining of an extent, by calling **getExtent()** on a persistence manager, to actually read instances from the database. Only when an **Iterator** is obtained and its **next()** method invoked does the data retrieval process commence. Therefore it is quite legitimate to obtain a particular extent at the beginning of an application, and use it to obtain **Iterator**s as required, and in different transactions, until the application is closed. Of course, if you take this approach you should be doubly sure to close each **Iterator** as soon as you've finished with it in order to conserve system resources. These **Iterator**s are closed through the **close()** methods of the **Extent**.

[handwritten margin note: performance — Close Extent Iterators.]

Extent of an interface

In some implementations, it may be possible to obtain the extent of an interface. This may require the interface to have been enhanced. Iterators obtained from such an extent would yield all of the persistent JDO instances that implement the chosen interface.

In theory, the extent of the **SellableItem** interface could be used to list items that can be placed on an order. However, this is not quite as useful as it might seem. Since interfaces have only methods and not true attributes, there can be no concept of the "persistent fields" of an interface. The JDO Query Language (JDOQL) requires that persistent fields be supported within query filters; arbitrary method invocations are not supported. Thus it may be impossible to execute meaningful JDOQL queries against such extents in a portable manner. For more information about JDOQL, see Chapter 8.

Support for the extent of an interface should be considered non-standard unless it is explicitly included in a future version of JDO.

We have already used extents in several examples when iterating through all persistent instances of a candidate class. However, the primary purpose of an extent is to provide a candidate collection of instances to a query. The query will then apply its filtering semantics to the extent. The result of query execution is a collection that is a subset of the extent containing only those instances that match the specified filter criteria.

How do queries actually use extents?

Although, logically, a query applies a filter to an extent, it is not expected to do this merely by iterating from start to finish. In most cases, information from the extent will merely be used to create an equivalent query in the data store's native query language. Implementations will compete amongst each other in an effort to provide the most efficient query resolution possible, by maximizing the capabilities of the underlying data store in this regard.

We discuss JDOQL and the Query interface in detail in Chapter 8.

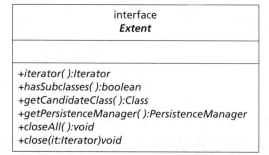

Figure 6.3 UML for extent interface

The extent interface (Figure 6.3) contains the following methods.

boolean hasSubclasses()

True is returned if subclasses were included in the call to **getExtent()**.

Note that this does not mean that the extent necessarily contains any instances of subclasses. Consider the code extract below:

```
Extent e = pm.getExtent(BusinessPartner.class, true);
System.out.println("Has Subclasses: " + e.hasSubclasses());
```

The output printed will be:

```
Has Subclasses: true
```

However, the extent will contain subclasses of **BusinessPartner** only if such persistent instances actually existed in the data store.

If **hasSubclasses()** returns **true**, the extent can be considered complete (any persistent instances of subclasses will be present). If **false** is returned, the extent might not be complete.

Class getCandidateClass()

This method returns the class descriptor of the candidate class (the class identified in the call to the persistence manager's **getExtent()** method).

The example below uses this to determine further information about an extent.

```
public void printExtentInfo(Extent e) {
    System.out.println("Candidate Class: " +
      e.getCandidateClass().getName());
    System.out.println("Has Subclasses: " +
      e.hasSubClasses());
}
```

If invoked with the extent of **BusinessPartner** constructed above, the output would be:

```
Candidate Class: BusinessPartner
Has Subclasses: true
```

PersistenceManager getPersistenceManager()

This method returns a reference to the persistence manager from which the extent was obtained.

void close(Iterator i)

This method closes an **Iterator** previously obtained from the **Extent**. Subsequent to this, the iterator's **hasNext()** method will return **false**. However, the extent can still be used to obtain further iterators or as the candidate collection for queries.

void closeAll()

This method closes all open (i.e. not yet closed) **Iterator**s that have been previously obtained from the extent.

Iterator iterator()

The **Iterator** returned from this method can be used to iterate through the contents of the extent. The objects returned at each call to the iterator's **next()** method will be persistent JDO instances of the candidate class or subclasses thereof.

6.6   PersistenceCapable

JDO is split into two packages. Package **javax.jdo** is the API and contains classes and interfaces that applications will use. Package **javax.jdo.spi** is the SPI containing those classes and interfaces internal to JDO implementations. The **PersistenceCapable** interface, which is implemented by hand coding or by enhancement by all persistence-capable classes, is part of the SPI.

The operations present in the **PersistenceCapable** interface all have names beginning with "jdo". Thus, to avoid potential conflicts, you should not use this prefix for methods in your persistence-capable classes. These methods allow the persistence infrastructure to interrogate and manipulate persistent field values and perform a number of administrative functions, such as state interrogation.

Application developers should never make use of the **PersistenceCapable** interface. All of the functionality they require is available through the **PersistenceManager** interface and the **JDOHelper** class. Indeed, even the name and structure of the **PersistenceCapable** interface represent implementation choices internal to JDO. The principle of encapsulation dictates that applications maintain a clear separation between the external and internal interfaces of components, and no dependency of an application on **PersistenceCapable** should be tolerated.

What's next?

In the next chapter we consider transaction management and the JDO **Transaction** interface. Specific focus is given to optimistic transaction strategies.

Transaction management 7

Effective transaction management is a critical aspect of object persistence. This chapter discusses JDO transactions in the context of the non-managed environment. Chapter 11, contains in-depth discussions of transaction management in the managed environment.

7.1 Transactions

A transaction is a grouping together of work – typically changes to persistent data – that must be completed in its entirety or not at all. The fundamental aim of a transaction is to ensure that partial completion, where some data changes persist in the data store and others in the same transaction don't, does not occur. This so-called *atomic* property of transactions is integral to the maintenance of data integrity.

Another fundamental property of transactions is that they must be *isolated*, to a given degree, from each other. Isolation levels dictate the consistency with which data, being manipulated in one transaction, is presented, in the context of another transaction.

Experienced database programmers will be familiar with the four transaction isolation levels that are recognized by JDBC: Read Uncommitted, Read Committed, Repeatable Read, and Read Serializable. Some database products, particularly object databases, define much richer sets.

JDO does not explicitly specify the isolation level that will be applied. instances may have fields read at different times and, conceivably, from different data sources. Developers should not rely on any isolation level greater than Read Committed. For reference, Read Committed is defined as:

> This isolation level does not allow other transactions to see state changes made by this transaction until a commit has been issued.

Nothing in JDO actually specifies that the locking of data in the data store should take place. Locking strategies do, however, account for the most common method of implementing the Read Committed level of isolation.

7.2   Transaction interface

A JDO persistence manager has at most one active transaction at any point in time. The **PersistenceManager** interface defines the **currentTransaction()** method, which returns an instance of the transaction interface. This transaction instance is the application developer's means for demarcating transaction boundaries within JDO.

From the time a persistence manager is obtained until the time it is closed, calls to **currentTransaction()** will return the identical **Transaction** instance. Thus it is common practice, in single-threaded client-server applications that typically maintain a single persistence manager instance for an extended period, to obtain the transaction as soon as the persistence manager is available. This object is then used for transaction demarcation until the persistence manager is finally closed. During this time many independent JDO transactions may be started and completed – one after the other – through the single Transaction instance.

Those applications that require multiple independent transactions to be active simultaneously must employ a corresponding number of persistence managers. Finally, JDO does not support the concept of "nested" transactions.

The UML notation of the transaction interface is shown in Figure 7.1.

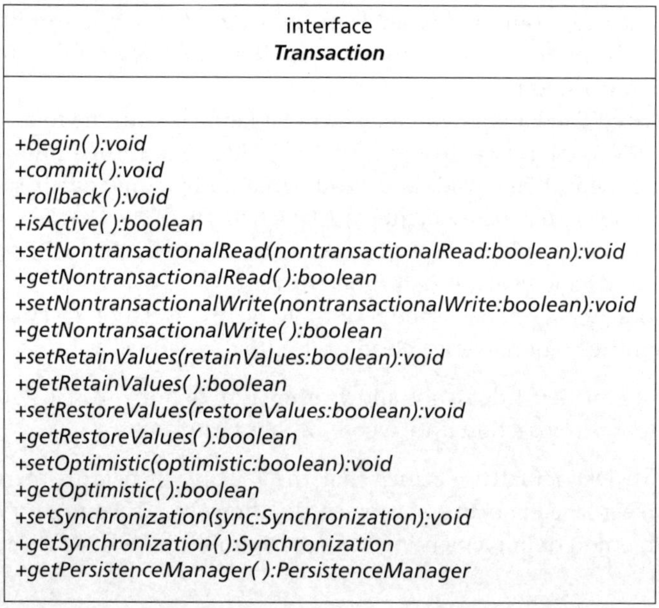

interface *Transaction*
+begin( ):void +commit( ):void +rollback( ):void +isActive( ):boolean +setNontransactionalRead(nontransactionalRead:boolean):void +getNontransactionalRead( ):boolean +setNontransactionalWrite(nontransactionalWrite:boolean):void +getNontransactionalWrite( ):boolean +setRetainValues(retainValues:boolean):void +getRetainValues( ):boolean +setRestoreValues(restoreValues:boolean):void +getRestoreValues( ):boolean +setOptimistic(optimistic:boolean):void +getOptimistic( ):boolean +setSynchronization(sync:Synchronization):void +getSynchronization( ):Synchronization +getPersistenceManager( ):PersistenceManager

Figure 7.1 UML for Transaction interface

7.3   Transaction strategies

JDO supports two specific transaction strategies. *Pessimistic transactions* are a required feature of the specification, and are therefore supported by all compliant implementations. *Optimistic transactions* are an optional feature of the specification. They will be supported by many, but not all, implementations. Support for this feature does not depend on native support for optimistic transactions in the underlying data store – vendors may choose to simulate this feature where such native support is lacking.

7.3.1   Pessimistic (data store) transactions

Pessimistic transactions are the default in JDO. They are suitable when the transaction is very short-lived, typically because there is no user interaction or other blocking activity between the transaction's start and end. When data is read or changed during a pessimistic transaction, other transactions are excluded from accessing that data until the first transaction has been completed. Pessimistic JDO transactions are usually implemented through native pessimistic transactions in the underlying data store.

We have already seen examples of pessimistic transactions in previous chapters – any transaction begun with the optimistic property of the transaction set to **false** is a pessimistic transaction.

In the example below, a pessimistic transaction is used to undertake an element of work. If any exceptions occur while the work is being performed, the transaction is rolled back if it is still active.

```
Transaction t = pm.currentTransaction();
t.setOptimistic(false); // I'm being explicit in case it was
                        // previously set true
t.begin()
try {
    // do some work here which does not involve significant
    // delays, therefore
    // this is a short-lived transaction
    // eg. Obtain a BusinessPartner and immediately update it
}
catch (Exception e) {
    // rollback the transaction if it is still active
    if (t.isActive()) t.rollback();
}
finally {
    try {
        // commit the transaction if it is still active
        if (t.isActive()) t.commit();
    }
```

```
        catch (JDOException je) {
            // transaction rolled back - advise the user or take
            // other appropriate action
        }
    }
```

Long-lived transactions typically occur when transaction demarcation is dependent upon intervening user activity. An example would be a transaction that is held open whilst a user enters data. In such cases the use of pessimistic transactions may cause excessive locking to occur in the data store, thereby reducing the overall concurrency of the system.

Although pessimistic transactions can be used in such cases, optimistic transactions provide an extremely useful alternative.

7.3.2   Optimistic transactions

When working with long-lived transactions, it is often unacceptable to physically lock data in the data store for the duration. Optimistic transactions stem from an approach to increase concurrency (reduce locking) in such instances.

The basis for doing this is a set of optimistic concurrency assumptions; it is presumed that any data altered in the optimistic transaction will not actually be altered by any other transaction until the first has been committed. Since in many cases this assumption is indeed true 99% or more of the time, there is no need to physically lock the underlying data. The only thing that needs to be done is to verify that the assumptions are indeed true before our changes are actually written to the data store.

A typical optimistic transaction under which a **BusinessPartner** is to be changed, and which is executed against a database that does not provide native support for optimistic transactions, would have the following steps (for those data stores which do support optimistic transactions, these steps would conceptually still apply but the implementation would be much simpler):

1 Read the business partner from the data store and obtain some piece of information by which we can later tell whether this object has had changes committed to the data store; this typically involves a timestamp or an object version number. Where the database schema has been previously dictated it may not be possible for such version number or timestamp information to be added to the tables. In these cases the entire state of the data store entity may be used for comparative purposes. (Where the data store natively supports optimistic transactions there will be no need for this additional information.)

2 Allow the business partner to be updated. These updates may occur over a period of time, during which the corresponding data store entity is not locked.

3 When the transaction is finally committed, a short-lived pessimistic transaction is started on the underlying data store. The data store is checked to determine whether the business partner object has been changed. This check verifies the optimistic concurrency assumptions and locks the underlying entity.

4 Assuming that the data store entity has not been changed, the updated data is synchronized to the data store and the short-lived pessimistic transaction is immediately committed.

5 The results of this commit are relayed back to the application. Thus, if the pessimistic transaction was rolled back for any reason, the application would be informed through an appropriate exception.

6 The optimistic concurrency assumptions would be **false** if the data was changed by someone else after the business partner was read, but before the optimistic transaction was committed. In this case, the short-lived pessimistic transaction would be rolled back and an appropriate exception thrown to the application.

So that's how it works internally. Let's take a look at a code example of an optimistic transaction:

```
Transaction t = pm.currentTransaction();
t.setOptimistic(true);
t.begin()
try {
    // do some work here which might take an extended time,
    // hence the use of optimistic locking. e.g. obtain a
    // BusinessPartner, show the field values to the user
    // and wait for the user to alte the data and press a
    // "save" button, before which the user might go out
    // for lunch!
}
catch (Exception e) {
    // rollback the transaction if it is still active
    if (t.isActive()) t.rollback();
}
finally {
    try {
        // commit the transaction if it is still active
        if (t.isActive()) t.commit();
    }
    catch (JDOUserException je) {
        // transaction rolled back - advise the user that
        // the work they did has not been saved and must
        // be done again
    }
}
```

The only significant code differences between the two locking strategies are the setting of the **Optimistic** transaction property to **false**, and the catching of **JDOUserException** after **commit()**.

Here we now see the fundamental difference between the two approaches. In the pessimistic case, an exception at commit time might mean that the user entered data that violated integrity constraints or was otherwise invalid. If the user's data had been valid, the commit would have been successful (system failures aside).

In the optimistic case, even valid data changes might be rolled back at transaction completion time, simply because the data had been changed by someone else in the interim. The user must review the now-changed data, and then perform the required changes again if they still apply.

Given that the likelihood of concurrency assumptions failing is usually small, such rework is unlikely to be required often. In some cases this is acceptable – if a user does go out for lunch whilst updating a business partner's details, they increase the risk of having to redo the work. They should complete the task at hand before leaving!

In other cases, however, such strategies are not acceptable. Almost all server-side transactions will be pessimistic (except those which must be open across user interaction on a remote client). It is up to the designer to make an appropriate choice based upon the concurrency requirements of the system, and the "cost" (in terms of staff time and morale as well as any financial implications) of work needing to be redone should optimistic concurrency assumptions fail.

7.3.3   Optimistic transactions and refresh

Before we look at more advanced transaction management features, I'd like to mention two potential uses of the persistence manager's **refresh()** methods within optimistic transactions.

7.3.3.1 Last commit wins

When an instance is passed as an argument to one of the persistence manager's **refresh()** methods, the field values are restored to those currently in the data store. After an instance has become part of an optimistic transaction, there is a possibility that the persistent entity will have been changed before the optimistic transaction is committed, causing optimistic concurrency assumptions to fail and the transaction to be rolled back.

The incidence of this can be reduced if field values in an optimistically locked instance are refreshed immediately before they are updated. By retrieving field values, the optimistic currency assumptions are reset to reflect the current state of the instance. If **refresh()** is invoked immediately before the instance is updated and the transaction committed, then the likelihood of concurrency assumptions proving to be incorrect is greatly reduced.

A code example of this is shown below:

```
Transaction t = pm.currentTransaction();
t.setOptimistic(true);
t.begin()
try {
    String bpKey = "123"; // some valid key value
    BusinessPartner bp = (BusinessPartner)
        pm.getObjectById(bkKey);
    String name = bp.getName();
    // bp transitions to Persistent-Nontransactional

    // do some work here which might take an extended time;
    // display the name
    // to the user and allow them to change it, before which
    // the user might go out for lunch!

    // retrieve the instance and update
    pm.refresh(bp); // bp remains Persistent-Nontransactional
    bp.setName(name); // bp transitions to Persistent-Dirty
}
catch (Exception e) {
    // rollback the transaction if it is still active
    if (t.isActive()) t.rollback();
}
finally {
    // commit the transaction if it is still active
    try {
        // commit the transaction if it is still active
        if (t.isActive()) t.commit();
    }
    catch (JDOUserException je) {
        // transaction rolled back - advise the user that
        // the work they did has
        // not been saved and must be done again
    }
}
```

The instance is refreshed immediately before it is updated. The chance of concurrency assumptions being invalid is greatly reduced. However, what we have is no longer a true optimistic transaction strategy – instead we have a "last commit wins" situation. This is equivalent to using one short-lived pessimistic transaction to read an instance, allowing the read data to be updated non-transactionally, and then committing that to the database without any regard for changes that may have occurred in the interim.

7.3.3.2 Reacting to optimistic concurrency assumption failures

The premise of optimistic transactions is that the data probably will not change during the transaction. The risk of this happening is justified by the increased concurrency afforded by an optimistic strategy.

Occasionally, however, the data associated with an optimistic transaction is changed by another (optimistic or pessimistic) transaction. The application must be able to cope with this.

Highly evolved applications may attempt some form of data reconciliation, essentially merging changes with the now updated persistent instance values. However, such strategies are inherently complex, and their implementation depends heavily on the business domain being modeled.

The simplest form of resolution involves telling the user their changes could not be saved and must be done again. The instances are refreshed from the data store, and these values are presented to the user.

7.3.3.3 Example without explicit refresh

Before we consider the mechanics of such a policy, let us closely examine the intricacies of optimistic transaction failure. For this purpose, presume that we are working with the **Product** class. Our transaction will update the `description` field.

To start with, presume we have two products: one with a description of "Green Chairs" and the other "Green Tables." We are going to examine the potential conflict of two transactions. For ease of reference we will refer to two users, User1 and User2, although the issue also pertains to situations where a single user has multiple transactions simultaneously active through different persistence managers in the same JVM.

User1 starts an optimistic transaction within which both products, "Green Chairs" and "Green Tables," are read. The instances will transition Persistent-Nontransactional at this point since they have been read in an optimistic transaction. User1 now goes to lunch without completing the transaction.

User2 begins a new transaction – optimistic or pessimistic, it doesn't matter which. Both products are read and their descriptions updated to "Red Chairs" and "Red Tables" respectively. The transaction is committed, and the commit is successful. The persistent data has now been changed.

User1, having returned from lunch, changes the description of the second product to "Blue Tables." That instance transitions to Persistent-Dirty. By pressing the Save button (imagine a carefully crafted Swing interface if you will!), the transaction commit is attempted. However we know that the transaction will fail, as the underlying data store entities have been altered by another transaction. According to the state transition tables of the JDO specification, the dirty instance will transition back to Hollow. Note that, according to the same state tables, the unaltered instance remains in the Persistent-Nontransactional state.

Now we see the problem. A **JDOUserException** is thrown by the JDO implementation when the commit of the optimistic transaction was attempted. I presume that the application will redisplay the data and invite User1 to make his changes again (manual resolution). When the fields of the Hollow instance are read and displayed, the values will be retrieved from the data store, and the description "Red Tables" will be shown. However, the Persistent-Nontransactional instance will likely yield an outdated description of "Green Tables."

Thus, in response to an optimistic transaction failure, the user is being presented with transactionally inconsistent data. (This specific problem arises when an instance is read in an optimistic transaction and is not altered within that transaction, but is altered by another transaction.)

Some implementations may choose to invalidate all instances involved in a failed optimistic transaction, essentially making them Hollow. This is not strictly correct, but – as has been illustrated above – would be extremely helpful.

7.3.4   Resolution using explicit refresh

The solution to the quandary described above is to explicitly refresh each instance involved in an optimistic transaction failure before the data is redisplayed to the user. Unfortunately there is no means to achieve this automatically through the JDO API, which requires the application to maintain a list of instances involved in an optimistic transaction expressly for this purpose. Since the code which handles commit failures may not be part of the code that manipulates instances within the transaction, this problem may be non-trivial.

Most of the JDO vendors agree that optimistic transactions are under-specified in JDO, and will be adding additional API calls to handle cases such as this. No doubt a future version of JDO will combine their best efforts under a revision of the standard API.

7.4   Advanced transaction options

We now look at ways in which applications can access persistent data outside the context of an active transaction. Recall that persistence and transactionality can be applied to instances in any combination. We say that the two concepts are *orthogonal*; just because the instance is persistent does not mean that it is necessarily transactional.

7.4.1   NontransactionalRead and Write

If the **NontransactionalRead** flag on a **Transaction** is **true**, then the field values of Hollow and Non-transactional instances can be read without an active transaction.

If the **NontransactionalWrite** flag on a **Transaction** is **true**, then the field values of Persistent-Nontransactional instances can be updated without an active transaction.

Each of these capabilities is an optional feature in the JDO specification.

7.5   Transaction modes to improve efficiency

JDO defines two additional transaction modes intended to improve efficiency. These are **RestoreValues** and **RetainValues**. Note that the setting of these flags only affects instances in memory, and does not alter the effect of commit or rollback processing on the data store.

7.5.1   RestoreValues

The setting of the **RestoreValues** flag affects the treatment of instances in memory as a result of transaction rollback.

If the **RestoreValues** flag is **true**, instances involved in a transaction that is rolled back will have their field values restored to their original values. These were cached when the transaction was begun.

If the **RestoreValues** flag is **false**, instances involved in a transaction that is rolled back will be transitioned to Hollow. In such a state they do not have field values loaded, and thus the field values do not need to be restored to their original values. This allows JDO vendors to optimize their implementations so that instance values are not cached in the first place. If the now Hollow instance is accessed by the application, persistent fields will be loaded from the data store at that time.

Setting **RestoreValues** to **false** can yield significant performance improvements if your application does not refer to instances after transaction rollback.

7.5.2   RetainValues

This flag determines what action is taken by the persistence manager on persistent instances in memory after a transaction has been *successfully* committed.

If **RetainValues** is **false** (the default setting), instances are automatically evicted on transaction commit, transitioning to Hollow. This limits the size of the instance cache and improves performance.

If **RetainValues** is **true**, this automatic eviction does not take place. The persistent instances remain cached in the Persistent-Nontransactional state until they are once again used transactionally, or evicted. Eviction may be performed explicitly by the developer, or implicitly by the persistence manager to free up cache resources. This setting can improve performance of applications that work with the same set of instances across a number of independent transactions, at the expense of greater resource utilization by the persistence manager.

Improving upon RetainValues

As it is currently defined, **RetainValues** applies globally to the entire contents of the persistence manager's cache. There is scope for this concept to be improved in future versions of JDO, so that instances of some specific persistence-capable classes can be retained but not others. Persistence-capable classes that represent infrequently changed reference data could then be retained in the cache, in order to reduce unnecessary data store access. A more advanced specification could facilitate timeouts for instances cached in this manner, so that the data store would indeed be checked if the instance was accessed after the designated period had elapsed.

7.6   Synchronization with JDO transactions

It is sometimes useful for an application to be notified when a transaction is about to be committed or has been completed (successfully or not). The transaction interface facilitates this by providing for the registration of a user-provided callback object. The callback object must implement the **javax.transaction.Synchronization** interface. Its **beforeCompletion()** and **afterCompletion()** methods will be called to notify the application of these events.

The synchronization interface is shown in Figure 7.2.

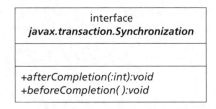

Figure 7.2 UML for javax.transaction.Synchronization interface

An instance of an application class that implements the **Synchronization** instance may be registered for transaction callbacks via the **Transaction** interface's **setSynchronization()** method.

setSynchronization(javax.transaction.Synchronization sync)

Replaces the previously registered synchronization object with the object sync. If the reference is null, then no object will receive transaction completion callbacks.

The synchronization object's **beforeCompletion()** method will be invoked during the transaction's commit processing. If the method throws a

JDOUserException, the transaction will be rolled back. The method is not called if a rollback is instigated instead of commit.

The synchronization object's **afterCompletion(int status)** method will be called once the transaction is complete. The status parameter indicates the success or failure of the transaction, and will have one of two values:

javax.transaction.Status.STATUS_COMMITTED

javax.transaction.Status.STATUS_ROLLEDBACK

Validation during commit

There are two different ways in which instances may be validated before they are committed to the data store. The first is to have the instances implement the **InstanceCallbacks** interface, and perform the validation in the **jdoPreStore()** method. The second is to register a callback object using the transaction interface's **setSynchronization()** method, and to perform the validation from its **beforeCompletion()** method.

I am not particularly in favor of the first approach, since it is less than transparent to the domain object model; the **InstanceCallbacks** interface is specific to JDO. Also, the **jdoPreStore()** method may be called multiple times on one instance in a single transaction, as it is invoked whenever the implementation flushes data to the data store.

Use of synchronization objects may seem to be an easy alternative. However, the synchronization object must maintain a list of dirty instances to be validated. Instances may be involved in other transactions where no synchronization object is registered, and so critical validation cannot be guaranteed in this way.

For the time being, therefore, **jdoPreStore()** may actually be the better of the two alternatives. This is an area that will be the subject of much debate as JDO becomes more widely used. I anticipate that, in a future version of JDO, persistence descriptor tags will be defined to provide declarative support for validation. These may include Delete Restrict and Delete Cascade functionality, as well as the identification of a validation method for each persistence-capable class, to be automatically invoked on instances during the commit process.

What's next?

In the next chapter, I introduce the new query language, JDOQL, which provides a Java-like syntax for the efficient querying of persistent data through JDO.

Queries with JDOQL 8

JDO's transparent persistence allows applications to navigate through the persistent fields of an instance that are references to other persistent instances. As the application de-references these objects, those that are not present in the persistence manager's cache are loaded from the data store. This gives the application the impression that the entire inter-connected graph of persistent instances is immediately available in memory.

The issue remains as to how an application should obtain the first persistent instance. Three methods are available.

1 The application can use the persistence manager's **getObjectById()** method if it is able to construct the Object ID instance. The Object ID may have been previously stored by the application for this purpose. Alternatively, an instance of the Object ID for a class with application identity may be constructed based on data input by the user. This is the most efficient way to retrieve a single specific instance.

2 The application could obtain an **Iterator** from the **Extent** of a persistence-capable class and iterate through the persistent instances. This approach might be used when it is the application's intention that every instance be processed. However, it is probably inefficient when trying to retrieve a single specific instance or a small group of instances.

3 The application can employ the **Query** interface and the new JDOQL. This employs a Java-like syntax for query definition, allowing the developer to specify filter criteria. Queries are implemented using the most efficient execution methods available in the target data store.

This chapter describes JDOQL in detail.

8.1 Query architecture

The JDO specification provides the **Query** interface and the JDOQL Query definition as an object-oriented and data-store independent means for the definition and execution of queries. By utilizing these features, application query requirements can be met without compromising the portability of the application amongst different implementations.

JDOQL is intended to be neutral to the native query language of the underlying data store. Most implementations will map the elements of JDOQL into the data store's native query language. Of course, some data stores do not have their own query language, e.g. file systems and XML documents, and in such cases the implementation will have to provide client-side query execution functionality.

The philosophy of JDOQL revolves around the concept of a so-called *candidate collection* of instances to which the query's filter criteria will be applied. The result of query execution is an unmodifiable **Collection**, comprised of those members of the candidate collection for which the filter criteria evaluated to **true**.

Queries can include parameterized values. They can also define and use local reference variables to which values are assigned during query execution, and by which the query filter may traverse connected instances.

Queries consist of the following mandatory elements:

- The candidate class. All instances of the candidate collection will be instances of this class. The unmodifiable collection returned after query execution will contain only instances of the candidate class. Polymorphism is fully supported, so "instances of" implicitly includes any subclasses of the candidate class.

- The candidate collection. This may be a true **Collection** object containing zero or more objects, all of which must be instances of the candidate class. Alternatively this may be the **Extent** of the candidate class, implicitly including all persistent instances as candidates for the query. (The extent may optionally include or exclude subclasses of the candidate class.)

- The query filter. This is expressed as a Java-like **boolean** expression. The result of query execution will include only those candidates for which the expression evaluates to **true**.

Queries may additionally contain:

- parameter declarations, comprising one or more pairs of identifier names and types;

- parameter values, provided at execution time, which are bound to the declared parameter identifiers. Values are usually assigned to declared identifiers as "positional parameters," but can also be passed as "named parameters" depending on the application's requirements;

- variable declarations, comprising one or more pairs of identifier names and types. Variables are typically used to hold references that allow query filters to span graphs of connected instances;

- import declarations, used to import non-standard class names that are to be used as types for parameters or variables;

- an ordering specification allowing arbitrary ordering of the query results.

Queries also include the notion of namespaces. A given identifier name may not be defined more than once in a particular namespace. There are two namespaces for each query:

- Type Namespace. All type names used by the query reside in this namespace. Thus a query may not use two different types that have the same name. The candidate class and all public types in the **java.lang** package are implicitly imported into this namespace. Other types must be imported explicitly as required through the import declaration for the query.

- Identifier Namespace. All parameter names, variable names, and persistent field names reside in this namespace. The persistent field names include all persistent fields of all classes referenced in the query. Thus it is not legal to define a parameter or variable with the same name as a persistent field of the candidate class or other persistence-capable class referenced in the query. Nor is it legal to define both a parameter and a variable with the same name.

JDOQL is very Java-like in syntax and therefore easy for Java developers to master. Nevertheless, the query interface has been designed so that it can be used with an alternative query language if the application so chooses, presuming that this alternative language is supported by the implementation.

8.2   Constructing queries

A persistence manager acts as the factory for queries, and provides a set of `newQuery()` methods by which an application can construct queries. These methods are detailed below.

`Query newQuery()`

Constructs a new query instance, bound to the current persistence manager. All of the query's properties can then be set directly, including the query language.

`Query newQuery(Object query)`

Constructs a query instance from another query. The new query shares the original query's elements except for the candidate collection or extent. The new query is bound to the persistence manager on which `newQuery()` was executed, even though the original query may have been obtained from a different persistence manager. This, combined with the requirement that all query implementation classes are serializable, facilitates the construction of a new query based on one earlier constructed against a different JDO implementation.

This method presumes that the implementation's default query language (typically JDOQL) is to be used.

`Query newQuery(String language, Object query)`

Constructs a new query from an existing query using the specified query language.

`Query newQuery(Class cls)`

Construct a new query with the specified candidate class.

`Query newQuery(Extent cln)`

Construct a new query with the candidate class derived from the **Extent**, and a candidate collection comprised of all persistent instances of the **Extent**.

`Query newQuery(Class cls, Collection cln)`

Construct a new query with the specified candidate class and candidate collection. The collection may contain zero or more objects, all of which must be instances of the candidate class.

`Query newQuery(Class cls, Collection cln, String filter)`

Construct a new query with the specified candidate class, candidate collection, and filter expression. The collection may contain zero or more objects, all of which must be instances of the candidate class.

`Query newQuery(Extent cln, String filter)`

Construct a new query with the candidate class derived from the **Extent**, a candidate collection comprised of all persistent instances of the **Extent**, and the specified filter expression.

`Query newQuery(Class cls, String filter)`

Construct a new query with the specified candidate class and filter expression.

8.3 Query interface

The object returned from the query factory methods of a persistence manager is an instance of the Query interface. The UML for the Query interface is shown in Figure 8.1.

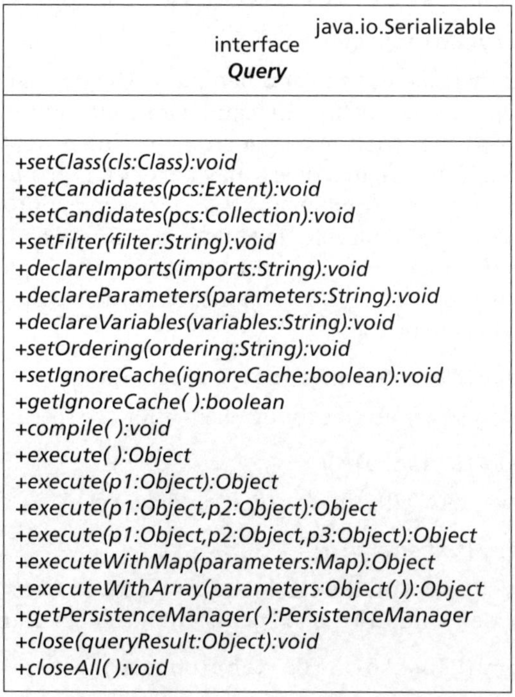

```
                              java.io.Serializable
                    interface
                      Query


 +setClass(cls:Class):void
 +setCandidates(pcs:Extent):void
 +setCandidates(pcs:Collection):void
 +setFilter(filter:String):void
 +declareImports(imports:String):void
 +declareParameters(parameters:String):void
 +declareVariables(variables:String):void
 +setOrdering(ordering:String):void
 +setIgnoreCache(ignoreCache:boolean):void
 +getIgnoreCache( ):boolean
 +compile( ):void
 +execute( ):Object
 +execute(p1:Object):Object
 +execute(p1:Object,p2:Object):Object
 +execute(p1:Object,p2:Object,p3:Object):Object
 +executeWithMap(parameters:Map):Object
 +executeWithArray(parameters:Object( )):Object
 +getPersistenceManager( ):PersistenceManager
 +close(queryResult:Object):void
 +closeAll( ):void
```

Figure 8.1 UML for Query interface

I will describe each of the Query interface's methods briefly before we look at our first JDOQL examples.

PersistenceManager getPersistenceManager()

Returns a reference to the persistence manager with which the query is associated.

void setClass()

Sets the candidate class for the query.

void setCandidates(Collection candidateCollection)

Sets the candidate collection for the query.

void setCandidates(Extent candidateExtent)

Sets the candidate class and candidate collection for the query, from the values encapsulated in the **Extent**.

void setFilter(String filter)

Sets the filter criteria for the query. The filter should be valid according to the chosen query language.

void declareImports(String imports)

Provides an import declaration. This will import classes into the "type" name-space, so that these types can be used for the declaration of query parameters and variables.

void declareVariables(String variables)
void declareParameters(String parameters)
void setOrdering(String ordering)

Provide the variable, parameter and ordering declarations for the query.

void setIgnoreCache(boolean ignoreCache)
Boolean getIgnoreCache()

These methods access the value for the **IgnoreCache** query property. If the property is set to **true**, the query might be executed such that changed instances in the persistence manager cache but not yet committed to the data store are ignored, and the currently persistent versions of those instances are queried instead.

This may improve query execution speeds with some JDO implementations, at the expense of generating only approximate query results. As such it should probably be applied only to read-only transactions, within which data is queried but never altered.

void compile()

JDOQL does not require queries to be compiled. However, compilation of queries has two advantages. Firstly, any syntactic errors can be reported in advance of query execution. Secondly, a compiled query may execute more quickly than an uncompiled equivalent, although this is entirely implementation-dependent.

Query compilation is generally recommended when the same query will be executed multiple times (albeit with different parameter values), or when queries are defined and then stored for later execution.

8.3.1 Query execution

The following methods of the Query interface are used to execute a query, each with a different argument list for incoming query parameter values.

The methods are all defined to return Object for flexibility in future enhancements to JDOQL. However, under the current version of JDO, all executions result in an unmodifiable collection object. The returned reference should be manually cast to collection by the application developer.

```
Object execute()
Object execute(Object p1)
Object execute(Object p1, Object p2)
Object execute(Object p1, Object p2, Object p3)
```

Execute a query taking zero, one, two, or three parameters. Parameters are "positional," and must be passed in the order in which they were declared.

```
Object executeWithArray(Object[] parameters)
```

Execute a query that takes any number of parameters (zero or more). Parameters are "positional," and must appear in the array in the order in which they were declared in the query.

```
Object executeWithMap(Map parameters)
```

Execute a query that takes any number of parameters (zero or more). Parameters are "named" instead of "positional". The map contains key and value pairs. Each parameter of the query will be assigned the value corresponding to the map entry with the parameter name as key.

8.3.2 Closing query results

```
void close(Object queryResult)
```

Close the resources associated with a given query result.

```
void closeAll()
```

Close the resources associated with all query results obtained from executions of this query.

8.4 Query examples

Although we have yet to discuss the syntax of query filters, we are now in a position to examine some simple queries.

8.4.1   Query without filter

Our first example is a query that lists all instances of the **BusinessPartner** class. I have presented this as a small application with a **main()** method which can be run from the command line, although future query examples will be shown as code snippets.

SimpleQuery.Java

```
package com.ogilviepartners.jdobook.app;

import java.util.Collection;
import java.util.Iterator;
import javax.jdo.*;

public class SimpleQuery
{
    public static void main() {
        JDOBootstrap bootstrap = new JDOBootstrap();
        PersistenceManagerFactory pmf =
            bootstrap.getPersistenceManagerFactory();
        PersistenceManager pm = pmf.getPersistenceManager();
        Transaction t = pm.currentTransaction();

        t.begin();

        Extent partnerExt = pm.getExtent(
          BusinessPartner.class, true);
        Query q = pm.newQuery(partnerExt);
        Collection c = (Collection) q.execute();

        Iterator i = c.iterator();
        System.out.println(
          "Listing all BusinessPartner instances:");
        while(i.hasNext()) {
            Object o = i.next();
            System.out.println(o);
        }
        System.out.println("Done.");

        q.close(c);
        t.commit();
    }
}
```

The above example is indeed very simple. There is no filter defined, nor are there any parameter, variable, import, or ordering declarations. The candidate collection is the entire extent of **BusinessPartner** (including subclasses). It is important to note that the objects being returned each time **next()** is called on the **Iterator** are in fact instances of the concrete subclasses of **BusinessPartner**: **Company**, **Charity**, and **Individual**.

8.4.2   Query with ordering

The next step is to add a simple ordering declaration. The example below orders the query results according to name, and then according to **partnerId** descending. Thus if multiple partners had the same name they would appear in the descending sequence of their **partnerId**s.

```
Extent partnerExt = pm.getExtent(BusinessPartner.class, true);
Query q = pm.newQuery(partnerExt);
q.setOrdering("name ascending, partnerId descending");
Collection c = (Collection) q.execute();
```

The ordering declaration comprises any number of persistent field names, each paired with the keyword **ascending** or **descending** as appropriate. These pairs are separated with commas.

8.4.3   Query with filter

For our next example, let's apply a simple filter to the query. We will discuss the full suite of available filter operators shortly. For now we will use the **==** operator to select only those business partners with a specific name.

```
Extent partnerExt = pm.getExtent(BusinessPartner.class, true);
String filter = "name == \"Ogilvie Partners\"";
Query q = pm.newQuery(partnerExt, filter);
q.setOrdering("name ascending, partnerId descending");
Collection c = (Collection) q.execute();
```

We are now using a different **newQuery()** method that returns a query with the filter declaration assigned. The filter declaration is a **String** containing the **boolean** expression. Although this expression is based on Java syntax there are significant differences, such as the use of the **==** operator for testing string equivalence above. In the next section we examine the capabilities and syntax of filter expressions in detail.

8.5   Query filter expressions

The filter expression for a query is optional. If no filter is set, the filter will be deemed to evaluate to **true** in all cases, and the query result will be the whole candidate collection.

Query filters are expressions that evaluate to a **boolean** value. They are structured as zero, one, or more **boolean** expressions separated by logical NOT (complement), AND, and OR operators, in that order of evaluation. Parentheses may be used to alter the default order of evaluation.

For readers well versed in formal grammars, the grammar for JDOQL is reproduced in Appendix E, in Backus-Naur Form (BNF).

8.5.1   Supported operators

Five logical operators are defined. These are listed and described in Table 8.1.

Table 8.1 Logical operators

Operator	Description
!	NOT (complement) Negates the logical expression to its right
&	Unconditional AND Causes the expressions to its left and right to be evaluated, and returns the result of a logical AND operation of the resulting boolean values
&&	Conditional AND Causes the evaluation of the expression to its left. If this is **false**, the result of the AND expression is **false**; otherwise the expression on its right is evaluated, the result of the AND expression being the result of the right-hand boolean expression
|	Unconditional OR Causes the expressions to its left and right to be evaluated, and returns the result of a logical OR operation of the resulting boolean values
||	Conditional OR Causes the evaluation of the expression to its left. If this is **true**, the result of the OR expression is **true**; otherwise the expression on its right is evaluated, the result of the OR expression being the result of the right-hand boolean expression

JDOQL filters must be non-mutating, which means that their evaluation will have no side effects. Thus there is no justification for using the unconditional logical operators (**&**, **|**), and the conditional ones (**&&**, **||**) should be used as a matter of course. Indeed, many JDO implementations replace **&** with **&&** and **|** with **||** during query execution.

JDOQL supports a complete set of comparative operators. These return **boolean** values based on evaluating the results of the left and right-hand expressions. They are shown in Table 8.2.

Table 8.2 Comparative operators

Operator	Description
==	Equal
!=	Not equal
>	Greater than
<	Less than
>=	Greater than or equal
<=	Less than or equal
+	Numeric addition and string concatenation
*	Multiplication
/	Division

JDOQL supports the casting and de-referencing of fields that are reference types. Both are performed using the familiar Java operators, shown in Table 8.3.

Table 8.3 Reference operators

Operator	Description
(Class)	Object casting
.	De-reference a reference type field (as in field1.field2)

Finally JDOQL supports the following unary operators, which apply to the expression immediately to their right (Table 8.4).

Table 8.4 Unary operators

Operator	Description
~	Integral bit-wise complement
−	Numeric sign inversion

8.5.2   Supported keywords

The keyword **this** is a reserved word in JDOQL. It is used in filter expressions to refer to the instance of the candidate collection for which the filter expression is currently being evaluated. It can also be used to differentiate between persistent fields of the candidate class and identically named query parameters. An example of such usage is given under section 8.6.1.

8.5.3   Differences between JDOQL and Java operators

There are a number of differences between the usage of these operators in JDOQL and their usage in Java. Many of the differences serve to streamline the query language, making it more intuitive.

8.5.3.1 Method invocation

JDOQL is a language for querying persistent instances from a data store. It is not, as some people have believed, a fully fledged object query language. This is borne out by the restriction that method invocations are largely illegal in JDOQL filters.

This restriction means that a JDO implementation is not required to instantiate an instance in order to determine whether it matches the given query filter criteria. Query performance is therefore greatly improved.

Four legal method invocations are defined. The filter may apply the following invocations to persistent fields of **Collection** type:

isEmpty()

Returns **true** if the persistent field is null or references a **Collection** that contains no elements.

contains(Object o)

Returns **true** if the persistent field references a **Collection** that contains the identified persistence-capable object. The object **o** must be a persistence-capable instance. Equality between persistent instances always uses JDO identity, and is irrespective of any **equals()** method that may be defined.

Conceptually the **contains(Object o)** method is used to iterate the local variable o over the elements of a **Collection**. It is used as the left-hand side of a **boolean** expression, and evaluates to **true** if any one element of the **Collection** satisfies that expression.

The filter may apply the following invocations to persistent fields of **String** type:

startsWith(String s)

Returns **true** if the persistent field to which the method is applied starts with the designated string.

endsWith(String s)

Returns **true** if the persistent field to which the method is applied ends with the designated string.

Vendors may add support for other method invocations as long as these are non-mutating. A non-mutating method is one that does not alter the state of any objects. Such additions will be well documented, but should not be considered portable across implementations. A few vendors are already supporting the **String** methods **indexOf()** and **toLower()**, with support for further invocations to follow.

8.5.3.2. Equality

The equality operator **==** can be used between primitives and instances of the corresponding wrapper types. Thus, if an identifier (field or parameter) called **intPrimitive** is of type **int**, and identifier **intWrapper** is of type **Integer**, the following comparison is legal in JDOQL (but would be illegal in Java):

```
intPrimitive == intWrapper
```

This is also extended to equality of **String** and **Date** objects.
Note that equality comparisons (**==** and **!=**) between floating point values are inherently inexact and should be used with caution. The results of such comparisons may vary across different JDO implementations.

8.5.3.3 Ordering

As with equality, the ordering operators (**>**, **<**, **>=**, **<=**) can be used between primitives and instances of the corresponding wrapper types. With the identifiers defined above, the following comparison is legal in JDOQL (but would be illegal in Java):

```
intPrimitive > intWrapper
```

This is again extended to ordering of **String** and **Date** objects.

8.5.3.4 Assignment

A query filter may not do anything that might change the value of a persistent field. Specifically the assignment operators (**=**, **+=**, **/=**, etc.) and the pre/post increment/decrement operators (**++** and **--**) are illegal.

Implementations may optionally permit the invocation of methods, on persistence-capable or system classes, as long as these methods are themselves non-mutating.

8.5.3.5 Navigation

JDOQL explicitly supports navigation from one instance to another, by use of the de-reference operator (the period). Queries can navigate from one instance to another through a singleton (non-collection) reference. Queries can also navigate through multivalued **Collection** fields by using the **Collection.contains()** method.

Attempted navigation through a null reference causes that subexpression to evaluate to **false**. Other subexpression evaluations, combined with the logical operators, may still cause the instance to be included in the query's result.

8.6   Further examples

Now that you know a bit more about JDOQL's capabilities and syntax, let's look at some slightly more complicated examples.

8.6.1   Parameterization

Our previous example employed the simple JDOQL filter

```
name == "Ogilvie Partners"
```

Now we'll add parameterization. The test will no longer be against the string literal "Ogilvie Partners," but against an incoming string parameter.

```
Extent partnerExt = pm.getExtent(BusinessPartner.class, true);
String filter = "name == searchName";
Query q = pm.newQuery(partnerExt, filter);
q.declareParameters("String searchName");
q.setOrdering("name ascending, partnerId descending");
Collection c = (Collection) q.execute("Ogilvie Partners");
```

The filter has been changed, so that **name** is compared with **searchName**. In turn, **searchName** is declared as a parameter to the query. Finally a **String** is passed to the query execution method.

It is permissible for the query parameter to have the same name as a persistent field. In such cases, the keyword **"this"** is used to differentiate between the two, as per the example below.

```
Extent partnerExt = pm.getExtent(BusinessPartner.class, true);
String filter = "this.name == name";
Query q = pm.newQuery(partnerExt, filter);
q.declareParameters("String name");
q.setOrdering("name ascending, partnerId descending");
Collection c = (Collection) q.execute("Ogilvie Partners");
```

There is only one parameter in this case. If there had been multiple parameters, the parameter declaration would be comma-delimited. Parameters would be bound to values at runtime according to the sequences with which parameter declarations and values were given. In this regard they are "positional parameters."

Here is an example with multiple parameters:

```
Extent partnerExt = pm.getExtent(BusinessPartner.class, true);
String filter =
  "name == searchName && address ==
searchAddress";
Query q = pm.newQuery(partnerExt, filter);
q.declareParameters("String searchName, String searchAddress");
q.setOrdering("name ascending, partierId descending");
Collection c;
c = (Collection) q.execute("Ogilvie Partners", "Milton Keynes");
```

Now that it has multiple parameters, the query execution can be rewritten to show the meaningful use of named parameters. This is particularly useful when the code executing the query is separate from the code constructing the query and requesting parameter values. Here we use a **HashMap** to hold the parameters:

```
Extent partnerExt = pm.getExtent(BusinessPartner.class, true);
String filter
    = "name == searchName && address == searchAddress";
Query q = pm.newQuery(partnerExt, filter);
q.declareParameters("String searchName, String searchAddress");
q.setOrdering("name ascending, partnerId descending");

Map m = new HashMap();
m.add("searchAddress", "Milton Keynes");
m.add("searchName", "Ogilvie Partners");

Collection c = (Collection) q.executeWithMap(m);
```

Notice that the order in which parameters are added to the map is insignificant. I have deliberately shown the reverse order being used to reinforce this concept.

8.6.2   Singleton field navigation

The next item to illustrate is the de-referencing of persistent fields that refer to other persistent objects. Let's write a query that retrieves all business partners with a credit limit greater than a parameter value. Notice that the credit limit is stored on the **Customer** instance.

```
Extent partnerExt = pm.getExtent(BusinessPartner.class, true);
String filter = "customer.creditLimit > searchCredit";
Query q = pm.newQuery(partnerExt, filter);
q.declareParameters("double searchCredit");
Double credit = new Double(1000);
Collection c = (Collection) q.execute(credit);
```

The above query de-references a singleton field. The customer field either references a single Customer object, or it is null. If the field is null, then attempts to de-reference it will cause that filter subexpression to evaluate to **false**. Since there is only one such subexpression, the filter will evaluate to **false**. Thus, **BusinessPartner**s that are not **Customer**s will be excluded from the query results.

8.6.3   Collection field navigation

Our final query example illustrates navigation through collections. Here we identify the list of **BusinessPartner**s that have at least one **Order** that has not yet been dispatched. This requires the definition of a variable to reference each **Order** that is examined.

```
Extent partnerExt = pm.getExtent(BusinessPartner.class, true);
String filter =
   "customer.orders.contains(o) && o.dispatched == false";
Query q = pm.newQuery(partnerExt, filter);
q.declareVariables("Order o");
Collection c = (Collection) q.execute();
```

The filter criteria could also be legally written using the logical complement operator (!) as follows:

```
customer.orders.contains(o) && !o.dispatched
```

Conceptually, **o** is set to each contained **Order** in turn and **!o.dispatched** is then evaluated. In practice, queries are usually translated into the native query language of the underlying data store in order to take best advantage of the available indexing and query tuning strategies. Thus explicit serial evaluation of individual order entities is unlikely.

8.7   Unconstrained query variables

The primary purpose of JDOQL variables is as identifiers for use in **contains()** clauses, facilitating the iteration through persistent fields of **Collection** type. However, the JDO specification does allow for the definition of query variables that are subsequently referenced in the filter expression, but not subject to a **contains()** clause. Such identifiers, known as *unconstrained query variables*, conceptually iterate across the entire extent (including subclasses) of their persistence-capable type.

The specification is particularly vague about the portability of query filters using unconstrained variables, and I will not discuss the concept further here. It has, however, been the subject of several threads of discussion at JDOcentral, and will certainly be clarified in the next version of the specification document.

8.8   Dynamic Query Window

You will have noticed that all query elements are passed as strings. This has one disadvantage; query syntax is checked only at query compilation or execution time. In most cases, query errors will be detected only during the running of the application. However, it does facilitate the writing of applications that execute ad hoc queries, the details of which are not known at compile time.

An example is the Dynamic Query Window, shown in Figure 8.2. This is a relatively simple Swing application. It uses the **JDOBootstrap** class to initialize JDO, so all of the configuration parameters can go into the **jdo.properties** file. It then allows the user to enter the various query element strings. Upon pressing the Prepare button, a new **Query** is obtained from the persistence manager and the user's query elements bound to it. The Execute button parses the list of parameter values, constructs the appropriate array of parameters, and executes the query. Queries may optionally be compiled before they are executed.

Query results are shown by iterating through the returned **Collection** and invoking the **toString()** method of each object reference.

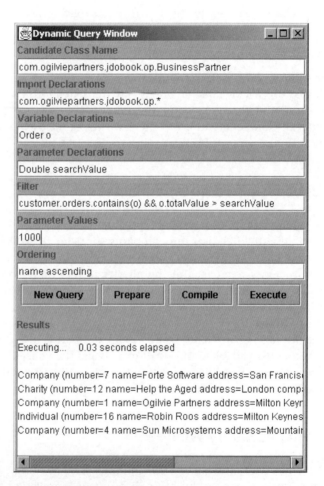

Figure 8.2 Dynamic Query Window

Dynamic Query Window enhancements

The Dynamic Query Window was written by Ogilvie Partners and is available in the downloadable distribution. It gives developers an excellent way to learn and experiment with JDOQL. It may also prove useful for manually tuning complex queries.

We plan an enhancement to generate the JDO-compliant code for each query at the user's request. This is intended as a means to coding JDOQL queries more efficiently and accurately.

Refer to http://www.OgilviePartners.com for further details.

What's next?

In the next chapter we briefly examine JDO's exception strategy, the exception classes JDO defines, and situations that might give rise to their being thrown.

JDO exceptions 9

JDO defines a number of exceptions to represent error conditions that might arise in the various layers of an implementation. These are all defined to be runtime exceptions. Since the compiler does not check such exceptions, the application is free to catch only those exceptions that warrant a particular response. This philosophy allows JDO to be more transparently applied to existing domain models and application components than would have been the case if checked exceptions were employed.

In this chapter we look at the JDO exception hierarchy, examine the base class exceptions and their subclass exceptions, and look at a selection of situations that might give rise to them.

Why runtime and not checked exceptions?

The choice of whether to use checked or runtime (unchecked) exceptions in a new API is one which must be considered carefully, as each style of exception has its place.

For instance, in Remote Method Invocation (RMI), **RemoteException** is a checked exception. The choice was made deliberately so that developers would always know when they were executing a remote method call. This was deemed necessary, as remote calls are particularly slow.

In JDO, however, the primary focus is transparency. We aim to provide a persistence infrastructure that can be applied easily without the addition of JDO-specific code to domain classes.

Some methods of JDO instances, which work fine when the instance is in the transient state, might throw JDO exceptions from other states; for example, attempting to interact with a persistent instance when no transaction is active, or when the persistence manager has been closed. In order to retain the high level of transparency desired, all of the JDO exceptions are runtime exceptions.

9.1   JDO exception hierarchy

Exceptions arising through JDO fall into a number of categories. Exceptions may be fatal (the requested operation cannot be completed) or can be retried (the error can be corrected by the application and the operation attempted again). They may be caused by the application (user), by the data store, or by the JDO implementation itself. The exception hierarchy defines base classes to handle each of these situations (Figure 9.1).

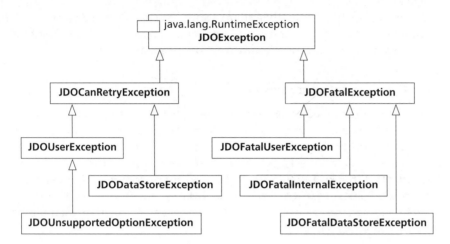

Figure 9.1 JDO exception hierarchy

When examining the hierarchy, note the following terminology that refers to the source of each exception:

User: the application/component invoking JDO persistence services.

DataStore: the underlying data store.

Internal: The JDO implementation.

implementations are free to define their own classes of exceptions that fit into this hierarchy by subclassing the appropriate base class. Alternatively they may throw instances of the base class exceptions themselves with appropriate identifying attributes.

9.2   Base exception classes

Here are detailed descriptions of each of the nine JDO base exception classes.

9.2.1   JDOException

This is the base class for all JDO exceptions. It extends **java.lang.Runtime Exception** so instances of this and all its subclasses do not have to be explicitly caught by the application.

When instantiated, the **JDOException** is given a descriptive string, an optional nested exception, and an optional failed object. All three of these can be accessed by the application if the exception is caught.

9.2.1.1 JDOException constructors

The constructors for **JDOException** are shown below, and equivalent constructors exist for every exception in the hierarchy. These are relevant to developers as it is occasionally necessary to throw instances of JDO exceptions from within persistence-capable objects. An example of this would be the use of the **InstanceCallbacks** interface to prevent an instance from being deleted in certain circumstances. The **jdoPreDelete()** method would throw a **JDOUserException** if deletion were to be prevented. Such an example has already been presented in Section 4.6.

JDOException()

This constructor takes no arguments.

JDOException(String msg)

This constructor takes a String message only.

JDOException(String msg, Throwable[] nested)

This constructor takes a message and an array of nested exceptions.

JDOException(String msg, Throwable nested)

This constructor takes a message and a single nested exception (which itself might contain further nested exceptions as necessary).

JDOException(String msg, Object failed)

This constructor takes a message and a reference to the "failed object."

JDOException(String msg, Throwable[] nested, Object failed)

This constructor takes a message, an array of nested exceptions, and a reference to the "failed object".

JDOException(String msg, Throwable nested, Object failed)

This constructor takes a message, a single nested exception, and a reference to the "failed object."

9.2.2 JDOFatalException

JDOFatalException is the base class for exceptions that cannot be retried. Occurrence of this exception (or a subclass thereof) generally implies that the transaction has been rolled back and should be abandoned by the application.

9.2.3 JDOCanRetryException

JDOCanRetryException is the base class for exceptions that can be retried after the application has attempted to address the cause of the exception.

9.2.4 JDOUserOptionException

This is the base class for all retriable exceptions that are caused by the user. The application must typically correct the problem causing the exception before attempting the operation again. Potential causes would include:

● attempts to make an instance with application identity persistent, with primary key fields that are identical to an already persistent instance. Correct the primary key field values and try again.

● attempts to fetch an instance by Object ID when no such persistent instance exists. Correct the Object ID and try again.

● attempts to get the extent of a class or interface for which the extent is not managed by JDO. Get the extent of a different class, or alter the persistence descriptor and enhance the chosen class so that its extent is managed by JDO.

9.2.5 JDOUnsupportedOptionException

A JDOUnsupportedOptionException is thrown when an application attempts to enable a particular optional feature that is not supported by the implementation. It is a subclass of JDOUserException.
    Potential causes would include:

● use of optimistic transaction management when not supported;

● the changing of an instance's primary key field values when not supported;

● use of Persistent-Nontransactional instances when not supported.

9.2.6 JDOFatalUserException

This is the base class for all fatal (cannot be retried) exceptions caused by the application. After a persistence manager has been closed, only its isClosed() method may be invoked. A JDOFatalUserException is thrown if any other method is invoked on the PersistenceManager, or on any Transaction, Query, Extent, or Iterator instances obtained from it.

9.2.7   JDOFatalInternalException

This is the base class for JDO implementation failures. instances of this exception should be reported to the JDO vendor.

9.2.8   JDODataStoreException

This is the base class for data store exceptions that can be retried.

9.2.9   JDOFatalDataStoreException

This is the base class for fatal data store exceptions that cannot be retried. It might be thrown if the data store transaction is rolled back other than at a commit/rollback request by the application.

9.3   Application exceptions

The discussion above has centered on JDO exceptions. However, it is also likely that an application will have its own cause to throw and catch domain-specific exceptions. These are referred to as *application exceptions*.

Application exceptions are designed along with the domain model, although they typically end up in a subpackage of the domain package. Domain objects throw and catch these exceptions according to the modeling of business processes by the designer. Persistent instances are capable of throwing and catching the same exceptions as their transient counterparts. No further effort is required of developers in this regard as a result of using JDO for object persistence.

What's next?

In the following chapter we take a detailed look at the structure of a persistence descriptor. Specific focus is given to the DTD that constrains these XML documents.

Persistence descriptor **10**

The persistence descriptor is used at enhancement time to identify classes to be made persistence-capable. Some of the information it contains may additionally be used by the implementation at runtime – particularly vendor-specific enhancements such as data store mapping information.

The persistence descriptor is an XML document. A brief overview follows for readers not yet familiar with XML.

10.1 XML overview

Markup languages, which allow text data to be structured using a set of prescribed tags, have been in use for many years. XML is a particularly simple markup language. It defines neither the tags nor the grammar according to which the tags can be combined.

Tag names for XML documents are defined by the document author in accordance with the information being marked up. This affords great flexibility. In a JDO persistence descriptor, the tags include **<jdo>**, **<package>**, and **<class>**. Tags are not case sensitive.

All XML documents must be *well formed*, in that each opening tag must be matched by a corresponding closing tag. Closing tags carry a preceding forward slash character, as in **</jdo>**, **</package>**, and **</class>**. The sequence in which tags are closed must match the sequence in which they were opened.

Pairs of opening and closing tags may have content between them. Often this content will include other tags as appropriate to the data being marked up. Additionally, tags may contain attributes. These are name–value pairs occurring within the opening tag. An example is the name attribute of the **<class>** tag:

```
<class name="Order">
  class tag content goes here
</class>
```

A tag that is opened and then closed with no intervening content may be written as a single *empty tag* for convenience. Empty tags may still contain attributes and are notated with a trailing forward slash character, as in **<class/>**. Thus

```
<class name="Order"/>
```

is equivalent to

```
<class name="Order"></class>
```

Whilst all XML documents must be well formed, they may optionally be *valid* according to a grammar. The grammar for an XML document is provided through a DTD. This is a text file that defines the valid attribute names for each tag, as well as the valid contents of each tag. Tag content is specified in terms of the allowable tags that may be included, and their respective cardinality.

For example, the **<class>** tag has an attribute called **name** that is mandatory. Between the opening tag **<class>** and the closing tag **</class>** a document may contain zero or more **<field>** or **<extension>** tags. The DTD specifies this as follows:

```
<!ELEMENT class (field|extension)*>
<!ATTLIST class name CDATA #REQUIRED>
```

The asterisk (*) represents a cardinality of "zero, one, or many." You will occasionally see the plus sign (+), which is used in DTDs to represent the cardinality of "one or many."

The DTD for JDO persistence descriptors is a file called **jdo.dtd**. Every persistence descriptor references the DTD through a **DOCTYPE** directive. An example is shown below. The actual path to jdo.dtd will vary according to your installation.

```
<?xml version="1.0" encoding="UTF-8" ?>
<!DOCTYPE jdo SYSTEM "file:///jdowork/dtd/jdo.dtd">
<jdo>
...
</jdo>
```

The full contents of **jdo.dtd** is shown in Appendix C. Hopefully the brief discussion above will be sufficient for you to read the DTD if you wish to do so. For further information about XML, and the Java APIs available to manipulate XML documents, I recommend *Java and XML* (McLaughlin, 2000).

10.2 Naming the persistence descriptor

A single persistence descriptor document should describe either a single class, or a single package. The descriptor should be named appropriately with either the class name or package name, followed by the extension ".jdo." This naming convention is recommended by the specification. However, it is unlikely that enhancement tools will enforce it, particularly since the DTD specifically provides for multiple packages to be described in a single descriptor.

10.3   Persistence descriptor elements

We will now consider the tags which are defined in the persistence descriptor DTD, and which are used in order to specify the persistence characteristics of persistence-capable classes.

10.3.1 <extension>

The **<extension>** element occurs at various places throughout the DTD. It is a placeholder facilitating the introduction of vendor-specific extensions into persistence descriptors whilst retaining conformance to the standard DTD.

It has three attributes: **vendor-name**, **key**, and **value**. This element will be illustrated at the end of the chapter.

10.3.2 <jdo>

jdo.dtd (extract)

```
<!ELEMENT jdo ((package)+, (extension)*)>
```

This is the root element of the document and must be present. It has no attributes. It must contain at least one **<package>** element, and may contain more than one. It may also contain zero, or more **<extension>** elements.

10.3.3 <package>

jdo.dtd (extract)

```
<!ELEMENT package ((class)+, (extension)*)>
<!ATTLIST package name CDATA #REQUIRED>
```

This element identifies a package from which some classes will be enhanced. It has one attribute, the name of the package, which must be fully qualified, as in the example below:

```
<PACKAGE NAME="com.ogilviepartners.jdobook.op">
...
</PACKAGE>
```

The **<package>** element must contain one or more **<class>** elements. It may also contain zero or more **<extension>** elements.

10.3.4 <class>

jdo.dtd (extract)

```
<!ELEMENT class (field|extension)*>
<!ATTLIST class name CDATA #REQUIRED>
<!ATTLIST class identity-type (application|datastore|none)
'datastore'>
<!ATTLIST class objectid-class CDATA #IMPLIED>
<!ATTLIST class requires-extent (true|false) 'true'>
<!ATTLIST class persistence-capable-superclass CDATA #IMPLIED>
```

This element identifies a single persistence-capable class. It has four attributes:

- The **name** attribute identifies the name of the class. The name is relative to the enclosing **<package>** element.

- The **identity-type** attribute specifies the required JDO identity, and must be one of **application**, **datastore**, and **nondurable**. The default identity is datastore.

- An **objectid-class** attribute must be specified only for classes with application identity. The identified Object ID class is relative to the enclosing package element. Inner classes are identified using the $ symbol following the standard set by the Java compiler. If the class is part of an inheritance hierarchy of persistence-capable classes, the Object ID class must be part of a corresponding inheritance hierarchy of Object ID classes.

- The **requires-extent** attribute specifies whether the extent of this class must be managed by JDO. The default is **true**. Persistence managers will only return the **Extent** of classes for which **requires-extent** is **true**.

The **<class>** element may contain zero or more **<field>** and **<extension>** elements.

10.3.5 <field>

jdo.dtd (extract)

```
<!ELEMENT field ((collection|map|array)?, (extension)*)?>
<!ATTLIST field name CDATA #REQUIRED>
<!ATTLIST field persistence-modifier
(persistent|transactional|none) #IMPLIED>
<!ATTLIST field primary-key (true|false) "false">
<!ATTLIST field null-value (exception|default|none) "none">
<!ATTLIST field default-fetch-group (true|false) #IMPLIED>
<!ATTLIST field embedded (true|false) #IMPLIED>
```

This element identifies the persistence characteristics of individual fields in a class. JDO assigns default persistence modifiers to each field defined in a persistence-

capable class based on the Java modifiers with which the field is defined. The
`<field>` element allows developers to override these defaults. The `<field>`
element has six attributes:

- The **name** attribute identifies the field and corresponds exactly to the field
name as defined in the class.

- The **persistence-modifier** attribute determines the extent to which JDO
will manage field values. It must have one of three values: **persistent**,
transactional, or **none**.
If the field is **persistent**, then it is by default transactional. JDO will synchronize the values of such fields of persistent instances with the data store.
This is done subject to transaction boundaries unless the instance is explicitly
made non-transactional. The persistence modifier **persistent** is the default
for fields of supported types or references to persistence-capable classes that are
not defined as **static**, **transient** or **final** in the un-enhanced class.
If the field's persistence modifier is **transactional**, its values will be cached
when the instance is first associated with a transaction, and the cached values
restored on transaction rollback. The cache is cleared on transaction commit.
However, JDO will not persist the field's value in the data store.
Fields with the persistence modifier **none** are not managed by JDO. This is
the default persistence modifier for fields declared as **static**, **transient** or
final in the un-enhanced class.
It is common practice to declare selected fields of a class with the Java modifier
transient in order to restrict the size of the object graph to which serialization would be applied. Such fields can then have their persistence modifier
explicitly set to **persistent** in the descriptor, overriding their default value of
none, so that their values will be transparently persisted to the data store.

- The **primary-key** attribute has values **true** or **false**, with **false** being the
default. It is used to identify those fields that comprise the Object ID of
classes with application identity.

- The **null-value** attribute has three possible values and is used to indicate
how null values should be handled by the implementation. The default
value is **none**, which requires the implementation to store null values as
such and throw a **JDODataStoreException** if the data store is not capable
of storing null values. The value **exception** requires the implementation to
throw a **JDOUserException** if the field contains a null value at the time it is
to be stored. The exception is more likely to occur at commit time than at
the time the null value is assigned.
The final value of **default** indicates that a null value should be replaced by
the field's default value prior to storage. If such a field's value is set to **null**
in an instance that is subsequently Persistent-New or Persistent-Dirty, the
application will typically see the default value after commit. (It is not necessary for the instance to be explicitly retrieved again by Object ID, extent
iteration or query execution.)

- The **default-fetch-group** attribute has values **true** or **false**. It specifies whether a particular field's value will be retrieved from the data store and populated into the instance's corresponding attribute when the instance itself is first read. This action typically takes place during a transition away from the Hollow state. The default value is **true** for fields of all Java primitive types, **Date** (from package **java.util**), **String** and **Number** (from package **java.lang**), **BigDecimal** and **BigInteger** (from **java.math**), and all array types. Note that although arrays are in the default fetch group by default, collections are not.

  Fields that are not part of the default fetch group are not read from the data store until their values are requested by the application.

- The **embedded** attribute has values **true** or **false**. If **true**, it is a hint to the implementation that the object referenced by that field should be stored as part of this instance instead of as a separate instance. Where supported by the implementation, the targets of such references are stored as second-class objects. Where not supported by the implementation, the targets of such references will be stored as first-class objects.

  The significant differences between first-class and second-class objects were discussed in Chapter 5. The default value is the same as that for the **default-fetch-group** attribute. Note that although arrays are embedded by default, collections are not.

10.3.6 <collection>

jdo.dtd (extract)

```
<!ELEMENT collection (extension)*>
<!ATTLIST collection element-type CDATA #IMPLIED>
<!ATTLIST collection embedded-element (true|false) #IMPLIED>
```

This element is used to identify fields of collection types as being collections of specific object types. By default all fields of collection types are deemed to be collections of **Object** type. All implementations are required to support such references of **Object** type but may restrict the class of instances that can be assigned to these references, throwing a **ClassCastException** as required.

Explicitly identifying the contained object type is recommended when storing references to other persistence-capable instances, as it removes the instance's dependency on the implementation being capable of storing such references as **Object** types. **ClassCastException**s will not then be thrown as long as the instances added to the collection are "instances of" the declared persistence-capable class.

The **<collection>** element has two attributes.

- The **element-type** attribute is the fully qualified name of the class, instances of which will be contained in the collection.

- The **embedded-element** attribute has values **true** or **false**. It identifies whether the objects contained by the collection should all be stored as part of the instance. If **embedded-element** is **true** and the implementation supports this behavior, all contained instances will be stored as second-class objects.

Support for second-class objects can improve the efficiency of the data store, as individual identities do not have to be maintained for such objects.

In the case of an order holding a collection of **OrderLine** instances, the collection itself is a separate object. Thus the order holds a reference to the collection, and the collection holds zero, one, or many references to **OrderLine** instances. Applications typically need to look up specific order instances by an Object ID, so these must be first-class objects. Designers may choose to assign **OrderLine** instances an Object ID as well, so that these can also be looked up individually. However, it is not necessary for the collection object to be looked up by an Object ID. Most implementations will treat such collection objects as second-class objects.

This is independent of the **embedded-element** attribute value, which indicates whether or not the contained objects will themselves be treated as second-class objects. If the designer determines that it is not necessary for individual **OrderLine** instances to be looked up independent of their containing **Order** instance, then the **orderLines** collection should have its **embedded-element** attribute set to **true**. This is illustrated below.

```
<field name="orderLines">
    <collection element-type="op.OrderLine"
                embedded-element="true"/>
</field>
```

The **embedded-element** attribute defaults to **false** for persistence-capable objects, and **true** for all other object types.

Serialization and second-class objects

It has previously been stated that second-class objects may be stored as part of their owning first-class object. One mechanism that implementations commonly use to achieve this is serialization. If the second-class object is serializable, its serialized form can be written into a single field of its owning first-class object's data store entity. This technique can easily be applied to singleton references or collections of objects.

The performance gains of retrieving the first-class object and all the embedded (second-class) objects it references in a single read from the data store, as opposed to multiple reads of related entities, are immense.

10.3.7 <map>

jdo.dtd (extract)

```
<!ELEMENT map (extension)*>
<!ATTLIST map key-type CDATA #IMPLIED>
<!ATTLIST map embedded-key (true|false) #IMPLIED>
<!ATTLIST map value-type CDATA #IMPLIED>
<!ATTLIST map embedded-value (true|false) #IMPLIED>
```

This element identifies a particular field as being a map, which stores key/value pairs. By default all map fields are persistent, and the key and value types are both object.

The **<map>** element has three attributes:

- The **key-type** attribute identifies the fully qualified class name of the objects that serve as keys in the map.

- The **value-type** attribute identifies the fully qualified class name of the objects that serve as values in the map.

- The **embedded-key** and **embedded-value** attributes identify whether keys and values should be stored as part of the containing instance (**true**) or as first-class objects in their own right (**false**). They default to **false** for persistence-capable objects, and **true** for all other object types.

10.3.8 <array>

jdo.dtd (extract)

```
<!ELEMENT array (extension)*>
<!ATTLIST array embedded-element (true|false) #IMPLIED>
```

The **<array>** element identifies a field that is an array. By default, array fields are persistent if a singleton reference of the same type would have been persistent.

The only attribute of an array is **embedded-element**, which identifies whether referenced instances will be stored as part of the containing instance (**true**) or as first-class objects in their own right (**false**). It defaults to **false** for persistence-capable objects, and **true** for all other object types.

10.4   Example – persistence descriptor "op.jdo"

Here is the complete persistence descriptor for our order processing domain. This illustrates many, although not all, of the persistence descriptor elements.

op.jdo

```xml
<?xml version="1.0" encoding="UTF-8" ?>
<!DOCTYPE jdo SYSTEM "file:///jdowork/dtd/jdo.dtd">
<jdo>
    <package name="com.ogilviepartners.jdobook.op">

        <class name="Customer"
                identity-type = "datastore">
            <field name="orders"
                    default-fetch-group="true">
                <collection element-type =
                    "com.ogilviepartners.jdobook.op.Order"/>
            </field>
        </class>

        <class name="BusinessPartner"
                identity-type="application"
                objectid-class=
"com.ogilviepartners.jdobook.op.pk.BusinessPartnerPK">
            <field name="partnerNumber"
                    primary-key="true"
                    default-fetch-group="false"/>
            <field name="customer"
                    embedded="false"/>
        </class>

        <class name="Individual"
                identity-type="application"
                persistence-capable-superclass=
"com.ogilviepartners.jdobook.op.BusinessPartner"
                objectid-class=
"com.ogilviepartners.jdobook.op.pk.BusinessPartnerPK" />

        <class name="Company"
                identity-type="application"
                persistence-capable-superclass=
"com.ogilviepartners.jdobook.op.BusinessPartner"
                objectid-class=
"com.ogilviepartners.jdobook.op.pk.CompanyPK" />

        <class name="Charity"
                identity-type="application"
                persistence-capable-superclass=
"com.ogilviepartners.jdobook.op.Company" />
```

```xml
        <class name="AbstractItem"
                identity-type="application"
                objectid-class=
"com.ogilviepartners.jdobook.op.pk.AbstractItemPK">
            <field name="itemId"
                    primary-key="true"
                    default-fetch-group="false"/>
        </class>

        <class name="Product"
                identity-type="application"
                persistence-capable-superclass=
"com.ogilviepartners.jdobook.op.AbstractItem"
                objectid-class=
"com.ogilviepartners.jdobook.op.pk.ProductPK" />

        <class name="ServiceContract"
                identity-type="application"
                persistence-capable-superclass=
"com.ogilviepartners.jdobook.op.AbstractItem"
                objectid-class=
"com.ogilviepartners.jdobook.op.pk.ServiceContractPK" />

        <class name="OrderLine"
                identity-type="datastore" >
        </class>

        <class name="Order"
                identity-type="application"
                objectid-class=
"com.ogilviepartners.jdobook.op.pk.OrderPK">
            <field name="orderNumber"
                    primary-key="true" />
            <field name="orderLines"
                    default-fetch-group="true">
            <collection element-type=
"com.ogilviepartners.jdobook.op.OrderLine" />
            </field>
        </class>

    </package>
</jdo>
```

10.5   Facilities for vendor-specific extensions

The experts behind JDO recognize that vendors will wish to add functionality which goes beyond that detailed in the specification – typically mapping strategies – to their implementations. Furthermore, some of this functionality will require meta-data defined in the persistence descriptor and therefore available to the implementation at runtime. JDO defines the **<extension>** element specifically to facilitate the storage of vendor-specific, and therefore non-standard, information in the descriptor.

10.5.1   <extension>

jdo.dtd (extract)

```
<!ELEMENT extension (extension)*>
<!ATTLIST extension vendor-name CDATA #REQUIRED>
<!ATTLIST extension key CDATA #IMPLIED>
<!ATTLIST extension value CDATA #IMPLIED>
```

By putting all non-standard data into **<extension>** elements, persistence descriptors that contain such information can still be considered valid according to the DTD.

The DTD defines the **<extension>** element so that a valid document can contain it in a number of places. In fact, zero, one, or many **<extension>** elements may appear as content within any persistence descriptor tag. Indeed, an **<extension>** tag may itself contain any number of further **<extension>** tags in its own content. The **<extension>** tag has three attributes:

- The **vendor-name** attribute identifies the JDO vendor to which the particular extension relates.

- The **key** attribute identifies the particular extension. Each JDO vendor documents the set of supported keys for its implementation.

- The **value** attribute identifies the value to be associated with the **key**.

The use of **<extension>** elements is best illustrated with an example.

10.6   Example – deletion semantics

By definition, the JDO specification does not identify any valid extensions. Extensions are intended for use by JDO vendors who wish to implement features above and beyond the standard, and require the application of such features to be declared in the persistence descriptor. This book is intended to address JDO in a vendor-independent manner, but I trust that you will appreciate the need for a vendor-specific example here.

In JDO it is possible to have one persistence-capable instance reference another instance that is subsequently deleted. Once the **deletePersistent()** method has completed and the transaction committed, JDO dictates that the deleted instance will be transient. However, it does not dictate what should have happened to fields that were previously referencing the now-deleted instance.

In Prism Technology's JDO implementation "OpenFusion JDO," an extension has been added to the **<field>** tag that identifies the deletion semantics for that field. Three options are permitted, as illustrated on Table 10.1.

Table 10.1 The three options for deletion semantics in OpenFusionJDO

Deletion semantics	Description
Null	If the field is referencing an instance that is subsequently deleted, set the field to null.
Exception	If the field is referencing an instance which is subsequently deleted, throw a **JDOUserException**.
None	If the field is referencing an instance that is subsequently deleted, do nothing. The field will still reference the instance, which will be in a transient state after commit.

The default behavior is **none**, which is consistent with the JDO specification. Thus one needs to specify only the deletion semantics for a field if the **null** or **exception** behaviors are required. This extension is implemented in the deployment descriptor with the vendor name "prismt," the key "deletion-semantics," and the appropriate attribute value; "null," "exception," or "none".

Here is an example in which the default deletion semantics are overridden, preventing the deletion of a **Customer** instance that is referenced by the **customer** field of a **BusinessPartner** instance.

BusinessPartner.jdo

```
<jdo>
  <package name="com.ogilviepartners.jdobook.op">
    <class name="BusinessPartner">
      <field name="customer">
        <extension vendor-name="prismt"
                   key="deletion-semantics"
                   value="exception">
      </field>
    </class>
  </package>
</jdo>
```

What's next?

We have now covered all of the information you need in order to use JDO in a non-managed environment, i.e. outside a J2EE application server. The next chapter looks in detail at the integration of JDO with server-side J2EE components such as Enterprise JavaBeans.

J2EE integration   **11**

his chapter deals with the so-called *managed environment*, in which JDO is used by components executing as part of a J2EE-compliant application server. Examples are provided of JDO access by EJB components (entity, session, and message-driven beans) and web components (servlets and JavaServer Pages).

11.1   The managed environment

All of the examples in the preceding chapters presume JDO to be used in a non-managed environment. This is where the application is itself responsible for bootstrapping JDO and for demarcating transactions.

However, given the prevalence of the J2EE component architecture, JDO was designed so that it could integrate seamlessly into J2EE application servers. J2EE strives to abstract the component developer from having to explicitly write code in support of infrastructure services. Instead, these services are provided by the application server's container, within which the components execute. The term *managed environment* applies to the use of JDO from the context of a J2EE container.

11.2   J2EE overview

J2EE is a specification for application server technology supporting the middle tiers of an application architecture. J2EE specifically addresses two tiers: the web tier and the EJB tier. The web tier contains components that service hypertext transfer protocol (HTTP) requests from web browsers and dynamically generate hypertext markup language (HTML) content in response. The EJB tier contains components that are transactional, scalable, secure, and which facilitate the encapsulation of and access to data entities. Application architectures are free to employ components from either tier or from both, as warranted by the application.

11.2.1   Enterprise JavaBeans tier

The EJB specification enables server-side application component developers to focus on the application logic their components will provide. The developers are abstracted from issues such as transactions and security, and code does not normally have to be written to interface with these services. After components have been written and compiled, they are assembled into server-side applications prior to deployment into the application server. At assembly time a deployment descriptor is constructed. This XML document identifies the components comprising the application and specifies their requirements regarding transactions, security, and (occasionally) persistence. The fact that these services can be configured declaratively without recourse to component recompilation, let alone source code access or editing, is a major benefit of the J2EE model.

The clients of EJBs may be applications running outside the J2EE application server (e.g. Java/Swing clients, or potentially non-Java clients using the CORBA protocol IIOP), web components in the web tier, or other EJB components.

The following types of EJB components are defined.

11.2.1.1 Session beans

These components are intended to encapsulate processing which must occur on the server in response to a client's request. They represent an interactive session between the server and a client. Session beans can be pooled by the application server to reduce instantiation delays when one is requested by a client. They operate as dedicated client resources, in that only one client can make use of a particular session bean instance at one time.

Two types of session bean exist. *Stateful* session beans are dedicated to a single client for as long as the client requires. All method invocations by that client occur on the same session bean instance. This allows the session bean to build up and maintain a conversational state based on the client's previous method invocations. *Stateless* session beans are dedicated to a single client only for the duration of individual method invocations. Stateless beans do not maintain conversational state across client invocations. Thus successive invocations by one client may be serviced by different session bean instances. As soon as one method invocation on a session bean is complete, the bean instance is returned to a pool of free instances and is immediately available to handle another request from any client.

Bean-managed transactions

EJB components typically rely on the application server for transaction demarcation. This relieves the component developer of having to code `begin()`, `commit()`, and `rollback()` invocations. The transaction demarcation specifics are instead defined in the deployment descriptor on a per-method basis, and transaction demarcation is delegated to the container. This policy is known as container-managed transactions (CMT).

As an alternative to employing CMT, a *stateful* session bean may be declared to have bean-managed transactions (BMT). In such cases the session bean itself undertakes to demarcate transactions programmatically. The resulting transactions may extend beyond a single method invocation and encompass multiple invocations (roundtrips) between the client and server.

11.2.1.2 Entity beans

Entity beans were designed to present a remote interface to data entities. This allows remote clients to have direct access to the entity bean and thence the data store. Entity beans usually obtain their data from a relational database.

The class of an entity bean identifies the type of data it can provide to the client, so a product entity bean would provide product data. Each particular instance of an entity bean in use by a client is associated with a primary key identifying the particular data (e.g. the particular product) that the bean encapsulates.

Entity beans must have their transactions managed by the container (CMT). However, they may choose whether to implement persistence management programmatically with bean-managed persistence (BMP) or declaratively with container-managed persistence (CMP).

All entity beans must implement methods for the creation, loading, storing, and removal of data from the data store. If the bean uses BMP, these methods will contain the code required to perform the corresponding operations on the data store. If the bean uses CMP, these methods are merely callback methods that, although present, are usually empty. Instead, the deployment descriptor is complemented with sufficient information for the container to undertake the persistence of data on behalf of the component.

11.2.1.3 Message-driven beans

Message-driven beans are an application of the Java Message Service (JMS) to enterprise components. They represent server-side processing that will be invoked in response to the receipt of an asynchronous JMS message. This is in contrast to session beans, which are invoked synchronously by clients.

The code written for a message-driven bean must deal only with the actions to be taken on receipt of a message. Other properties, such as the source of messages (a JMS destination) and the transactional nature and durability of its connection to the underlying messaging service, are specified declaratively through the deployment descriptor.

For further information about JMS I recommend the thorough treatment in *Java Message Service* (Monson-Haefel and Chappel, 2001).

11.2.1.4 Developer-provided enterprise bean interfaces and classes

EJB components are made up of interfaces and classes provided by the bean developer in accordance with the EJB specification. All components require a *bean class*. This provides implementations of callback methods invoked by the bean's lifecycle, and business methods invoked at the discretion of a client. Session and entity beans require a *home interface* that provides factory methods by which clients can obtain bean instances, and a *remote interface* that describes the methods that clients may execute on these instances. Entity beans additionally need to have a *primary key class* (Table 11.1).

Table 11.1 Interfaces and classes the developer must provide for each EJB type

Bean type	Home interface	Remote interface	Bean class	Primary key class
Session	✔	✔	✔	✘
Entity	✔	✔	✔	✔
Message-driven	✘	✘	✔	✘

For further information on EJB I recommend *Enterprise JavaBeans*, (Monson-Haefel, 2001).

11.2.2   Web tier

The web tier is comprised of components that enhance web server functionality with the ultimate aim of producing dynamic content for web browsers and executing business transactions in response to web-based requests. Web components may execute in a servlet engine or as components within a web-aware application server. The former is typically used where an application makes no use of EJB, and the latter where the application is comprised of components from both tiers. Two types of web-tier component are defined: Servlets and JavaServer Pages (JSP).

11.2.2.1 Servlets

Servlets are process-centric components that receive HTTP requests and ultimately produce an appropriate response. The actual format of the response will depend upon the nature of the client. HTML content is the most common, but servlets are also being used to generate XML content which might be consumed directly by an XML-aware client, or transformed to HTML as a separate step prior to being rendered by a web browser.

During execution, the servlet instance can access parameters passed with the request, and can make use of the full spectrum of Java APIs in order to respond to the request correctly. This includes accessing and invoking EJB components if required.

11.2.2.2 JavaServer Pages

Servlets are process-centric, and might contain `println()` method calls to output HTML content. This requires that any embedded quotation marks in the desired output be correctly escaped. It also requires that any edits to HTML content be undertaken by a suitably qualified Java developer. Finally, the presentation generated by a servlet cannot be edited in an HTML editor.

JSP's are components which serve to address these restrictions. They are text files containing presentation markup (usually HTML, but potentially XML or something else) and scripting elements in a target language (only Java is supported to date). Web designers without Java expertise can edit JSPs in HTML editors. The scripting elements can either be hidden or be wrapped up into custom tag libraries to ease such manipulation.

All JSPs are ultimately transformed into temporary servlet code by the runtime environment and then compiled and executed as Servlets. The markup content is placed into **println()** statements and special characters escaped as necessary. Script code is placed verbatim into the generated servlet and facilitates the declaration of attributes, methods, local variables, and execution logic.

For further information on web components I recommend *Core Servlets and JavaServer Pages* (Hall, 2000).

11.3 Serialization of JDO instances

J2EE components communicate with their clients (actual clients or other J2EE components) using RMI. To improve interoperability, most application servers channel their RMI calls over the IIOP protocol. RMI facilitates the passing of objects by value through serialization. This technique is widely employed by middle-tier Java designers, and is likely to be applied to persistence-capable objects. This section examines the serialization of persistent instances.

The serialization process can be invoked explicitly on any object implementing the **Serializable** interface. However, it is more common for it to occur implicitly, as happens whenever a **Serializable** object is included as an argument to or return value from an RMI. The object is transformed into a stream of bytes that is transferred across the network, where a new object of the same class is constructed and initialized from the contents of the byte stream.

Java contains the **transient** modifier with which developers can mark certain attributes as *non-serializable*. Non-serializable attributes will not form part of the byte stream and will acquire default values in the remote copy of the object.

JDO implements serialization such that transient and persistent instances can be serialized and de-serialized into their corresponding un-enhanced classes. This prevents clients from needing to have the enhanced classes present when they do not intend to invoke JDO services directly.

Serialization and closure of instances

When an instance is serialized, the result is a byte stream representing the complete object graph of all connected serializable instances. The persistence manager will retrieve these instances from the data store and fully populate all persistent fields. The graph of instances will subsequently be made transient (preventing any subsequent changes to them from affecting the data store and eliminating their reliance on supporting JDO infrastructure). It is these transient objects that are then converted to their serialized form for transmission across the network.

By default, *non-serialized* fields, i.e. those declared with the Java modifier **transient**, will not be persisted by JDO. This setting can, however, be overridden by ascribing a persistence modifier of **persistent** to such fields in the persistence descriptor. The field values will then be synchronized in the data store since they are declared persistent. However, the instances to which they refer will not form part of the serialized object graph, since the references are non-serializable. (The Java modifier **transient** still applies.)

With careful application of Java's **transient** modifier, designers can reduce the size of object graphs involved in the serialization process. This is achieved without compromising "transparent persistence," since navigation through persistent but non-serialized fields will still transparently retrieve referenced objects from the data store as required.

By way of example, consider the **BusinessPartner** class. It contains a reference to a **Customer** object, which in turn references a collection of **Order** objects. For business partners which are customers and for which many orders exist, the object graph that is involved when the **BusinessPartner** object is serialized could be very large. To minimize this a designer might decide to make the **Customer**'s reference to its collection of **Order** objects transient. Thus the serialization process would not include any **Order** objects. In order to keep the **orders** field persistent it would have to have its persistence-modifier set explicitly in the persistence descriptor. Here is an extract from the altered class and its descriptor.

Projects w/ many tasks, roles ...

But we use DTO's.

Customer.java (extract)

```
public class Customer {

    protected transient Collection orders;
        .
        .
        .
}
```

Customer.jdo

```
<jdo>
  <package name="com.ogilviepartners.jdobook.op">
    <class name="Customer"
      <field name="orders"
      persistence-modifier="persistent"/>
        <collection element-type=
          "com.ogilviepartners. jdobook.op.Order" />
      </field>
    </class>
  </package>
</jdo>
```

11.4   JDO vs. J2EE transactions

Each of J2EE and JDO provide their own mechanisms for managing transactions. In JDO this is the **javax.jdo.Transaction** object returned to applications from the persistence manager's **currentTransaction()** method. In J2EE it is the **javax.transaction.UserTransaction** object. The **UserTransaction** is made available to EJBs through their session, entity or message-driven context objects, and to other J2EE components through JNDI lookups.

In the managed environment, JDO implementations can synchronize their transactions with the distributed J2EE transactions. This design feature is central to JDO's ability to operate in these tiers. Where the container is managing transactions on behalf of a component, transaction demarcation methods may not be invoked by that component. This applies to all entity beans, and to those session beans and message-driven beans for which CMT is selected. Where session beans or message-driven beans have BMT selected, the component developer programmatically provides transaction demarcation. In these cases either J2EE **UserTransaction** or JDO **Transaction** objects may be used for this purpose.

If a persistence manager is obtained from a factory before the J2EE transaction is established, the **begin()**, **commit()**, and **rollback()** methods of the JDO transaction object may be used for demarcation. During this process the persistence manager will start and complete the associated J2EE transaction appropriately.

If a persistence manager is obtained from a factory once a J2EE transaction is already active, the demarcation methods of the JDO transaction *must not be used*. All transaction demarcation should be performed through the **UserTransaction** object, with which JDO will synchronize.

JDO Transaction vs. J2EE UserTransaction

There are two approaches for transaction demarcation, but when should each be used?

Since the **UserTransaction** object is readily available to most J2EE components and is the standard by which they accomplish transaction demarcation, I generally use this method in preference to demarcation with JDO's **Transaction** object.

However, if a particular web component has no need of J2EE's distributed transaction services and merely requires transactional access through JDO, JDO transactions can and should be used. This avoids the unnecessary lookup of a **UserTransaction** through JNDI, which may not be supported in some lightweight servlet engines.

11.5   JDO integration with EJB

The essential philosophy of JDO integration with EJB containers is as follows. A **PersistenceManagerFactory** will be looked up through JNDI early on in the bean's lifecycle, and the reference retained as an attribute of the class. I typically look up the factory during the **setSessionContext()**, **setEntityContext()**, and **setMessageDrivenContext()** methods.

For all components (except stateful session beans with BMT) the persistence manager should be obtained from the factory during each business method that actually uses JDO. It should always be closed before that method returns. Judicious use should be made of the **finally** clause in **try** blocks to ensure that the persistence manager is closed, even in the case of an exception being thrown from the method before its usual end point.

In the CMT case, the persistence manager must be closed because transaction demarcation is not the component's responsibility and therefore it should not presume that any two method calls would necessarily be part of the same transaction. Technically, a stateless session bean with BMT could maintain a single persistence manager instance for its entire lifecycle. However, doing so would subvert the pooling of persistence managers by the factory. It may also tempt developers to leave transactions open across business method boundaries, which is illegal for stateless beans.

Stateful session beans with BMT use persistence managers for longer periods of time. If the J2EE **UserTransaction** object is being used for transaction demarcation, the persistence manager should be obtained *after* the call to its **begin()** method and closed *before* the call to its **commit()** method. If JDO **Transaction** objects are to be used, the persistence manager is naturally obtained before the transaction is begun and closed only after the transaction has been completed. Indeed, there is no way to obtain the **Transaction** object except through the persistence manager itself.

11.6   JDO integration with stateless session beans

Although entity beans were originally designed to encapsulate data access, it is far more common for session beans to manipulate data directly without doing so through entity beans.

Session beans may be either stateless or stateful, and employ CMT or BMT. For stateless beans, BMTs hold no benefit unless it is a requirement that a single method invoked on the session bean invokes several serial transactions. Therefore the stateless session bean example will use CMTs.

The bean implementation will not programmatically demarcate transactions, and the persistence manager will be obtained after the J2EE transaction has started. Since the application server's container will commence transactions before invoking the session bean's methods, the persistence manager can indeed be obtained at the start of each method that uses JDO. It is essential that such methods have an appropriate transaction attribute set in the EJB deployment descriptor so that they are invoked transactionally.

The stateless session bean lifecycle is illustrated in Figure 11.1.

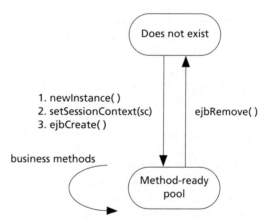

Figure 11.1 Stateless session bean lifecycle

After a session bean has been instantiated, its **setSessionContext()** and **ejbCreate()** methods are called before it is placed into the method-ready pool. A number of client-initiated business method invocations may occur (although only one at a time). Finally, the bean's **ejbRemove()** method is invoked before the instance is destroyed.

Our example is an **OrderDispatcher** bean. This stateless bean provides facilities for dispatching and canceling orders. As it is stateless, only a single **create()** method, with no arguments, is provided in the home interface.

OrderDispatcherHome.java

```
package com.ogilviepartners.jdobook.op.j2ee;

import javax.ejb.*;
import java.rmi.RemoteException

interface OrderDispatcherHome extends EJBHome {
    OrderDispatcher create() throws CreateException,
    RemoteException;
}
```

The remote interface defines the business methods that this bean exposes to its clients. These allow the dispatch or cancellation of an order, which is identified by its Object ID.

OrderDispatcher.java

```
package com.ogilviepartners.jdobook.op.j2ee;

import javax.ejb.*;
import com.ogilviepartners.jdobook.op.pk.*;
import com.ogilviepartners.jdobook.op.ex.*;
import java.rmi.RemoteException;

interface OrderDispatcher extends EJBObject {
    void dispatchOrder(OrderPK orderKey) throws
    RemoteException;
    void cancelOrder(OrderPK orderKey) throws
    OrderStatusException, RemoteException;
}
```

Finally the bean class implements the callback and business methods. Take note of the following:

- The persistence manager factory is looked up in the **setSessionContext()** method.
- CMTs are used so no transaction demarcation code is present in the bean.
- Persistence managers are obtained, used, and closed within every business method that requires persistence services.

OrderDispatcherBean.java

```java
package com.ogilviepartners.jdobook.op.j2ee;

import javax.ejb.*;
import com.ogilviepartners.jdobook.op.*;
import com.ogilviepartners.jdobook.op.ex.*;
import com.ogilviepartners.jdobook.op.pk.*;
import javax.jdo.*;
import javax.naming.*;

public class OrderDispatcherBean implements SessionBean
{
    SessionContext sc;
    PersistenceManagerFactory pmf;
    Context env;

    public void setSessionContext(SessionContext sc) {
        this.sc = sc;
        try {
            Context ic = new InitialContext();
            env = (Context) ic.lookup("java:comp/env");
            pmf = (PersistenceManagerFactory)
            env.lookup("jdo/OrderProcessingPMF");
        }
        catch (Exception e) {
            throw new EJBException(e);
        }
    }


    public void dispatchOrder(OrderPK orderKey) {
        PersistenceManager pm = null;
        try {
            pm = pmf.getPersistenceManager();
            Order o = (Order) pm.getObjectById(orderKey, true);
            o.despatch();
        }
        catch (Exception e) {
            throw new EJBException(e);
        }
        finally {
            if (pm != null && !pm.isClosed()) pm.close();
        }
    }
```

```
public void cancelOrder(OrderPK orderKey) throws
                             OrderStatusException {
    PersistenceManager pm = null;
    try {
        pm = pmf.getPersistenceManager();
        Order o = (Order) pm.getObjectById(orderKey, true);
        o.cancel();
    }
    catch (Exception e) {
        throw new EJBException(e);
    }
    finally {
        if (pm != null && !pm.isClosed()) pm.close();
    }
}
public void ejbCreate() {}
public void ejbRemove() {}
public void ejbPassivate() {}
public void ejbActivate() {}
}
```

11.7   JDO integration with stateful session beans

Stateful session bean instances are dedicated to one client for a number of method invocations, and can maintain conversational state across these methods. Stateful session beans can also employ BMTs in order to keep a transaction open over such a series of invocations. The stateful session bean lifecycle is illustrated in Figure 11.2.

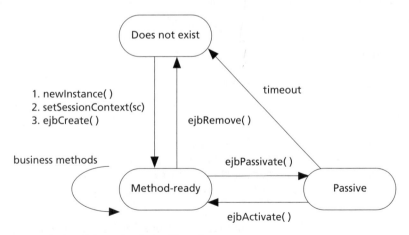

Figure 11.2 Stateful session bean lifecycle

The stateful session bean lifecycle is similar to that of the stateless session bean. Notable differences are that once in the method-ready state, it is assigned to a single client. The **activate()** and **passivate()** invocations are used by the application server when temporarily destroying the bean in order to free up system resources.

Our example of a stateful session bean is called the order entry bean and uses BMT. It provides clients with methods to create an order, add products to the order, and complete or discard the order. A transaction is commenced when the order is created and committed only when the order is completed. The transaction is explicitly rolled back if the order is discarded. Since the bean maintains a reference to the current order internally, the **addProduct()** method needs only a product Object ID and a quantity, and does not require a separate order Object ID parameter.

The home interface contains a **create()** method identifying the business partner for which orders will be created.

OrderEntryHome

```
package com.ogilviepartners.jdobook.op.j2ee;

import javax.ejb.*;

import java.rmi.RemoteException;
import javax.ejb.EJBHome;
import javax.ejb.CreateException;
import com.ogilviepartners.jdobook.op.pk.BusinessPartnerPK;

interface OrderEntryHome extends EJBHome{
    void create(BusinessPartnerPK bpKey) throws
    RemoteException, CreateException;
}
```

The remote interface contains methods that a client uses in order to add products to the order and complete or discard the order.

OrderEntry.java

```
package com.ogilviepartners.jdobook.op.j2ee;

import java.rmi.RemoteException;
import com.ogilviepartners.jdobook.op.pk.ItemPK;
import javax.ejb.EJBObject;

interface OrderEntry extends EJBObject {
    void addProduct(ItemPK pKey) throws RemoteException;
    void completeOrder() throws RemoteException;
    void discardOrder() throws RemoteException;
}
```

The bean class contains implementations of business methods and callback methods.

Take note of the following:

- The persistence manager factory is looked up from JNDI during the **setSessionContext()** method, and its reference saved for later use.

- Transaction demarcation begins in the **ejbCreate()** method. The **UserTransaction** object is used for transaction demarcation. Transactions begin in the **ejbCreate()** method and are completed in the **completeOrder()** and **discardOrder()** methods.

- The persistence manager is obtained when the transaction has been commenced, and its reference retained until the transaction is about to be completed. All JDO invocations within the transaction take place on the same persistence manager instance.

OrderEntryBean.java

```
package com.ogilviepartners.jdobook.op.j2ee;

import javax.ejb.*;
import javax.jdo.*;
import javax.naming.Context;
import javax.naming.InitialContext;
import javax.transaction.UserTransaction;
import com.ogilviepartners.jdobook.op.*;
import com.ogilviepartners.jdobook.op.pk.*;

public class OrderEntryBean implements SessionBean
{
    PersistenceManagerFactory pmf;
    PersistenceManager pm;
    Context env;
    Order o;
    UserTransaction ut;
    SessionContext sc;

    public void setSessionContext(SessionContext sc) {
        this.sc = sc;
        try {
            Context ic = new InitialContext();
            env = (Context) ic.lookup("java:comp/env");
            pmf = (PersistenceManagerFactory)
                env.lookup("jdo/OrderProcessingPMF");
            ut = sc.getUserTransaction();
        }
        catch (Exception e) {
            throw new EJBException(e);
        }
    }
```

```
public BusinessPartnerPK ejbCreate(BusinessPartnerPK
               bpKey, int newOrderNumber) {
    try {
        ut.begin();
        pm = pmf.getPersistenceManager();
        BusinessPartner bp = (BusinessPartner)
            pm.getObjectById(bpKey,false);
        o = bp.getCustomer().createOrder(newOrderNumber);
        pm.makePersistent(o);
    }
    catch (Exception e) {
        throw new EJBException(e);
    }
    return (BusinessPartnerPK) pm.getObjectId(o);
}

public void ejbPostCreate(OrderPK k) {}

public void addProduct(ItemPK k, int quantity) {
    try {
        Product p = (Product) pm.getObjectById(k, true);
        o.addItem(p, quantity);
    }
    catch (Exception e) {
        throw new EJBException(e);
    }
}

public void completeOrder() {
    try {
        pm.close();
        ut.commit();
    }
    catch (Exception e) {
        throw new EJBException(e);
    }
}

public void discardOrder() {
    try {
        pm.close();
        ut.rollback();
    }
    catch (Exception e) {
        throw new EJBException(e);
    }
}
```

```
      public void ejbRemove() {}
      public void ejbActivate() {}
      public void ejbPassivate() {}
}
```

11.8   JDO integration with entity beans

Entity beans must employ CMTs, and so they contain no transaction demarcation code.

Entity beans may delegate their persistence to the container. This is known as container-managed persistence (CMP). In such cases the bean no longer contains code to synchronize its attributes with the data store.

JDO as the underlying technology for CMP implementations

Incidentally, an EJB container may utilize JDO internally in support of its CMP implementation. However, that is of architectural significance only and makes no difference to the bean implementation.

The rest of this discussion centers on bean-managed persistence. To implement a BMP entity bean with JDO, the bean should hold a reference to one (or more) JDO instances. The `ejbLoad()`, `ejbStore()`, `ejbCreate()`, and `ejbRemove()` methods manipulate this instance through a persistence manager. The business methods, generally providing accessor (get) and mutator (set) services for these data items, are then implemented to directly invoke the instance. The entity bean lifecycle is particularly complex, as illustrated in Figure 11.3.

Whilst a client is maintaining a reference to a bean proxy (EJB object) for a particular primary key, there may or may not be a bean instance associated with that primary key in the application server. The passivation and activation lifecycle transitions allow one instance of an entity bean to encapsulate data corresponding to a number of different primary keys in its lifetime, transcending transaction boundaries. The implementation of JDO within an entity bean is correspondingly complex. I have chosen to describe it in conjunction with the example source code below.

The following example is of a product entity bean. The home interface details the create methods available to clients wishing to insert new products into the data store, and to find methods for retrieving already persistent instances.

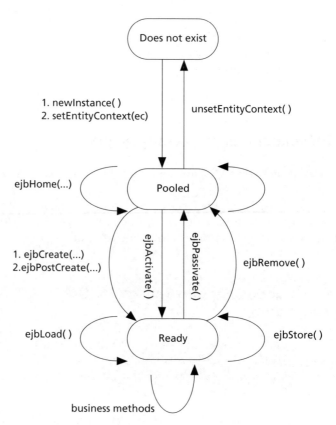

Figure 11.3 Entity bean lifecycle

ProductEntityHome.java

```java
package com.ogilviepartners.jdobook.op.j2ee;

import javax.ejb.*;

import com.ogilviepartners.jdobook.op.pk.ItemPK;
import java.util.Collection;
import java.rmi.RemoteException;

public interface ProductEntityHome extends EJBHome {
    // create methods
    ProductEntity create(String itemId) throws
                        RemoteException, CreateException;

    ProductEntity create(String itemId, String description,
            double price,String color) throws RemoteException,
                                        CreateException;
```

```
    // finder methods
    ProductEntity findByPrimaryKey(ItemPK itemKey)
                    throws RemoteException,FinderException;
    Collection findAll() throws RemoteException,
                                        FinderException;
}
```

The remote interface lists the business methods with which clients may alter the data.

ProductEntity.java

```
package com.ogilviepartners.jdobook.op.j2ee;

import javax.ejb.*;
import java.rmi.RemoteException;

public interface ProductEntity extends EJBObject
{
    public String getDescription() throws RemoteException;
    public void setDescription(String description)
                                    throws RemoteException;

    public double getPrice() throws RemoteException;
    public void setPrice(double price)
                                    throws RemoteException;

    public String getColor() throws RemoteException;
    public void setColor(String color)
                                    throws RemoteException;

    public String getItemId() throws RemoteException;
}
```

The entity bean class provides implementations of the business and callback methods. It begins with the normal imports, etc.

ProductEntityBean.java

```
package com.ogilviepartners.jdobook.op.j2ee;

import javax.ejb.*;
import com.ogilviepartners.jdobook.op.Product;
import com.ogilviepartners.jdobook.op.pk.ItemPK;
import javax.jdo.PersistenceManager;
import javax.jdo.PersistenceManagerFactory;
import javax.jdo.JDOHelper;
import javax.jdo.Extent;
import java.util.Iterator;
```

```
import java.util.Vector;
import java.util.Collection;
import javax.naming.Context;
import javax.naming.InitialContext;
public class ProductEntityBean implements EntityBean
{
```

The class defines attributes in which to store the persistence manager as well as its factory. Also note the reference to a persistence-capable class, in this case **Product**. More complex entity beans might manage graphs of persistence-capable objects.

```
private PersistenceManagerFactory pmf;
private PersistenceManager pm;
private Product product;
private EntityContext ec;
private Context env;
```

Every entity bean has a no-argument constructor used by the server when populating the free pool.

```
public ProductEntityBean() {}
```

The **setEntityContext()** method is invoked only once in an entity bean instance's lifecycle. It is an appropriate place for one-time initialization. Storage of the **EntityContext** object is standard practice. In the implementation below we also look up the component's environment within JNDI and subsequently look up the persistence manager factory.

```
public void setEntityContext(EntityContext ec) {
    this.ec = ec;
    try {
        InitialContext ic = new InitialContext();
        env = (Context) ic.lookup("java:comp/env");
        pmf = (PersistenceManagerFactory)
                      env.lookup("jdo/OrderProcessingPMF");
    }
    catch (Exception e) {
        throw new EJBException(e);
    }
}
```

The **ejbCreate()** and **ejbPostCreate()** method pairs are used when new data is inserted into the data store. This is potentially the first time this bean instance is using JDO in the current J2EE transaction scope, so we acquire the persistence manager from the factory before creating a transient instance and making it persistent. This bean allows creation with only an item ID or with additional description, price, and color information.

```
// create methods

public void ejbPostCreate(String itemId) {}

public ItemPK ejbCreate(String itemId) {
    // get the PM
    pm = pmf.getPersistenceManager();

    // construct transient object and make persistent
    product = new Product(itemId);
    pm.makePersistent(product);

    // obtain the key
    ItemPK productKey = (ItemPK)
                        JDOHelper.getObjectId(product);

    // return the Key
    return productKey;
}

public void ejbPostCreate(String itemId, String
               description, double price, String color) {}

public ItemPK ejbCreate(String itemId, String description,
                         double price, String color) {
    // get the PM
    pm = pmf.getPersistenceManager();

    // construct transient object and make persistent
    product = new Product(itemId, description, price, color);
    pm.makePersistent(product);

    // obtain the key
    ItemPK productKey = (ItemPK)
                        JDOHelper.getObjectId(product);

    // return the Key
    return productKey;
}
```

The **ejbLoad()** method is invoked by the container. It obtains a persistence manager, which will then be synchronized with the current J2EE transaction. JDO is then used to retrieve from the data store the persistent entity corresponding to the entity bean's primary key. The entity bean's primary key is obtained from the **EntityContext** reference **ec**.

```
public void ejbLoad() {
    // get the PM
    //get the PM
    if (pm == null || pm.isClosed())
        pm = pmf.getPersistenceManager();

    // construct key and obtain persistent object
    ItemPK productKey = (ItemPK) ec.getPrimaryKey();
    product = (Product) pm.getObjectById(productKey, true);
}
```

The **ejbStore()** method must synchronize the data store with the attribute values in the entity bean instance. Since the business methods of the bean have merely been altering the persistent instance, it will already have transitioned a dirty state if necessary. The persistence manager will synchronize this dirty instance to the data store when the J2EE transaction is committed. Therefore there is nothing JDO-specific for **ejbStore()** to do.

```
public void ejbStore() {
}
```

ejbStore()

Please note that **ejbStore()** should not close the persistence manager. The EJB specification allows for **ejbStore()** to be called multiple times without an intervening call to **ejbLoad()** or another method that might acquire a persistence manager from the factory.

If the persistence manager were to be closed during an **ejbStore()** invocation, a **JDOFatalUserException** might occur if the same persistence manager instance, or one of its JDO instances, was subsequently invoked.

Entity beans that do close the persistence manager at this point in their lifecycle may work in a particular application server but will not be portable.

Passivation occurs when this entity bean instance is being disassociated from its current primary key and J2EE transaction, to be potentially activated against a different primary key in the context of a different transaction. The **ejbPassivate()** method's action is to nullify the reference to the persistent product instance (to speed up the garbage collection process) and close the persistence manager.

```
public void ejbPassivate() {
    // nullify reference to persistent instance
    product = null;

    // close the PM and nullify its reference
    pm.close(); pm = null;
}
```

Activation occurs when this entity bean instance is being associated with a new entity bean primary key and J2EE transaction. The J2EE specification does not specify that ejbActivate() will be called within the context of an open transaction. Since persistence managers must be obtained within such a context, in order to be bound to the J2EE transaction, this is deferred to the ejbLoad() method. Thus ejbActivate() remains empty.

```
public void ejbActivate() { }
```

The removal of an entity bean corresponds directly to the deletion of data from the data store. This is implemented by the **ejbRemove()** method. In addition, the entity EJB is transitioned to its pooled state on **ejbRemove()**, so the persistence manager should be closed.

```
public void ejbRemove() {
    pm.deletePersistent(product);
    pm.close();
}
```

The final method in a bean's instance lifecycle is **unsetEntityContext()**, which signals to the bean that it is about to be discarded and subsequently garbage-collected. The only action we implement is to nullify the reference to the persistence manager factory. Once again this is done in order to speed up the garbage-collection process.

```
public void unsetEntityContext() {
    pmf = null;
}
```

The finder methods in an entity bean return individual primary keys or collections of primary keys to the container. Although entity beans are themselves inherently stateful, each finder method invocation occurs in a stateless fashion on an arbitrary bean of the appropriate class in the free pool. Thus a persistence manager must be obtained and closed within the scope of such methods.

Below we implement two finder methods for the product entity bean; one will find a single instance by primary key, and the other uses the **Extent** of products to return a collection of all persistent product Object IDs.

```
public Collection ejbFindAll() {
    // find all products and return a collection of
    // primary keys
    pm = pmf.getPersistenceManager();
    Vector v = new Vector();
    try {
        Extent e = pm.getExtent(Product.class, true);
        Iterator i = e.iterator();
        while (i.hasNext()){
            v.add(JDOHelper.getObjectId(i.next()));
        }
```

```
        }
        finally {
            pm.close();
        }
        return v;
    }

    public ItemPK ejbFindByPrimaryKey(ItemPK itemKey) throws
                                      FinderException {
        // find a single product corresponding to the entity
        // primary key
        try {
            pm = pmf.getPersistenceManager();
            Object o = pm.getObjectById(itemKey, true);
        }
        catch (Exception e) {
            e.printStackTrace();
            throw new FinderException("failed to locate
    object through JDO " + "with itemId=" + itemKey.itemId);
        }
        finally {
            pm.close();
        }
        return itemKey;
    }
}
```

Business methods merely invoke the persistence-capable class as required to fulfill their requirements.

```
// business methods

public String getDescription() {
    return product.getDescription();
}

public void setDescription(String description) {
    product.setDescription(description);
}

public double getPrice() {
    return product.getPrice();
}

public void setPrice(double price) {
    product.setPrice(price);
}
```

```
public String getColor() {
    return product.getColor();
}

public void setColor(String color) {
    product.setColor(color);
}

public String getItemId() {
    return product.getItemId();
}
```

This concludes the **ProductEntityBean** source code.

JDO vs. entity beans – the great debate

There has been much discussion recently on the pros and cons of entity beans vs. JDO. In fact, as I hope you will agree, the choice is now remarkably clear-cut.

Entity EJBs have been a part of J2EE since its 1.0 release, and support for them was made mandatory in J2EE 1.1. They can provide a remote interface to the data they encapsulate, which in some select situations is beneficial. Generally, however, architects choose to front remote entity bean access with a session bean façade. Local interfaces are available with EJB 2.0, but the difference between local (pass by reference) and remote (pass by value) invocation must be considered carefully.

Entity beans are not at all transparent to the domain object model, and support for inheritance is far from complete. With J2EE 1.3 (EJB 2.0), support is now provided for container-managed relationships between entity beans. However, this further complicates an already complex architecture.

JDO instances do not inherently provide a remote interface, but this can be achieved with a session bean façade in which instances are accessed directly from the session tier.

JDO provides full support for inheritance and implementation hierarchies. It is remarkably transparent to the domain object model, and provides all the benefits of transparent persistence that we have described. Many analysts have indeed commented that JDO is what entity beans should have been.

I expect to see the widespread use of JDO in the managed environment, and would be surprised if companies continued to use entity beans for significant numbers of new developments. Where an existing investment has already been made in entity beans as part of an application, JDO could be used as a strategy for BMP until such time as the entity beans might be replaced with JDO instances.

In the light of this, will entity beans be removed from the J2EE specification? I don't believe this will happen. However, with entity beans being used even less frequently, it will become apparent that application servers can be smaller, faster, easier to develop, less resource intensive, and ultimately cheaper if they do not support entity beans. I hope that the entity bean aspects of the EJB specification will be made optional, so that those application server vendors that choose not to support them can, nevertheless, have their products branded as J2EE-compliant.

11.9   JDO integration with message-driven beans

After the relative complexities of the entity bean lifecycle you will be pleased to know that the message-driven bean lifecycle is extremely straightforward – and JDO integration is much simpler too! Figure 11.4 shows the message-driven bean lifecycle.

A message-driven bean has a **MessageDrivenContext** object passed to its **setMessageDrivenContext()** method when the bean is introduced into the free pool. The **ejbCreate()** method is then invoked associating the instance with a particular JMS destination, subsequent to which its **onMessage()** method may be called zero, one, or more times to handle incoming messages. At some point the bean's **ejbRemove()** method is invoked to disassociate it from that particular JMS destination.

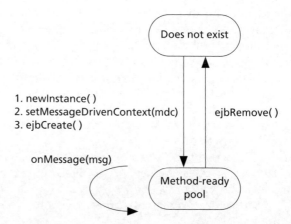

Figure 11.4 Message-driven bean lifecycle

To use JDO for persistence services from within a message-driven bean, the persistence manager factory is looked up during the **setMessageDrivenContext()** method. The **onMessage()** method should acquire a persistence manager from the factory. This will be synchronized with the J2EE transaction. The persistence manager should be closed before the method returns.

Our example is a message-driven bean called **ProductRecipient**. It receives new product descriptions as asynchronous messages and constructs, initializes, and persists product instances with these descriptions. It is evident that this is a simplification of a far more complicated process, which would usually involve the receipt of strings that are themselves entire XML documents. These, containing more comprehensive product information, would be parsed in order to initialize the product.

Message-driven beans only have a bean class and do not have any home or remote interfaces. The bean class is shown below.

ProductRecipientBean.java

```java
package com.ogilviepartners.jdobook.op.j2ee;

import javax.ejb.*;
import javax.jdo.*;
import javax.naming.*;
import javax.jms.*;
import com.ogilviepartners.jdobook.op.*;
import com.ogilviepartners.jdobook.op.pk.*;

public class ProductRecipientBean implements
                MessageDrivenBean {
    MessageDrivenContext ctx;
    PersistenceManagerFactory pmf;
    Context env;

    public void setMessageDrivenContext(MessageDrivenContext ctx)
{
        this.ctx = ctx;
        try {
            Context ic = new InitialContext();
            env = (Context) ic.lookup("java:comp/env");
            pmf = (PersistenceManagerFactory)
                env.lookup("jdo/OrderProcessingPMF");
        }
        catch (NamingException e) {
            throw new EJBException("JNDI Lookups Failed");
        }
    }

    public void ejbRemove() {}
    public void ejbCreate() {}
```

```
public void onMessage(Message m) {
    Object content;
    Product product;
    PersistenceManager pm;

    try {
        // only TextMessage types expected
        if (m instanceof TextMessage) {
            // retrieve message contents
            TextMessage tm = (TextMessage) m;
            String s = tm.getText();

            // get pm from pmf, synchronized to the
            // J2EE transaction
            pm = pmf.getPersistenceManager();

            // instantiate, initialize and persist the
            // new product
            product = new Product();
            product.setDescription(s);
            pm.makePersistent(product);
        }
        else throw new EJBException(
            "Message was not a TextMessage");
    }
    catch (Exception e) {
        throw new EJBException(e);
    }
    finally {
        if (pm != null && !pm.isClosed()) pm.close();
    }
}
```

That concludes our look at JDO integration with EJB components. We now turn our attention to the web tier.

11.10 JDO integration with the web tier

As with EJB components, servlets and JSP may use JDO for object persistence. From the web tier this is typically done in support of HTML websites, enabling the delivery of dynamic content to a client based on parameters in the incoming request, as well as the execution of business transactions in response to these requests.

11.10.1 Servlets

The servlet lifecycle starts with a call to the **init()** method after the instance has been constructed (Figure 11.5). Subsequently there may be zero, one, or many invocations of its service method in response to HTTP requests. These invocations will usually be on a multithreaded basis requiring explicit synchronization of access to attributes of the servlet class. If the servlet implements the **SingleThreadModel** interface, these invocations will be strictly in serial. The service method of an **HttpServlet** interprets the HTTP request and invokes the appropriate do method. This is usually **doGet()** or **doPost()**, although other request types exist.

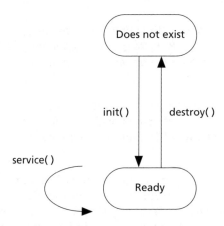

Figure 11.5 Servlet lifecycle

For servlets to use JDO, the reference to the persistence manager factory must be obtained in the **init()** method. The persistence manager should then be obtained upon a request and closed before the request is completed. However, it should be noted that servlets do not have transactions provided for them by the container. Thus it is necessary for servlet code to explicitly demarcate transactions through JDO or through J2EE.

The servlet example presented here is one that displays, in HTML format, a list of all business partners. This is given as an HTML table with columns labeled ID, Name, Address, and Type. The Type column contains the name of each partner's actual concrete subclass: **Company**, **Charity**, or **Individual**. Here's the code.

BusinessPartnerServlet.java

```
package com.ogilviepartners.jdobook.op.j2ee;

import javax.servlet.*;
import javax.jdo.*;
import op.Product;
```

```java
public class BusinessPartnerServlet extends HttpServlet
{
    PersistenceManagerFactory pmf;

    public void init(ServletConfig config) {
        super.init(config);
        Context ic = new InitialContext();
        Context env;
        env = (Context) ic.lookup("java:comp/env");
        pmf = env.lookup("OrderProcessingPMF");
    }

    public void doGet(HttpRequest request,
                      HttpResponse response) {
        processRequest(request, response);
    }

    public void doPost(HttpRequest request,
                       HttpResponse response) {
        processRequest(request, response);
    }

    private void processRequest(HttpRequest request,
                      HttpResponse response) {
        // get the persistence manager and begin transaction
        PersistenceManager pm = pmf.getPersistenceManager();
        Transaction t = pm.currentTransaction();
        t.begin();

        // get the extent of BusinessPartner including
        // subclasses
        Extent e;
        e = pm.getExtent(BusinessPartner.class, true);
        Iterator i = e.iterator();

        // commence output
        response.setContentType("text/html");
        PrintWriter out = response.getWriter();

        // page header
        out.println("<HTML><HEAD><TITLE>" +
            "Business Partners<?TITLE></HEAD>")
        out.println("<BODY>");
        out.println("<H1>List of Business Partners</H1>");

        // start of table
        out.println("<TABLE><TR><TH>ID</TH><TH>Name" +
            "</TH><TH>Address</TH><TH>Type</TH></TR>");
```

```
        while(i.hasNext()) {
            BusinessPartner bp = (BusinessPartner) i.next();
            out.println("<TR>");
            out.println("<TD>" + bp.getPartnerId() + "</TD>");
            out.println("<TD>" + bp.getName() + "</TD>");
            out.println("<TD>" + bp.getAddress() + "</TD>");
            out.println("<TD>" + bp.class.getName() + "</TD>");
            out.println("</TR>");
        }

        //end of table and document
        out.println("</TABLE></BODY></HTML>");

        // output complete
        out.flush();
        e.close(i);
        t.commit();
        pm.close();
    }
}
```

The above example employs JDO transactions, which does not rely on any specific J2EE transaction support from the servlet container. If the servlet were invoking EJB components for some of its processing, it would be unusual for it to access persistent objects directly as well. Instead, all access to JDO would typically be delegated to the EJB tier. However, if necessary, the servlet can look up the **UserTransaction** though JNDI and then demarcate J2EE transactions. With such an approach, the persistence manager must not be obtained from the factory until the J2EE transaction has been commenced.

That's all I wish to say regarding servlets. We now look briefly at the same example rendered as a JSP.

11.10.2 JavaServer Pages

In order to handle the JNDI lookup of the persistence manager factory, the JSP uses a bean called **PMFHolder**. This simple bean looks up the persistence manager factory according to the given JNDI name and then exposes a **getPersistenceManager()** method. The source code for the bean is shown below.

PMFHolder.java

```
package com.ogilviepartners.jdobook.op.j2ee;

import javax.jdo.*;
import javax.naming.*;
```

```
public class PMFHolder
{
    PersistenceManagerFactory pmf;

    public void setJNDIName(String jndiName) {
        Context ic = new InitialContext();
        Context env = ic.lookup("java:comp/env");
        pmf = (PersistenceManagerFactory)
                                    env.lookup(jndiName);
    }

    public synchronized PersistenceManager
                                getPersistenceManager() {
        return pmf.getPersistenceManager();
    }
}
```

Here then is the JSP page itself.

BusinessPartnerList.jsp

```
<%@ page import javax.jdo.* %>
<%@ page import com.ogilviepartners.jdobook.op.Product %>

<%! PersistenceManagerFactory pmf %>

<jsp:useBean id="OrderProcessingPMFHolder" scope="application"
class="com.ogilviepartners.jdobook.op.j2ee.PMFHolder">
    <% OrderProcessingPMFHolder.setJNDIName
                                ("OrderProcessingPMF"); %>
</jsp:useBean>

<HTML><HEAD><TITLE>Business Partners</TITLE></HEAD>
<BODY>
<H1>List of Business Partners</H1>
<TABLE>
<TR><TH>ID</TH><TH>Name</TH><TH>Address</TH><TH>Type</TH></TR>
<%

    PersistenceManager pm = OrderProcessingPMFHolder.
                                getPersistenceManager();
    Transaction t = pm.currentTransaction();
    t.begin();
    Extent e = pm.getExtent(BusinessPartner.class, true);
    Iterator i = e.iterator();
    while (i.hasNext) {
```

```
            BusinessPartner bp = i.next();
%>
<TR>
<TD><%= bp.getPartnerId() %></TD>
<TD><%= bp.getName() %></TD>
<TD><%= bp.getAddress() %></TD>
<TD><%= bp.class.getName() %></TD>
</TR>
<%
    }
    e.close(i);
    t.commit();
    pm.close();
%>
</BODY>
```

Note that a "proper" JSP should contain as little Java code as possible, instead delegating to helper classes through custom tag libraries. The above example ignores this precept for the sake of brevity.

It is possible that future versions of JDO will include a library of JSP tags specifically for persistence management.

11.11 Bootstrapping JDO in the managed environment

All of our discussions in this chapter have presumed that an appropriately configured **PersistenceManagerFactory** instance has already been instantiated and registered with the naming service, ready to be looked up through JNDI. But how is this achieved?

Unfortunately there is no standard method. If JDO were to be accepted as part of the next release of J2EE, provision would be made for this bootstrapping through the J2EE configuration file **resource.properties**.

In the interim, however, the mechanics of registering factories on application server startup must be addressed in conjunction with advice and documentation from the vendors of your chosen application server and JDO implementation products.

What's next?

In the next chapter I present a survey of the non-reference JDO implementations available as at March 2002.

JDO implementations 12

O ur examination of JDO 1.0 is now complete. This penultimate chapter gives the reader an introduction to some of the most important JDO Implementations and the companies behind them.

For each vendor there is a page or two about the company, their products, and the extent of their support for various data stores and application servers. Some of the products listed are object-relational mapping implementations which work with an underlying relational database. Others are themselves fully fledged object databases for which a JDO interface is provided.

Table 12.1 Optional feature support, as at March 2002

Product	Fast Objects		JRelay		Kodo JDO	IntelliBO	
Version			2.0	2.1	2.2	2.5	3.0
Status	GA	Plan	GA	Plan	GA	GA	Plan
TransientTransactional	✔	✔	✔	✔	✔	✘	✔
NontransactionalRead	✔	✔	✔	✔	✔	✔	✔
NontransactionalWrite	✔	✔	✔	✔	✔	✔	✔
RetainValues	✔	✔	✔	✔	✔	✔	✔
RestoreValues	✔	✔	✘	✘	✔	✘	✔
Optimistic	✘	✔	✔	✔	✔	✔	✔
ApplicationIdentity	✘	✘	✔	✔	✔	✔	✔
DatastoreIdentity	✔	✔	✔	✔	✔	✔	✔
NondurableIdentity	✘	✘	✘	✘	✔	✘	✔
ArrayList	✔	✔	✔	✔	✔	✔	✔
HashMap	✔	✔	✘	✔	✔	✔	✔
Hashtable	✔	✔	✘	✔	✔	✔	✔
LinkedList	✔	✔	✔	✔	✔	✔	✔
TreeMap	✔	✔	✘	✔	✔	✔	✔
TreeSet	✔	✔	✔	✔	✔	✔	✔
Vector	✔	✔	✔	✔	✔	✔	✔
Map	✔	✔	✘	✔	✔	✔	✔
List	✔	✔	✔	✔	✔	✔	✔
Array	✔	✔	✘	✘	✔	✔	✔
NullCollection	✔	✔	✘	✘	✘	✔	✔
ChangeApplicationIdentity	✘	✘	✔	✔	✘	✘	✔
JDOQL	✔	✔	✔	✔	✔	✔	✔

Table 12.1(Continued) Optional feature support, as at March 2002

Product	LiDO		Open Fusion		Orient		PE.:J	
Version	1.2	1.3	1.1	2.x	2.0	2.1	2.0	3.0
Status	GA	Plan	GA	Plan	GA	Plan	GA	Plan
TransientTransactional	✔	✔	✘	✔	✘	✔	✘	✘
NontransactionalRead	✔	✔	✘	✔	✔	✔	✔	✔
NontransactionalWrite	✔	✔	✘	✔	✔	✔	✘	✔
RetainValues	✔	✔	✘	✔	✘	✔	✔	✔
RestoreValues	✔	✔	✘	✘	✘	✔	✘	✘
Optimistic	✘	✔	✘	✔	✘	✔	✔	✔
ApplicationIdentity	✔	✔	✔	✔	✘	✘	✔	✔
DatastoreIdentity	✔	✔	✔	✔	✔	✔	✔	✔
NondurableIdentity	✔	✔	✘	✘	✘	✔	✘	✔
ArrayList	✔	✔	✔	✔	✔	✔	✔	✔
HashMap	✔	✔	✘	✔	✔	✔	✔	✔
Hashtable	✘	✔	✘	✔	✔	✔	✔	✔
LinkedList	✘	✔	✔	✔	✔	✔	✘	✔
TreeMap	✘	✔	✘	✘	✔	✔	✘	✔
TreeSet	✘	✔	✘	✘	✔	✔	✘	✔
Vector	✔	✔	✔	✔	✔	✔	✔	✔
Map	✔	✔	✘	✔	✔	✔	✔	✔
List	✔	✔	✔	✔	✔	✔	✔	✔
Array	✔	✔	✘	✔	✔	✔	✔	✔
NullCollection	✔	✔	✔	✔	✘	✘	✔	✔
ChangeApplicationIdentity	✔	✔	✘	✘	✘	✘	✔	✔
JDOQL	✔	✔	✔	✔	✘	✔	✔	✔

In addition to the textual information, each vendor was invited to supply a list of supported features for their GA release (general availability as at March 2002), and for their next planned release if they wished. Most vendors supplied this information, which is collated in Table 12.1. Since this information was sourced, two further JDO implementations have been announced. These are "JDOGenie" and "FrontierSuite for JDO", each of which is discussed during this chapter but does not feature in the comparison table.

This information is intended to raise awareness of the various companies and products that are active in the JDO community. It is interesting to note that, with JDO only recently finalized, many vendors already have commercial products that will shortly implement almost the entire specification. This is in stark contrast to previous efforts by the ODMG to standardize access to object databases, for which the vendors of the day provided only partial support.

Finally, please note that a number of factors must be borne in mind in choosing an implementation. Even though a vendor may claim that their implementation supports every optional feature in the specification, this does not mean that the features are efficiently implemented. Non-functional characteristics must also be considered, including, but not limited to, factors such as performance, scalability, support, ancillary services (e.g. training), and cost.

12.1   enJin™ by Versant

Contact addresses: www.versant.com and sales@versant.com
enJin™ is a trademark of Versant Corporation.

12.1.1 About Versant

Versant Corporation (NASDAQ: VSNT) has led the industry in highly scalable, reliable object management solutions for complex, enterprise-level systems since its founding in 1988.

The company's ODBMS serves as the core database for fraud detection, yield management, real-time data collection and analysis, operation support systems, and other large-scale applications in the telecommunications, financial services, transportation, and defense industries.

12.1.2 About enJin

Versant enJin speeds the development and performance of applications requiring transactional storage, distribution, and caching of objects from EJBs and JSPs/Servlets in the middle tier.

12.1.3 Supported data stores

Versant ODBMS.

12.1.4 Supported application servers

The following application servers are supported:

- IBM WebSphere
- BEA WebLogic.

12.2 FastObjects™ by Poet Software

Contact addresses: www.fastobjects.com and sales@fastobjects.com
FastObjects™ is a trademark of Poet Software Corporation.

12.2.1 About Poet software

Poet Software provide embedded database components for smart devices and turnkey software applications. FastObjects embedded databases improve the reliability and performance of sophisticated data-intensive applications. Unlike general-purpose data engines, FastObjects is built to meet the specific needs of OEMs with features that improve ease of operation and simplify lifecycle management of durable long-lived products.

12.2.2 About FastObjects

All FastObjects embedded databases share the following features:

- easily accepts any data structure;
- rapid data storage, search, and retrieval for Java;
- ensures consistency of data;
- fully automated maintenance;
- support for field-upgradable products;
- compliant with JDO standard.

12.2.3 Product family

Each member of the FastObjects product family augments the standard features as follows.

12.2.3.1 FastObjects j1

j1 is a JDO-compliant pure Java community edition object database.

- Free for non-commercial development.

12.2.3.2 FastObjects j2

j2 Is a JDO-compliant pure Java embedded object database for smart devices.

- Concurrent sharing of data for multithreaded applications.
- Pure Java.
- Small footprint – 450KB.
- Fault tolerance for mission-critical applications.

12.2.3.3 FastObjects e7

e7 is a JDO-compliant embedded object database for large-scale computer-controlled equipment.

- Secure sharing of data between processes.
- User authorization.
- Security add-on for data encryption.

12.2.3.4 FastObjects t7

t7 is a JDO-compliant multi-tier object database for large distributed applications.

- Secure sharing of data between hosts.
- User authorization.
- Client-side caching of objects.
- Pre-fetching of object graphs.
- Security add-on for data encryption.
- Fault-tolerance add-on for mission-critical applications.

12.2.4 Supported data stores

FastObjects databases are specifically built to work in non-managed "embedded" environments. Typical FastObjects applications are turnkey software applications and computer-controlled equipment.

12.2.5 Supported application servers

FastObjects t7 is a multi-tiered version that works within J2EE application servers. Example application servers include JBoss and Borland AppServer.

12.3   FrontierSuite for JDO™ by ObjectFrontier

Contact addresses: www.ObjectFrontier.com and sales@ObjectFrontier.com
FrontierSuite for JDO™ is a trademark of ObjectFrontier Inc.

12.3.1   About ObjectFrontier

ObjectFrontier is a provider of component and service oriented enterprise software. ObjectFrontier's products focus on transparent persistence for Java objects
and have been providing persistence solutions for the J2EE and J2SE platforms
for the past several years. FrontierSuite, the company's flagship product, is a
powerful JCA compliant persistence engine and a Model Driven Architecture
(MDA) based development environment for designing, developing, and deploy-
ing enterprise applications. FrontierSuite has a mature persistence technology
for both the J2SE and J2EE (both EJB 1. 1 and EJB 2. 0) environments.

   ObjectFrontier brings the mature persistence technology and the experience
gained in providing persistence in various platforms into FrontierSuite for JDO,
claiming it to be the first product with a comprehensive development environment for building JDO applications.

12.3.2   About FrontierSuite for JDO

FrontierSuite for JDO provides four modules for building and running JDO
applications using different approaches.

12.3.3   Product Family

12.3.3.1 FrontierSuite for JDO (Forward Engineering)

In this approach, building a new JDO application from scratch is supported.
The input for this approach is a UML based project model for persistent objects.
The development environment provides tools for defining or importing
UML object models. It then automates the entire process of generating
PersistenceCapable classes from the object model through Frontier Builder, a
code generator tool. Finally, mapping of the classes to an underlying
RDBMS scheme is accomplished through Frontier Fusion, an object-relational
mapping tool.

12.3.3.2 Frontier ReModeler for JDO (Reverse Engineering)

This approach to JDO application building provides a migration path for enterprises moving to the JDO standards whilst re-using an existing database

schema. Enterprises can use this approach for migration to a JDO layer above the existing enterprise data layer for easy maintenance and robustness. The schema of the existing enterprise database is captured and an object model created automatically by Frontier ReModeler for JDO. From this object model, a JDO application that uses the existing database schema is created.

12.3.3.3 Frontier DeployDirect for JDO (Class Enhancement)

Normal non-persistent Java classes can be made persistence-capable through Frontier DeployDirect for JDO, which includes a JDO enhancer and a mapping tool for mapping the enhanced classes to a relational database schema. The mapping process is totally automated and GUI based and allows much flexibility in terms of fine-tuning the default mapping schema.

12.3.3.4 Frontier DeployDirect for JDO (Bridge Pattern)

Java Applications that use a database schema and that want to migrate to the JDO standard, while retaining the existing Java Code and the database schema, can use the Bridge pattern supported by Frontier DeployDirect for JDO. This approach provides a bridge between legacy applications and JDO standards by enhancing the existing Java classes to become persistence-capable and mapping these enhanced classes to the existing database schema through a GUI interface. This provides maximum reusability, wherein both the existing Java Code and the database schema are migrated to the JDO standard and become part of the new JDO application.

12.3.4 Supported data stores

FrontierSuite for JDO targets JDBC compliant relational databases, specifically:

- Oracle
- MS SQL Server
- DB2
- PointBase
- Cloudscape
- MS Access

12.3.5 Supported application servers

FrontierSuite for JDO currently supports the following J2EE application servers:

- Weblogic
- WebSphere

- Orbix E2A J2EE Server
- Jboss
- Oracle 9i
- HP AS
- Orion AS

12.4   IntelliBO™ by Signsoft

Contact addresses: www.signsoft.com and sales@signsoft.com
IntelliBO™ is a trademark of Signsoft GmbH.

12.4.1 About Signsoft

Signsoft offers software solutions and services for companies needing highly scalable and high-performance applications. The company's products offer high levels of integration, reliability and flexibility, and its aim is to ease the development and integration of complex software applications. Including the capability to integrate dynamic adoptions to applications. Signsoft makes products that support the growing requirements of scalability, performance, and availability of an IT infrastructure.

Signsoft has a solid, long-term experience in the field of software development. The outstanding knowledge of its developers makes Signsoft one of the foremost software developers. Its staff are at the front of new technologies, and have published a number of articles in well-known developer magazines. Its developers often give keynote speeches at important conferences and meetings, and have close contact with other experts worldwide. All this supports the development of high-quality and reliable software products.

12.4.2 About IntelliBO

Signsoft IntelliBO is a flexible and easy-to-use JDO implementation. It supports all the required and optional features of JDO, and is highly reliable. It has been tested in many environments and supports all JDBC-compliant databases. Many disparate databases can be used simultaneously. For a large number of databases there are special JDBC-support drivers which enhance the capabilities of the standard JDBC-drivers.

IntelliBO supports complex objects models and database schemas. It optimizes the queries sent to the database and supports mixed JDOQL/SQL queries, which developers can augment by defining their own functions and operators. Beside this, IntelliBO is able to handle all kinds of mappings to existing database schemas.

For improved performance, an extensive caching system is used and large result sets are loaded incrementally.

IntelliBO can be integrated seamlessly into J2EE application server environments. Additional tools that support development are provided, including:

- integrated development environment (IDE);
- Swing components;
- JBuilder integration;
- automatic creation of persistence-capable classes from tables;
- verification of persistence descriptors.

Signsoft runs a competent support team for its clients and provides help promptly in every phase of a client project.

12.4.3 Supported data stores

JDBC-compliant resources, including specific support for:

- JDBC/ODBC Bridge
- Oracle
- Sybase
- InterBase
- InstantDB
- Informix
- IBM DB2
- SAPDB.

12.4.4 Supported application servers

All J2EE 1.3-compliant application servers.

12.5   JDO Genie™ by Hemisphere Technologies

Contact addresses: www.hemtech.co.za and info@hemtech.co.za
JDO Genie™ is a trademark of Hemisphere Technologies.

12.5.1 About Hemisphere Technologies

Hemisphere Technologies is an independent software house specializing in Java and related technologies. The company has completed several Java projects using its in house Object/Relational mapping technology. JDO Genie incorporates this experience, accrued through real life projects.

12.5.2 About JDO Genie

JDO Genie is a JDO implementation for relational databases focusing on performance, flexible mapping, optimistic transactions and distributed persistence managers.

JDO Genie supports access to multiple physical data stores through a single persistence manager with one object model. Persistence managers may be in different virtual machines to the JDO server and communicate using RMI or SOAP. This makes JDO Genie ideal for rich client deployment, as clients no longer have to make session bean calls to access the object model.

JDO Genie supports many extensions for mapping and performance, including multiple fetch groups, flexible caching options and reference navigation using joins. All of these options are easily declared through the provided meta-data editing tool.

12.5.3 Supported data stores

JDO Genie targets JDBC -compliant databases. Specifically, the following:

- Oracle
- Sybase
- Informix
- Postgres
- Microsoft SQL Server

IBM DB2 will be supported in the next release, with support for XML data stores and LDAP anticipated in a subsequent release.

12.5.4 Supported application servers

JDO Genie uses JCA for operation in the managed environment. The following application servers are currently supported

- JBoss
- WebLogic

Support for Websphere will be provided soon.

12.6   JRelay™ by Object Industries

Contact addresses: www.objectindustries.com and sales@objectindustries.com
JRelay™ is a trademark of Object Industries GmbH.

12.6.1 About Object Industries

Object Industries provides highly optimized and sophisticated tools to speed up Java software development. The company's special competence lies in the field of persistence management, where the object-relational JDO persistence layer JRelay is positioned.

12.6.2 About JRelay

JRelay is a JDO implementation for relational database systems. It is based on the JDBC-API and therefore can be used with any RDBMS supporting that standard. JRelay is delivered with a JDO-compliant source-code enhancer and a powerful graphical mapping tool, the JRelay Workbench.

The JRelay Workbench supports flexible roundtrip engineering when mapping classes to database tables. This includes the generation of complete database models in one direction, and the mapping of existing tables to new or modified classes in the other direction.

The JRelay runtime is designed for performance optimization.

12.6.3 Supported data stores

JDBC-compliant resources.

12.6.4 Supported application servers

J2EE application server support is planned for JRelay 2.1.

12.7   Kodo JDO™ by SolarMetric

Contact addresses: www.solarmetric.com and sales@solarmetric.com
Kodo JDO™ is a trademark of SolarMetric Inc.

12.7.1 About SolarMetric

SolarMetric is a global company with corporate headquarters in Washington, D.C. A strong team of Java developers and experienced business leaders founded SolarMetric in 2001. The core technology team has been together since 1997, working on enterprise web applications and networking products for previous employers.

SolarMetric creates enterprise development products leveraging Sun's Java development language. SolarMetric's products are targeted towards enabling application developers to focus on their application logic rather than on deployment-specific details. SolarMetric's client base represents all major industries and includes customers in the European Union, Switzerland, Canada, Australia, Hong Kong, and the United States.

12.7.2 About Kodo JDO

Kodo JDO is SolarMetric's implementation of Sun's JDO specification for transparent persistence. Kodo JDO provides access to relational databases through the JDO specification, enabling Java developers to use existing relational database technology from Java without needing to know SQL or be an expert in relational database design. It can be used with existing database schemas, or can automatically generate its own schema.

12.7.3 Product family

There are two editions of Kodo JDO.

12.7.3.1 Kodo JDO Standard Edition

The Standard Edition is a complete solution for developers who need a fully functional JDO solution but aren't interested in using JDO in concert with a J2EE application server.

12.7.3.2 Kodo JDO Enterprise Edition

The Enterprise Edition is a fully spec-compliant JDO implementation. It is an appropriate choice for applications that will be run in a J2EE application server, such as BEA's WebLogic, IBM's WebSphere, or the open source JBoss. It facilitates the integration of JDO operations into globally managed transactions, letting all JDO transactional operations be governed by the application server.

12.7.4 Supported data stores

Kodo JDO targets JDBC-compliant relational databases. The following are currently supported:

- IBM DB2 UDB 7.2
- InstantDB 3.26
- Microsoft SQLServer 8.00
- MySQL 3.23.43
- Sybase ASE 12.5
- Oracle 8.1.7
- PostgresSQL 6.5
- Hypersonic SQL.

Support for other databases not on this list can easily be added to Kodo JDO, either by a third party or by SolarMetric's consulting team.

12.7.5 Supported application servers

Kodo JDO currently supports the following application servers:

- BEA WebLogic
- JBoss

12.8   LiDO™ by LIBeLIS

Contact addresses: www.libelis.com and sales@libelis.com
LiDO™ is a trademark of LIBeLIS.

12.8.1 About LIBeLIS

LIBeLIS, which stands for Liberty for Large Information Systems, delivers Java technologies focussed on highly scalable transactional systems. LIBeLIS is a member of the JDO Expert Group and a board member of the ObjectWeb consortium.

12.8.2 About LiDO

LiDO is the company's flagship product. It is a set of universal JDO drivers, focussed primarily on very high performance, and targetting production systems with tough quality of service requirements and heterogeneous data sources.

LiDO for RDBMS supports the reverse engineering of existing databases and automatic creation of new data models. LiDO implements all mandatory and optional lifecycle JDO states. It supports all JDK collections, including vectors, lists, maps, sets, arrays, and all attribute types including interface, object, abstract classes, second-class objects, and embedded objects.

LiDO proposes various strategies to map inheritance (flat and vertical models) and relationships (independent relation table, reverse foreign key, etc.). For performance reasons, LiDO can use a configurable pool of prepared statements and employ statement batching. LiDO supports the mapping of SELECT statements and the mapping of stored procedures. UPDATE statements only update modified attributes, and there it is possible to control how result sets are loaded into memory (one by one, using cursor size or complete). A trace mode allows developers to monitor LiDO's interaction with the server by viewing SQL statements that are issued, and so on.

12.8.3 Vendor-specific persistence descriptor extensions

LiDO supports some vendor extensions to indicate how inheritance, dates, and collections are mapped, and which indices to create. LiDO provides a smart and configurable naming feature to deal with table/column naming limitations.

12.8.4 Product family

12.8.4.1 LiDO Professional Edition

The Professional Edition is for RDBMS, Versant ODBMS and binary files (light-weight embedded database). Supports reverse mapping of existing databases. Includes NAViLIS, the GUI mapping tool, a JSP tag library, and JCA/J2EE support.

12.8.4.2 LiDO Standard Edition

The Standard Edition is for binary files and open source database management systems (DBMS) only. There is no support for JCA/J2EE and the mapping of existing databases.

12.8.4.3 LiDO Community Edition

The Community Edition is for open source DBMS only, but is free for non-commercial or education use.

12.8.4.4 NAViLIS

NAViLIS is a LiDO-based "business model" browser.

12.8.5 Supported data stores

LiDO currently supports most commercial and open source RDBMS products:

- Oracle
- SQL Server
- DB2 (UDB)
- Sybase
- Informix
- Cloudscape
- PointBase
- InstantDB
- MySQL
- PostgresSQL
- InterBase
- HyperSonicSQL.

Used in conjunction with its own binary file storage engine, LiDO provides a fully JDO-compliant, efficient, low-memory footprint persistence system for embedded systems.

The ODBMS support provides Versant users with standard APIs such as JDO, JTA, and JCA, making their applications fully portable. It is also much more efficient and complete than the original JVI/VEC product.

JCA connectors (CCI mapping) and support for data stores comprising XML files are being engineered. Any other data source can be supported quickly upon request.

12.8.6 Supported application servers

LiDO has been tested with:

- WebSphere
- WebLogic
- Borland AS
- JBoss
- JOnAS (ObjectWeb).

Being fully JCA compliant, it works with any other JCA-enabled J2EE application server.

12.9   OpenFusion JDO™ by PrismTechnologies

Contact addresses: www.prismtechnologies.com and
info@prismtechnologies.com
OpenFusion JDO™ is a trademark of Prism Technologies Ltd.

12.9.1 About Prism Technologies

Founded in 1992, PrismTech is a privately held company headquartered in the UK, with US and European operations. PrismTech is a leader in the provision of standards-based middleware to an impressive list of multinational companies worldwide, operating primarily in the telecommunications, defense, financial services, and manufacturing sectors.

PrismTech develops and markets the OpenFusion range of middleware software products that connect and integrate the leading standards-based distributed computing platform technologies: J2EE, CORBA, and web services. PrismTech's reputation for delivering high-quality, reliable, scalable, and highly-performant software is reflected in its worldclass customer base.

PrismTech's involvement with JDO began in late 2000 when the company was investigating technologies that could unify the disparate persistence mechanisms then used in its products. It identified JDO as the best approach. PrismTech has significant expertise in object-relational mapping, dating back to the early days of the company, and developed through collaborations with companies such as Oracle and Sybase, implementing complex data models and resolving the issues related to their use.

PrismTech has strongly supported the development of the JDO standard and members of its JDO development team, led by Steve Johnson, have been active participants of the JDO Expert Group.

12.9.2 About OpenFusion JDO

OpenFusion JDO is PrismTech's implementation of the JDO specification. It is an implementation for relational data stores only. OpenFusion JDO is written in Java and has been tested on Solaris 8, Linux, Windows NT/4 and Windows 2000. It is also usable on a wide range of Java platforms.

OpenFusion JDO supports the mandatory features of the JDO specification as well as some PrismTech additional functionality. The principal features of OpenFusion JDO are:

- Automatic creation of mappings from Java Objects to relational databases:
  - a default mapping style of one table per inheritance hierarchy is provided;
  - name and type mappings exposed in XML descriptors;
  - a vendor extension to the persistence descriptor enables indexes for specific fields to be generated.
- Support for both datastore and application identity.
- Configurable deletion semantics:
  - a PrismTech enhancement that allows developers to specify the behavior of an application when deleting an object;
  - supported options are nullify, no-action and exception.
- Simple command line interface:
  - simplifies use
  - easily integrated with IDEs;
  - Apache 'ant' task provided to simplify build management.
- Aligned with J2EE Connector Architecture
  - integrates with compliant application servers;
  - enables portable application code across multiple enterprise information server types.
- Robust implementation.

12.9.3 Supported data stores.

The following data stores are supported:

- HSQL, Version 1.61

- IBM DB2, Version 7.1
- Informix Dynamic Server 2000, Version 9.20
- Oracle 8i, Version 8.1.x
- Microsoft SQL Server 2000, Version 8.00.194
- MySQL, Version 3.23.36
- Sybase ASE, Version 11.9.2

Type mappings are exposed in an XML file, enabling users to add mappings for additional databases if required.

12.9.4 Supported application servers

All J2EE 1.3-compliant application servers. Specific details are available upon request.

12.10   Orient™ by Orient Technologies

Contact addresses: www.orientechnology.com and
sales@orientechnology.com
Orient™ is a trademark of Orient Technologies.

12.10.1 About Orient Technologies

Orient Technologies provides solutions based on its own fast Object Database engine. Orient was one of the first products to support the ODMG 3.0 standard for ODBMS. A partially JDO-compliant implementation of the Orient ODBMS was first made available in mid-2001.

Mr Luca Garulli, project leader for the Orient ODBMS products, is a member of the JDO Expert Group.

12.10.2 About Orient

Orient is a 100% pure ODBMS. It supports worldwide standards as Sun JDO 1.0, ODMG 3.0, and SQL. Orient is a pure object database and was built upon object oriented concepts rather than the relational model (tables, columns, and rows).

Its JDO implementation treats Java objects without conversion since Orient manages objects directly, instead of mapping them to table rows as would be the case for relational data stores. As a JDO implementation, Orient delivers high performance at low cost, when compared with alternative solutions comprising an object-relational JDO Implementation and a relational database.

12.10.3 Product family

12.10.3.1 Orient ODBMS Just Edition

The Just Edition works with a very small footprint (around 250Kb) and is perfect for embedded devices.

12.10.3.2 Orient ODBMS Enterprise Edition

The Enterprise Edition supports complex architectures with thousands of clients in a distributed environment, with many enterprise features such as load-balancing, fault-tolerance, and data replication.

12.10.4 Supported data stores

Orient ODBMS.

12.10.5 Supported application servers

Orient integrates with any application server that runs on JDK 1.3 or above, e.g. BEA WebLogic Server, IBM WebSphere, JBoss, etc.

12.11 PE:J™ The Productivity Environment™ for Java by HYWY Software

Contact addresses: www.hywy.com and sales@hywy.com
PE:J™ and Productivity Environment™ are trademarks of HYWY Software Corporation.

12.11.1 About HYWY Software

HYWY Software Corporation is a developer of Java productivity software. HYWY's products significantly reduce the complexity, cost, risk, and time-to-market of Java development. HYWY is a Sun Developer Connection Commercial Developer, a Forte™ for Java Framework Extension Partner, and an IBM PartnerWorld© member.

12.11.2 About PE:J

The PE:J Productivity Environment for Java is the first environment to deliver an integrated, standards-based, platform-independent product solution to enhance and automate the complete Java technology productivity lifecycle; from the conceptualization of a business idea to object model to scripted Java code.

Much more than a JDO implementation, PE:J boosts developer/analyst productivity with:

- code, schema and JSP application generation from UML specifications (forward engineering);
- UML diagram generation from code/schema (reverse engineering);
- intelligent merge to protect user code (roundtrip engineering);
- sample data and test harness generation.

With PE:J, developers can achieve an easy-to-extend, working, enterprise, object-relational (JDO), deployed JSP application from a diagram in several minutes. A free version of PE:J, limited only by a maximum number of user classes, is available for download from the HYWY website.

12.11.3 Product family

12.11.3.1 PE:J Developer

PE:J Developer Edition significantly lowers costs and time-to-market by boosting the productivity of existing developers and increasing the returns on prior investments in training and software, including:

- RDBMS servers
- J2EE application servers
- UML modeling tools
- Java IDEs.

PE:J increases functional accuracy by enabling end users and analyst/developers to participate in joint-application design sessions where they can quickly model, generate, try out, and refine an industrial-strength (J2EE) application, generated from UML specifications in minutes. PE:J features a very intuitive and easy-to-use interface that even Java novices can master quickly. Built on standards, and offering reverse engineering of existing systems, PE:J improves code quality and re-use of both new and existing systems.

12.11.3.2 PE:J Systems Engineering Edition

Please see the HYWY website for forthcoming details.

12.11.4 Supported data stores

PE:J supports all JDBC-compliant relational databases and is currently certified against:

- Oracle 8i
- Oracle 9i.

12.11.5 Supported application servers

PE:J supports all J2EE 1.3-compliant application servers and is currently certified against BEA WebLogic 6.1.

Epilogue   **13**

13.1   Beyond JDO 1.0

The first 11 chapters discussed JDO 1.0 in detail. Chapter 12 illustrated how comprehensively the specification is being adopted and implemented by the various JDO vendors. In this final chapter I wish to discuss a few areas where further refinement and extension of JDO can be anticipated in the future.

If you wish to contribute further ideas for enhancements or new features, an informal list is maintained by the moderators of the JavaDataObjects discussion forum at Yahoo!Groups (see 13.2.2).

13.1.1   Sequences

Sequence objects have been provided by relational database implementations for many years. They provide mechanisms for obtaining a sequence of numbers, and are often used to populate primary key fields in top-level domain objects, e.g. order numbers, invoice numbers, etc. (Some existing RDBMS-based applications use sequences for the construction of internal Object IDs. This functionality is provided in JDO by the use of datastore identity.)

JDO does not directly support sequence objects, but positions this as an issue to be solved by the domain object model. In the short term, JDO vendors may provide proprietary extensions by which sequence objects internal to the data store can be accessed. However, it is an area that is likely to be considered for specification as part of a future JDO release.

Conceptually, sequences can be used in two ways. Used *transactionally*, a sequence is associated with the active transaction each time a new value is requested. This ensures that, in the case of transaction rollback, the sequence object will not actually have been altered. Such assurance is imperative when assigning numbers such as check numbers or invoice numbers, where auditors would not accept "missing" entries in the sequence. This usage does, however, reduce overall concurrency since access to each individual sequence represents a potential bottleneck in the application.

Used *non-transactionally*, sequences do not become associated with transactions. When invoked they yield the next entry in the sequence, but are not affected by subsequent rollback events. This results in significantly higher concurrency, but is only appropriate when the occasional "hole" in the sequence is acceptable (e.g. for delivery numbers, which are not audited in the same way as invoice or check numbers).

13.1.2 Clarification of extent

The JDO 1.0 API provides for the construction of extents that include or exclude subclasses. The construction of extents that do not include subclasses is intended to facilitate performance improvements within those JDO implementations that map to underlying relational databases. By knowing that subclasses are to be excluded, the implementation can reduce the number of table joins in SQL queries based on that extent.

However, from an object oriented perspective, the concept of an extent that does not include subclasses is nonsensical. By definition, any instance of a subclass is ascribed the types of its superclass, and the Java **instanceof** operator will evaluate to **true** for each of them. Indeed, through its extensive support for polymorphism, Java itself does not recognize the notion of "an instance of this class but not any of its subclasses."

In the same way that the implementation of extents without subclasses can yield a performance improvement for RDBMS-based implementations, it can cause significant complications for ODBMS-based implementations.

Finally, any application developer who employs extents without subclasses is making the assumption, perhaps unwisely, that there will *never* be any subclasses. This goes against the tenets of object oriented design.

I believe that the notion of an extent without subclasses should be made a *hint* to the implementation. The implementation would be at liberty to include any instances of the extent's candidate class (even subclasses thereof). However, if it is beneficial in performance terms for the implementation to exclude subclasses, then it may do so. As such, extents without subclasses should be used only when it is known that no subclasses exist, and it is necessary to achieve the performance gains offered by a particular relational implementation.

This would maintain the object oriented "correctness" of JDO and give RDBMS-based implementations every chance of improving performance, whilst not burdening ODBMS-based implementations with unnecessary complications.

13.1.3 JDOQL

JDOQL holds the promise of being an efficient, vendor-neutral query language based on familiar Java syntax. Its restriction that only persistent fields may be accessed enables implementations to execute queries quickly. This is in contrast to "true" object query languages that require the instantiation of all candidate instances, many of which will fail the filter criteria before the filter can be evaluated.

However, the JDOQL we have with JDO 1.0 is just a beginning, and I list below some of the areas where enhancements and new features can be expected.

13.1.3.1 Projection

Presently JDOQL is only capable of returning a subset of the candidate collection or extent. If you give a query a collection of orders, it will return to you a subset of that collection – you still get just orders.

Imagine a situation where you have a collection of **Order**s and wish to identify each **Product** for which more than a designated quantity was ordered on a single **OrderLine**. Using JDOQL you can filter the original collection of orders to only those that contain individual **OrderLine**s with more than the designated quantity. However, you then have to iterate through the returned collection of **Order**s, and each **Order**s collection of **OrderLine**s, to programmatically locate the individual **Product** instances.

This would be easier if a JDOQL query could take one candidate class (**Order**) and return a collection of a different class (**Product**) according to the filter criteria. Such functionality, referred to as *projection*, is expected in a future release.

13.1.3.2 Aggregates

JDOQL does not define any aggregate functions (e.g. maximum, count, average, etc.). Queries to determine the maximum value of a persistent field, such as an order number, can be written to return the entire candidate collection in an appropriate sequence (e.g. by **orderNumber** descending). However, the definition of a maximum aggregate function would be far more flexible. Aggregates are expected in a future release.

13.1.3.3 Additional filter operators

It is also likely that the filter operators will be complemented in due course with an operator equivalent to the Java keyword **instanceof**. This could be used to restrict the result of a query to certain subbranches of inheritance or implementation hierarchies.

13.1.3.4 String-based query definition

It is already possible to define a query as a set of strings, as illustrated by the Dynamic Query Window presented in Chapter 8. However, there is no standard for a single string grammar encapsulating all query elements.

If such a grammar is defined, JDO query monitors could be written that would accept, compile, and execute queries in this form. For example, the query shown in the Dynamic Query Window in Figure 8.2 (page 144) might be typed into a JDO query monitor as:

```
EXECUTE-NEW-QUERY
CANDIDATE com.ogilviepartners.jdobook.op.BusinessPartner
IMPORTS com.ogilviepartners.jdobook.op.*
VARIABLES Order o
PARAMETERS Double searchValue
FILTER customer.orders.contains(o) && o.totalValue >
searchValue
ORDERING name ascending PARAMETER-VALUES 1000;
```

Or perhaps it would be useful to define a query and execute it in separate steps. This might even facilitate the chaining of query executions, illustrated below with a pipe | operator.

```
DEFINE-QUERY q1
CANDIDATE com.ogilviepartners.jdobook.op.BusinessPartner
IMPORTS com.ogilviepartners.jdobook.op.*
VARIABLES Order o
PARAMETERS Double searchValue
FILTER customer.orders.contains(o) && o.totalValue >
                                            searchValue
ORDERING name ascending;


EXECUTE-QUERY q1 PARAMETER-VALUES 1000 | q2
                            PARAMETER-VALUES ... ;
```

Please note that the above is not supported, or even suggested syntax, but should be sufficient to give the reader an idea of the possibilities for a standard string-based JDOQL representation.

13.1.3.5 Query object model

I have already pointed out that SQL suffers from loose typing and deferred compilation, which makes it easy to compile and deploy applications with syntactically incorrect queries. The current form of JDOQL reduces this risk significantly, since all mapping between JDO instances and the underlying data store is handled internally. However, it is still possible to write a query in JDOQL that will not execute correctly, but which will be compiled by the Java compiler. This is due to the presence of string elements within a programmatic query definition.

JDOQL will not have its current string elements (variable declaration, filter, ordering declaration, parameter declaration, etc.) removed, as their presence enables a wide variety of dynamic applications. However, it is likely that a future specification of JDOQL will provide the classes and methods necessary to describe a query in a purely programmatic manner, with no reliance on string data. This is known as a query object model (QOM). In the interim, vendors will be quick to provide tools for the generation and verification of queries and query strings in JDOQL.

13.1.4 Pre-fetch patterns

JDO currently defines the default fetch group. This is a grouping of fields which, in addition to primary key fields, will be retrieved from the data store when the instance is first read. However, it has been argued successfully that this simplistic treatment is inadequate in certain scenarios. It is possible that work in this area will provide application-level functionality for influencing the data that is initially retrieved for each instance. This functionality could then be employed on an as-required basis, although in most cases the default fetch group will remain adequate.

In the interim, look to the JDO vendors to implement their own enhancements ahead of any standardization in this area.

13.1.5 Optimistic transactions

Optimistic transactions are an optional feature of JDO 1.0, although this feature is under-specified, especially in the areas of isolation and failure recovery. In particular, there is no straightforward and portable way of discerning the instances for which optimistic concurrency assumptions have failed. Furthermore, the application remains responsible for refreshing all instances associated with failed optimistic transactions, a tedious task for which additional support should be provided.

As users of JDO employ optimistic transactions and vendors provide proprietary enhancements to make the task easier, the JDO Expert Group will be working to standardize the necessary features.

13.1.6 Standardized O-R mapping

JDO 1.0 does not state how the persistent fields of an instance are mapped to the rows and columns of pre-existing database schemas. This work is being undertaken independently by each RDBMS-based JDO vendor in order to achieve competitive superiority.

In due course the description of these mappings may be standardized, which would improve the portability of such mappings between implementations.

13.1.7 Event-driven "reactive" instances

Enterprise applications are making significant use of JMS for inter-component asynchronous communication. Increasingly, JMS is being employed in the business-to-business arena. The content of such messages typically needs to be persisted.

A message-driven bean can be constricted that will persist incoming data through JDO. This was illustrated in Chapter 11. However, this approach mandates the presence of a J2EE application server.

It is easy to conceptualize a JDO instance which itself reacts to incoming JMS messages, through a direct JMS/JDO connection which is independent of J2EE and the message-driven bean architecture. It will be interesting to see how JDO evolves in this area.

13.2 Sources of further information

Further information about JDO is available in a number of online forums that are updated regularly.

13.2.1 Ogilvie Partners Ltd

The author maintains a website which is dedicated to JDO:

```
http://www.OgilviePartners.com
```

Ogilvie Partners offer vendor-independent JDO consultancy, training, and mentoring. The website includes useful downloads such as FAQs and presentations
on JDO which I have delivered at conferences and user groups worldwide.

13.2.2 JavaDataObjects at Yahoo!Groups

The JavaDataObjects discussion forum at Yahoo!Groups is lively and enjoys
contributions from many high-profile members of the JDO community:

```
http://groups.yahoo.com/group/JavaDataObjects/
```

The moderators maintain a JDO suggestions document and the group regularly
debates proposals for future inclusion in JDO.

13.2.3 JDOcentral.com

If you prefer not to receive regular email but to go online for information about
JDO, you should try JDOcentral. This comprehensive forum contains discussions about JDO as well as news from the community, a calendar of
forthcoming JDO-related events, and other features. A newsletter is emailed
monthly to subscribers.

```
http://www.JDOcentral.com
```

Properties for JDOHelper bootstrap

A

The following are the standard property names for use when constructing a persistence manager factory through the following **JDOHelper** method:

```
getPersistenceManagerFactory(Properties props)
```

Each JDO vendor may add other properties for their implementation, which will be described in the product-specific documentation. For a detailed discussion of each of these properties please refer to the "JDOHelper" section in Chapter 6.

```
javax.jdo.PersistenceManagerFactoryClass
javax.jdo.option.Optimistic
javax.jdo.option.RetainValues
javax.jdo.option.RestoreValues
javax.jdo.option.IgnoreCache
javax.jdo.option.NontransactionalRead
javax.jdo.option.NontransactionalWrite
javax.jdo.option.Multithreaded
javax.jdo.option.ConnectionDriverName
javax.jdo.option.ConnectionUserName
javax.jdo.option.ConnectionPassword
javax.jdo.option.ConnectionURL
javax.jdo.option.ConnectionFactoryName
javax.jdo.option.ConnectionFactory2Name
```

Strings for supported options

B

The **supportedOptions()** method of a persistence manager factory returns a **Collection** of **Strings**. The presence of particular strings in that collection indicates support for the corresponding optional feature of the JDO specification. In the same way, the absence of a string indicates that the corresponding feature is not supported by the implementation.

The strings used for each optional feature are standardized by the JDO specification, and are listed here for quick reference. For further information, please refer to section 6.3.1 on page 104.

```
"javax.jdo.option.TransientTransactional"
"javax.jdo.option.NontransactionalRead"
"javax.jdo.option.NontransactionalWrite"
"javax.jdo.option.RetainValues"
"javax.jdo.option.RestoreValues"
"javax.jdo.option.Optimistic"
"javax.jdo.option.ApplicationIdentity"
"javax.jdo.option.DatastoreIdentity"
"javax.jdo.option.NonDurableIdentity"
"javax.jdo.option.ArrayList"
"javax.jdo.option.HashMap"
"javax.jdo.option.Hashtable"
"javax.jdo.option.LinkedList"
"javax.jdo.option.TreeMap"
"javax.jdo.option.TreeSet"
"javax.jdo.option.Vector"
"javax.jdo.option.Map"
"javax.jdo.option.List"
"javax.jdo.option.Array"
"javax.jdo.option.NullCollection"
"javax.jdo.option.ChangeApplicationIdentity"
"javax.jdo.query.JDOQL"
```

JDO persistence descriptor DTD

C

jdo.dtd

```
<?xml version="1.0" encoding="UTF-8"?>
<!ELEMENT jdo ((package)+, (extension)*)>
<!ELEMENT package ((class)+, (extension)*)>
<!ATTLIST package name CDATA #REQUIRED>
<!ELEMENT class (field|extension)*>
<!ATTLIST class name CDATA #REQUIRED>
<!ATTLIST class identity-type
(application|datastore|nondurable) #IMPLIED>
                <!ATTLIST class objectid-class CDATA #IMPLIED>
<!ATTLIST class requires-extent (true|false) 'true'>
<!ATTLIST class persistence-capable-superclass CDATA #IMPLIED>
<!ELEMENT field ((collection|map|array)?, (extension)*)?>
<!ATTLIST field name CDATA #REQUIRED>
<!ATTLIST field persistence-modifier
                    (persistent|transactional|none) #IMPLIED>
<!ATTLIST field primary-key (true|false) 'false'>
<!ATTLIST field null-value (exception|default|none) 'none'>
<!ATTLIST field default-fetch-group (true|false) #IMPLIED>
<!ATTLIST field embedded (true|false) #IMPLIED>
<!ELEMENT collection (extension)*>
<!ATTLIST collection element-type CDATA #IMPLIED>
<!ATTLIST collection embedded-element (true|false) #IMPLIED>
<!ELEMENT map (extension)*>
<!ATTLIST map key-type CDATA #IMPLIED>
<!ATTLIST map embedded-key (true|false) #IMPLIED>
<!ATTLIST map value-type CDATA #IMPLIED>
<!ATTLIST map embedded-value (true|false) #IMPLIED>
<!ELEMENT array (extension)*>
<!ATTLIST array embedded-element (true|false) #IMPLIED>
<!ELEMENT extension (extension)*>
<!ATTLIST extension vendor-name CDATA #REQUIRED>
<!ATTLIST extension key CDATA #IMPLIED>
```

PersistenceManagerFactory

D

This appendix is provided as a quick reference to the get/set methods for the
`PersistenceManagerFactory` interface's configuration properties (Table D.1).
It is more common to construct appropriately configured factories through the
`JDOHelper` class than to configure each property through the
`PersistenceManagerFactory` interface directly.

Table D.1 get/set methods for configuration properties

Property	Type	get	set
ConnectionUserName	String	✔	✔
ConnectionPassword	String	✘	✔
ConnectionURL	String	✔	✔
ConnectionDriverName	String	✔	✔
ConnectionFactoryName	String	✔	✔
ConnectionFactory	Object	✔	✔
ConnectionFactory2Name	String	✔	✔
ConnectionFactory2	Object	✔	✔
Multithreaded	boolean	✔	✔
Optimistic	boolean	✔	✔
RetainValues	boolean	✔	✔
RestoreValues	boolean	✔	✔
NontransactionalRead	boolean	✔	✔
NontransactionalWrite	boolean	✔	✔
IgnoreCache	boolean	✔	✔
MaxPool	int	✔	✔
MinPool	int	✔	✔
MsWait	int	✔	✔

JDOQL BNF   E

Grammar notation

The grammar notation is taken from the Java Language Specification. Terminal symbols are shown in bold in the productions of the lexical and syntactic grammars, and throughout this specification whenever the text is directly referring to such a terminal symbol. These are to appear in a program exactly as written.

Non-terminal symbols are shown in italic type. The definition of a non-terminal is introduced by the name of the non-terminal being defined followed by a colon. One or more alternative right-hand sides for the non-terminal then follow on succeeding lines.

The suffix "opt", which may appear after a terminal or non-terminal, indicates an optional symbol. The alternative containing the optional symbol actually specifies two right-hand sides, one that omits the optional element and one that includes it.

When the words "one of" follow the colon in a grammar definition, they signify that each of the terminal symbols on the following line or lines is an alternative definition.

Parameter declaration

This section describes the syntax of the **declareParameters()** argument.

```
DeclareParameters:
    Parameters ,opt
Parameters:
    Parameter
    Parameters , Parameter
Parameter:
    Type Identifier
```

Variable declaration

This section describes the syntax of the **declareVariables()** argument.

```
DeclareVariables:
    Variables ;opt
Variables:
```

```
        Variable
        Variables ; Variable
    Variable:
        Type Identifier
```

Import declaration

This section describes the syntax of the **declareImports()** argument.

```
DeclareImports:
    ImportDeclarations ;opt
ImportDeclarations:
    ImportDeclaration
    ImportDeclarations ; ImportDeclaration
ImportDeclaration:
    import Name
    import Name.*
```

Order specification

This section describes the syntax of the **setOrdering()** argument.

```
SetOrdering:
    OrderSpecifications ,opt
OrderSpecifications:
    OrderSpecification
    OrderSpecifications , OrderSpecification
OrderSpecification:
    Identifier ascending
    Identifier descending
```

Filter expression

This section describes the syntax of the **setFilter()** argument.

Basically, the query filter expression is a Java boolean expression, where some of the Java expressions are not permitted. Specifically, pre- and post-increment and decrement (++ and – –), shift (>> and <<), and assignment expressions (+=, –=, etc.) are not permitted.

The description follows the structure of the grammar for Java expression in Chapter 19.12 of the *Java Language Specification* (Joy et al., 2000). The description is bottom-up, i.e. the last rule expression is the root of the filter expression syntax.

Please note, the grammar allows arbitrary method calls (MethodInvocation), where JDO only permits calls to the methods **contains()**, **isEmpty()**, and a number of string methods. This restriction cannot be expressed in terms of the syntax and has to be ensured by a semantic check.

```
Primary:
    Literal
    this
    ( Expression )
    FieldAccess
    MethodInvocation
ArgumentList:
    Expression
    ArgumentList , Expression
FieldAccess:
    Primary . Identifier
MethodInvocation:
    Name ( ArgumentListopt )
    Primary . Identifier ( ArgumentListopt )
PostfixExpression:
    Primary
    Name
UnaryExpression:
    + UnaryExpression
    - UnaryExpression
    UnaryExpressionNotPlusMinus
UnaryExpressionNotPlusMinus:
    PostfixExpression
    ~ UnaryExpression
    ! UnaryExpression
    CastExpression
CastExpression:
    ( Type ) UnaryExpression
MultiplicativeExpression:
    UnaryExpression
    MultiplicativeExpression * UnaryExpression
    MultiplicativeExpression / UnaryExpression
    MultiplicativeExpression % UnaryExpression
AdditiveExpression:
    MultiplicativeExpression
    AdditiveExpression + MultiplicativeExpression
    AdditiveExpression - MultiplicativeExpression
RelationalExpression:
    AdditiveExpression
    RelationalExpression < AdditiveExpression
```

```
    RelationalExpression > AdditiveExpression
    RelationalExpression <= AdditiveExpression
    RelationalExpression >= AdditiveExpression
EqualityExpression:
    RelationalExpression
    EqualityExpression == RelationalExpression
    EqualityExpression != RelationalExpression
AndExpression:
    EqualityExpression
    AndExpression & EqualityExpression
ExclusiveOrExpression:
    AndExpression
    ExclusiveOrExpression ^ AndExpression
InclusiveOrExpression:
    ExclusiveOrExpression
    InclusiveOrExpression | ExclusiveOrExpression
ConditionalAndExpression:
    InclusiveOrExpression
    ConditionalAndExpression && InclusiveOrExpression
ConditionalOrExpression:
    ConditionalAndExpression
    ConditionalOrExpression || ConditionalAndExpression
Expression:
    ConditionalOrExpression
```

Types

This section describes a type specification, used in a parameter or variable declaration or in a cast expression.

```
Type:
    PrimitiveType
    Name
PrimitiveType:
    NumericType
    boolean
NumericType:
    IntegralType
    FloatingPointType
IntegralType: one of
    byte short int long char
FloatingPointType: one of
    float double
```

Literals

A literal is the source code representation of a value of a primitive type, the String type, or the null type. Please refer to the *Java Language Specification* (Joy et al., 2000) for the lexical structure of IntegerLiterals, FloatingPointLiterals, CharacterLiterals, and StringLiterals.

```
IntegerLiteral: ...
FloatingPointLiteral: ...
BooleanLiteral: one of
    true false
CharacterLiteral: ...
StringLiteral: ...
NullLiteral:
    null
Literal:
    IntegerLiteral
    FloatingPointLiteral
    BooleanLiteral
    CharacterLiteral
    StringLiteral
    NullLiteral
```

Names

```
Name:
    Identifier
    QualifiedName
QualifiedName:
    Name . Identifier
```

Glossary

ACID Atomic, Consistent, Isolated and Durable – properties of a transaction

aggregate functions Functions which can be used as part of a query and which generate a result based on the application of that function across the query results; currently unavailable in JDOQL

API Application programming interface – programming interface used by the application developer, as opposed to the service provider.

application exception An exception defined by the application developer, as opposed to the standard JDO exceptions present in the `javax.jdo` package

application identity A JDO identity type whereby the identity of an instance is determined by the value of its so-called *primary key* fields

bean class (EJB) One of the classes that make up an EJB component, specifically the class that provides concrete implementations of the lifecycle and business methods of the component

BMP Bean-managed persistence – whereby EJB entity beans contain code to programmatically manage write/read data to/from the data store

BMT Bean-managed transactions – whereby EJB components contain code to programmatically demarcate transactions

BNF Backus-Naur form – a formal grammar for notating programming syntax

bootstrapping The process of starting up, or initializing, a software service

candidate class (JDOQL) Every JDOQL query has a candidate class; the collection or extent over which the query executes must contain only instances of this class; the unmodifiable collection returned by query execution will contain only instances of this class; JDO is inherently polymorphic, and "instances of" implicitly includes subclasses

candidate collection (JDOQL) The collection of instances of the candidate class, over which a query is to execute

candidate extent (JDOQL) The extent of the candidate class, over which a query is to execute

CMP Container-managed persistence – whereby persistence management is delegated to the J2EE application server's container (entity beans only)

CMT Container-managed transactions – whereby transaction management for EJB components is delegated to the J2EE application server's container

CORBA Common Object Request Broker Architecture

datastore identity A JDO identity type whereby the identity of an instance is determined entirely by the data store

DBMS Database management system

DDL Data Definition Language – general term for languages that define the data representation of entities in data stores, SQL being the most common example

deletion The removal of the state of a persistent instance from a data store, such that the instance is no longer persistent

detachment The removal of an object from an object graph, such that the removed object is no longer referenced by any other objects in the graph; if the object was a persistent JDO instance, this is not the same as deletion since the object's state will still exist in the data store and the object itself can potentially be retrieved by its Object ID through iteration of its class's extent, or through JDOQL

domain object model A definition of one or more classes and their structural relationships (inheritance, implementation, association), specifically designed to represent abstractions of the business domain and containing classes that represent concepts recognizable to project stakeholders familiar with that business domain

DTD Document Type Definition – used to constrain XML documents

EAI Enterprise Application Integration

EJB Enterprise JavaBean – a server-side component written according to the J2EE specification

EJBQL Enterprise JavaBean Query Language – used to specify the persistence of CMP entity beans

equality Two object references are equal if they reference the same single object

equivalence Two object references are equivalent if the (potentially different) objects that they reference represent the same thing

GA General availability – applies to JDO implementations that are commercially available and supported in deployment

GUI Graphical user interface

hint A request, or part of a request, passed to a persistence manager that may legitimately be ignored by a JDO-compliant implementation

Hollow (JDO state) The state that applies to any JDO instance that exists in the persistence manager's cache and contains the instance's JDO identity, but has not had any further persistent field values read from the data store

home interface One of the interfaces that make up an EJB component, specifically the interface that provides factory methods for the client-managed lifecycle of the bean instance

HTML Hypertext Markup Language

HTTP Hypertext Transfer Protocol

IDE Integrated development environment

IIOP Internet Inter-ORB Protocol

J2EE Java 2 Enterprise Edition – a collection of Java APIs that must be supported by compliant application server products

J2ME Java 2 Micro Edition – the specification of Java for embedded (low-resource) platforms

JCA Java Connector Architecture

JCP Java Community Process –facilitates broad industry involvement in the specification of new Java APIs

JDBC Java Database Connectivity – a Java API that facilitates access to SQL-based (generally relational) databases

JDK Java Development Kit

JDO Java Data Objects – the new Java API for the transparent persistence of Java Objects

JDO implementation A set of classes that implement the JDO service providers' interface (package javax.jdo.spi) and provide support for JDO with a specified underlying data store

JDO instance An instance of a persistence-capable Java class, whether or not that particular instance is persistent

JDO vendor The provider of a JDO implementation

JDOQL Java Data Objects Query Language – a dynamic language for querying JDO instances

JMS Java Message Service – a Java API for asynchronous messaging, supporting publish-subscribe and point-to-point semantics

JNDI Java Naming and Directory Interface

JSP JavaServer Page – text document containing marked-up text and optionally embedded Java constructs, which is translated into a Java servlet and executed in the web server tier

JTA Java Transaction Architecture

JVM Java Virtual Machine – software that executes Java byte-code and, by virtue of its implementation for many disparate computer platforms, ascribes portability to the Java language

managed environment Usage of JDO by components executing in a J2EE application server

NASDAQ Listing of technology stocks traded on the New York stock exchange, see www.nasdaq.com

nondurable identity A JDO identity type whereby uniqueness is not maintained in the data store, thus facilitating the rapid persistence of new instances

non-managed environment Usage of JDO independent of a J2EE application server

non-serialized fields Fields (attributes) of a class that are marked with the Java keyword transient, and which do not form part of the serialized form instances of that class

object An instance of a Java class; the class defines the attributes and methods of the object, and each object of that class encapsulates the specific field values (state) that it represents

Object ID An object that uniquely identifies a JDO instance, and is unique to that instance across the entire data store

Object ID class The class from which an Object ID is instantiated for a particular persistence-capable class; for datastore identity the Object ID class is internal to the JDO implementation, whereas for application identity the Object ID class is named by the developer (and implemented by the developer or by the enhancer)

object model A definition of one or more classes and their structural relationships (inheritance, implementation, association)

object persistence The storage of object state in some data store from which the objects can later be reconstituted; specifically we presume that the lifetime of object state in the data store will extend beyond the lifetime of the process from which the object was persisted

ODBMS   Object Database Management System – a data store that natively persists objects

ODMG   Object Data Management Group

OEM   Original equipment manufacturer

optional JDO features   Features detailed in the JDO specification, but which an implementation is not obliged to support in order to be JDO-compliant

O-R   Object-Relational – applies to any mechanism that maps between object technology and relational technology, and specifically to JDO implementations that support an underlying relational database

orthogonal   Concepts are orthogonal if they are independent of each other (the Greek actually means "at right angles"); transactionality and persistence are orthogonal concepts, and thus an instance may be transactional or not transactional regardless of whether it is persistent or non-persistent

persistence by reachability   The recursive algorithm by which transient instances referenced by a persistent instance are themselves made persistent

persistence-capable   A class that implements the PersistenceCapable interface and which is identified to the implementation as such (as a persistence-capable class) in the persistence descriptor

persistence descriptor   An XML document that identifies the persistence-capable classes to a JDO implementation, and facilitates the overriding of default persistence modifiers and the specification of further persistence-relevant information for such classes

persistent   Stored beyond the lifetime of a single JVM process – objects (and object graphs) which are persistent, represent data that is stored in the data store

Persistent-Clean (JDO state)   The state that applies to any JDO instance that has some of its field values loaded, but which has not been changed in the current transaction

Persistent-Deleted (JDO state)   The state that applies to any JDO instance that was persistent before this transaction, but has been deleted in the current transaction

Persistent-Dirty (JDO state)   The state that applies to any JDO instance that was persistent before this transaction, but has been changed in the current transaction

Persistent-New (JDO state)   The state that applies to any JDO instance that has been made persistent in the current transaction

Persistent-New-Deleted (JDO state)   The state that applies to any JDO instance that has been made persistent and subsequently deleted, all within the current transaction

Persistent-Nontransactional (JDO state) The state that applies to any JDO instance that represents a persistent data store entity, but which is not guaranteed to be transactionally consistent with that entity

persistent object model 1. The set of restrictions placed on an object model in order for it to be persistable through JDO, and the implications of persisting an object model through JDO

2. An object model comprising persistence-capable classes

primary key class (EJB) One of the classes that make up an entity bean component, specifically the class that provides identity for the entity bean; EJB primary key classes can be replaced by JDO Object ID classes if the underlying BMP mechanism is JDO

primary key class (JDO) The Object ID class for a persistence-capable class with application identity is sometimes referred to as the class's primary key class

projection The capability of a query language to return a result comprising objects that are not instances of the candidate class; not currently available in JDOQL

provisionally persistent A transient instance to be made persistent through persistence by reachability is actually made provisionally persistent until the transaction commits; on commit the instance becomes persistent if and only if it is still reachable from a persistent instance (i.e. it has not been detached from the object graph in the interim)

QOM Query object model

RDBMS Relational database management system – a data store that natively persists data as tables of rows and columns; storage of objects requires that they be decomposed into constituent field values, each of which is stored as a column value

remote interface (EJB) One of the interfaces that make up an EJB component, specifically the interface that identifies those business methods that the client may invoke on the component

required JDO features Features detailed in the JDO specification that an implementation must support in order to be JDO-compliant

RMI Remote Method Invocation – a Java API for distributed programming

SPI Service providers' interface – programming interface used by the service provider, as opposed to the application developer

SQL Structured Query Language

SQL-92 Structured Query Language (1992 standard)

stateful (session bean) A stateful component is dedicated to a single client for the duration of the client's reference to that component; it can usefully maintain client-specific state across method invocations

stateless (session bean) A stateless component is dedicated to a single client only for the duration of an individual method invocation by that client on the component; it cannot meaningfully maintain client-specific state across method invocations

transient 1. A keyword in Java that specifies attributes as being non-serialized
2. An object that does not represent persistent data

transient (JDO state) The state that applies to any JDO instance that does not represent a data store entity, as is typical of instances newly instantiated with the new keyword

Transient-Clean (JDO state) The state that applies to any JDO instance that is transactional, but which has not been changed in the current transaction

Transient-Dirty (JDO state) The state that applies to any JDO instance that is transactional, and has been changed in the current transaction

transparent persistence Everything that JDO undertakes in order to abstract applications from the underlying complexity of object persistence, specifically:
1. persistence by reachability
2. automatic change tracking of JDO instances
3. automatic mapping of Java data types to the native data types of the underlying data store
4. automatic mapping of persistence-capable classes to data structures in the underlying data store
5. automatic mapping of relationships between persistent instances: references, collections and, if supported, arrays
6. automatic support for inheritance hierarchies of persistence-capable classes and, if supported, interface implementation hierarchies as well
7. automatic translation of JDOQL syntax to the native query language of the underlying data store if appropriate

UML Unified Modeling Language – a set of standard notations by which software systems, and elements thereof, can be diagrammed

uniquing The process by which a JDO implementation ensures that there is at most one JDO instance with a given JDO identity (Object ID) in the persistence manager's cache at one time

URL Universal resource locator

valid (XML) Some XML documents are constrained by a Document Type

Definition (DTD); XML documents constrained by a DTD and which conform to the grammar defined by the DTD and are said to be valid

well formed (XML)   All XML documents must be well formed, in that they must obey the basic document structure and close all tags in the reverse of the order in which they were opened

XML   eXtensible Markup Language – a markup language specification that defines the structure of a document, but leaves the choice of tag names to be agreed by the document authors and readers

Bibliography

Coad, Peter, Mayfield, Mark and Kern, Jon *Java Design*, 2nd edition (Yourdon Press, 1999) ISBN 0-13-911181-6.

Coad, Peter, Lefebvre, Eric, and De Luca, Jeff, *Java Modeling in Color with UML: Enterprise Components and Process* (Prentice Hall, 1999) ISBN 0-13-011510-X.

Hall, Marty, *Core Servlets and JavaServer Pages* (Sun Microsystems Press, 2000) ISBN 0-13-089340-4.

Joy, Bill, Steele, Guy, Grosling, James, Brache Gilad, *Java Language Specification*, 2nd edition (Addison-Wesley, 2000) ISBN 0-201-31008-2.

McLaughlin, Brett, *Java and XML* (O'Reilly, 2000) ISBN 0-596-00016-2.

Monson-Haefel, Richard, *Enterprise JavaBeans*, 3rd edition, (O'Reilly, 2001) ISBN 0-596-00226-2.

Monson-Haefel, Richard, and Chappel, David A., *Java Message Service* (O'Reilly, 2001) ISBN 0-596-00068-5.

Nicola, Jill, Mayfield, Mark, and Abney, Mike, *Streamlined Object Modeling: Patterns, Rules, and Implementation* (Prentice Hall PTR, 2002) ISBN 0-13-066839-7.

Index

JavaSpaces ™
In Practice
Philip Bishop and Nigel Warren

"Phil Bishop and Nigel Warren have been pioneers in the use of JavaSpaces (tm) to build real systems that solve real problems. This book is an excellent distillation of their accumulated wisdom on this subject, and will save any programmer using the technology far more time than it will take to read. It is also well written and clearly presented, a rarity in technical books these days. I learned a lot reading it."

~ Jim Waldo, *Distinguished Engineer at Sun Microsystems, lead architect for the Jini networking technology and JavaSpaces.*

This book will show you how to use JavaSpaces to build practical, scalable distributed systems. It will increase your understanding of where JavaSpaces are applicable, and how to use them effectively within your system architecture.

JavaSpaces in Practice is structured in three parts:

- Part One focuses on patterns for designing and evolving entries from the basics to advanced distributed data structures.
- Part Two covers designs and idioms associated with remote events, code mobility, and both transient and persistent spaces.
- Part Three highlights some practical applications including implementing smart proxies, location-based services and agent systems, together with guidelines and tips for testing and tuning JavaSpaces.

Developers and Programmers with some experience in Java will learn by example a set of idioms that make distributed systems more dynamic and flexible.

ISBN 0 321 11231 8

Visit us on the world wide web at
www.it-minds.com
www.awprofessional.com

Realizing eBusiness with Components
Paul Allen

Unfortunately, there is a great deal of hype and over-expectation surrounding e-business. Many organizations are jumping on the e-business bandwagon without understanding what they are getting into. Lack of planning and analysis, resulting in inflexible solutions that are unable to integrate with existing systems, are all too common. At the same time, e-business calls for a closer relationship between those involved in business development and those required to support these initiatives within the company's information technology infrastructure.

This book is designed to provide practical advice for planning, analysis and design of e-business systems using component-based development (CBD). Just as e-business is more than a series of web pages, so CBD is not just an approach to problem-solving using software building blocks. It includes architectures, processes, modeling techniques, economic models and organizational guidelines, all of which are well placed to ease migration of large organizations to e-business.

The author defines the key concepts relating to CBD, and introduces component standards, component frameworks, middleware and all the relevant internet technologies. The book also deals with issues such as the business case for adopting CBD, pragmatic approaches to modeling business requirements, putting CBD to work using the Catalysis process, migrating to CBD from legacy systems, and the issues associated with sourcing components from off-the-shelf purchasing to bespoke design.

This book shows you:

- how to obtain commitment for a CBD strategy at board level
- how to deploy catalysis modeling techniques and other commercial approaches
- how to use component modeling techniques to create innovative eBusiness solutions
- how to gain competitive advantage with TNBT and Collaborative Commerce

The core of the book is an extensive example that tracks the experiences of a typical company, with a traditional set of business processes and supporting software systems, through various stages along the road to e-business.

ISBN 0 201 67520 X

Visit us on the world wide web at
www.it-minds.com
www.awprofessional.com

Find more information about the **Component Software Series** at
www.awprofessional.com/series/index.asp

UML and the Unified Process
Jim Arlow and Ila Neustadt

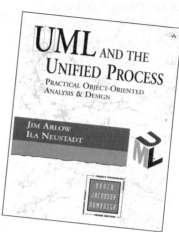

This book provides an indispensable guide to the complex process of object-oriented analysis and design using the Unified Modeling Language (UML). It describes how the process of OO analysis and design fits into the software development lifecycle, as defined by the Unified Process (UP).

UML and the Unified Process contains a wealth of practical and useful techniques that can be applied immediately. You will learn OO analysis and design techniques, UML syntax and relevant aspects of the UP as you progress through the text. It also provides an accessible, accurate and succinct summary of both UML *and* UP from the point of view of the OO analyst and designer.

This book provides:

- Chapter roadmaps, detailed diagrams and margin notes allowing a rapid overview, enabling you to focus on your needs
- Outline summaries for each chapter making it ideal for revision and a comprehensive index, so the book can be used as a reference

*The accompanying website (***www.umlandtheunifiedprocess.com***) provides:*

- A complete worked example of a simple e-commerce system
- Useful links to Open Source and proprietary software

ISBN 0 201 77060 1

Visit us on the world wide web at
www.it-minds.com
www.awprofessional.com

Find more information about the **Object Technology Series** at
www.awprofessional.com/series/index.asp

Developing Software with UML
Object-Oriented Analysis and Design in Practice
Second Edition
Bernd Oestereich

Are you a software developer or project manager looking to exploit the power of object technology in your development process for the first time? Do you need a practical, example-driven introduction to object-oriented analysis and design? If so, look no further.

This book explains the benefits of using the object-oriented approach for software development as well as providing a state-of-the-art account of the technology available. Employing numerous real-life examples to illustrate its application, the use of the Unified Modeling Language (UML) in object-oriented analysis and design is explained systematically by an experienced practitioner.

This book:

- Takes the reader step-by-step through the development process
- Uses one continuous example to show how each principle and concept is applied in practice
- Explains the basics of UML in detail, with individual examples
- Uses cross-references, allowing readers to follow the software development example, learning the appropriate features of UML as they become relevant
- Can be used as a tutorial on the application of UML
- Uses Java for coded examples
- Covers the Object Constraint Language (OCL).

New to the second edition of *Development Software with UML:*

- All chapters comprehensively updated
- Contains two chapters on analysis and design
- Is fully compliant with UML 1.4
- Offers solutions to problems that cannot be solved by UML alone.

ISBN 0 201 75603 X

Visit us on the world wide web at
www.it-minds.com
www.awprofessional.com

Find more information about the **Object Technology Series** at
www.awprofessional.com/series/index.asp

The Java Series:

The Java™ Series is supported, endorsed, and authored by the creators of the Java technology at Sun Microsystems, Inc. It is the official place to go for complete, expert, and definitive information on Java technology. The books in this Series provide the inside information you need to build effective, robust and portable applications and applets. The Series is an indispensable resource for anyone targeting the Java™ 2 Platform.

ADDISON-WESLEY

Effective Java™ Programming Language Guide

Joshua Bloch   0201310058

Josh Bloch designed, implemented, and maintained many of the Java platform libraries. Here he shares 57 'nuggets' – rules and code examples showing what works, what doesn't, and how to use the language to best effect. Accessible by anyone who knows the language, and food for thought even for advanced programmers.

The J2EE™ Tutorial

Stephanie Bodoff et al.
0201791684

You're familiar with Java™ programming, but now it's time for you to take it to the next level and begin creating enterprise applications with the Java™ 2 Platform, Enterprise Edition (J2EE™).

The Java™ Web Services Tutorial

Eric Armstrong et al
0201768119

The Java™ Web Services Tutorial is a comprehensive, example-driven, 'roll up your sleeves and dive-in' guide to building Web services applications in Java™ Technlogy.

The Java™ Developers Almanac 1.4

Volume 1
Patrick Chan
0201752808

The Java™ Developers Almanac 1.4 is the most up-to-date and complete quick reference for the Java Class Libraries, JDK™ v1.4. This resource is loaded with over 500 examples, and covers the use of over 2000 members.

The Java™ Programming Language

Third Edition
Ken Arnold, James Gosling
and David .Holmes   0201704331

These expert authors describe the latest version of the language, as defined in the Java Language Specification, Second Edition, and implemented in version 1.2 of the Java™ 2SDK Standard Edition. The book serves as a tutorial introduction to the language and essential libraries, as well as a reference.

Designing Enterprise Applications with the J2EE Platform

Second Edition.
Inderjeet Singh, Beth Stearns, Mark Johnson, and the Enterprise Team.   0201787903

Describes the key architectural and design issues in applications supported by the J2EE platform, and offers practical guidelines for both architects and developers. 'The Java™ Blueprints Team has done it again. This book is an indispensable asset to all J2EE

Concurrent Programming in Java™

Second Edition
Doug Lea
0201310090

Concurrent Programming in Java™, Second Edition delivers expert, thoroughly updated coverage of multithreading in the Java™ 2 platform, with new and expenaded coverage of the Java memory model, cancellation, portable parallel programming, utility classes for concurrency control, and more.

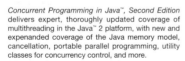

J2EE™ Connector Architecture and Enterprise Application Integration

Rahul Sharma et al.
0201775808

Written for application component developers, the book explains how to connect applications to one another and how to link to enterprise information systems and legacy systems.

Java™ Look and Feel Design Guidelines: Advanced Topics

Sun Microsystems, Inc.
0201775824

This title complements the first volume of the Look and Feel Guidelines. It provides advanced guidelines for developing user interfaces based on the Java™ Foundation Classes.

Applying Enterprise Javabeans™ – Component-Based Development for the J2EE Platform

Vlada Matena and Beth Stearns
0201702673

Written by the chief architect of the Enterprise JavaBean™ (EJB) specification, Applying Enterprise Javabeans™ provides complete, in depth, and authoritative information on the EJB technology.

Sun Microsystems Press

Sun Microsystems Press publishes, in conjunction with Prentice Hall PTR, official retail books on Sun Products and technologies that focus on real-world applications with tested solutions and source code examples. These books have become must-have volumes for the bookshelves of developers, system programmers, system administrators, application architects, and other technical staff.

Just Java™2 *Fifth Edition*
Van der Linden
0130320722

The fully updated and revised edition of Peter van der Linden's classic bestseller the painless way to master the fundamentals of Java™ and serverside programming.

Core Java™ 2 Volume 1 Fundamentals
Fifth Edition
Horstmann, Cornell
0130894680

The #1 bestselling book on Java™, and the experienced developer's guide to Java™ 2.

Core Java™ 2 Volume 2 Fundamentals
Fifth Edition
Horstmann, Cornell
0130927384

The experienced developer's guide to Java™ 2, fully updated for JDK 1.4

More Servlets and JavaServer™ Pages
Hall
0130676144

Perfect companion to the bestselling Core Servlets and Java™ Server Pages from Marty Hall.

Core J2ME Technologies
Muchow
0130669113

Complete indepth developers guide to J2ME technology version 1.0.2

JavaSpaces™ Example by Example
Halter
0130619167

The tutorial to JavaSpaces™, for developers and programmers that shows how to make the most effective use of JavaSpaces™ by providing a solid basis of examples.

Applied Design Patterns in Java™
Stelting, Maassen
0130935387

A handson guide to classic design patterns and their application in the Java™ Programming Language

Core J2EE Patterns
Crupi, Malks, Alur
0130648841

The advanced guide to creating scalable J2EE applications using J2EE patterns, principles, best practices and implementation strategies.

Advanced JavaServer™ Pages
Geary
0130307041

The advanced guide to Java™Server Pages.

Core Servlets and JavaServer™ Pages
Hall
0130893404

A complete guide to building interactive sites, dynamic pages, and Webenabled applications with the new J2EE version of servlets and Java™Server Pages.

Licensing Agreement

This book comes with a CD-ROM software package. By opening this package, you are agreeing to be bound by the following:

Concurrency & open amf

Client

settlement | Gateway — Can only deal w/ 1 at a time

Client get req/s